# MALINES: CONTINUING THE CONVERSATIONS

The Malines Conversations Group is an international group of Anglican and Roman Catholic theologians committed to dialogue and unity. The group takes its name and inspiration from the original Malines Conversations of the 1920s. These early informal conversations, held between a small group of British Anglicans and European Roman Catholics, were made possible because of the bonds of friendship between the members of the group.

The current Malines Conversations Group is under the patronage of Cardinal Jozeph De Kesel (Archbishop Emeritus of Mechelen-Brussels) and The Right Reverend and Right Honourable The Lord Williams of Oystermouth (former Archbishop of Canterbury), and meets with the blessing and support of the Dicastery for Promoting Christian Unity and Lambeth Palace. Like its predecessor, it is an informal group whilst also keeping in close contact with the official mandated ecumenical bodies in both communions; it includes members of the Anglican Roman Catholic International Commission (ARCIC) and the Anglican Roman Catholic Commission for Unity and Mission (IARCCUM).

The Group's Steering Committee is chaired by The Revd Dr Thomas Pott, O.S.B. of the Pontifical Atheneum Sant'Anselmo, Rome, along with The Revd Dr James Hawkey, Canon Theologian of Westminster Abbey, and The Revd Dr Keith Pecklers S.J., of the Pontifical Gregorian University, Rome.

Since 2013, the Malines Conversations Group has been gathering annually, always in early spring, alternately at Anglican and Roman Catholic venues.

# MALINES: CONTINUING THE CONVERSATIONS

Editors
Thomas Pott, O.S.B.
James Hawkey
Keith F. Pecklers, S.J.

with the assistance of
Tom McLean

First published in Great Britain in 2023

Society for Promoting Christian Knowledge
36 Causton Street
London SW1P 4ST
www.spck.org.uk

*British Library Cataloguing-in-Publication Data*
A catalogue record for this book is available from the British Library

ISBN 978-0-281-09035-8
eBook ISBN 978-0-281-09036-5

1 3 5 7 9 10 8 6 4 2

Typeset by Indian SPCK
First printed in Great Britain

# Contents

**Preface**
Bernard Longley                                                                    ix

**Introduction**

The Malines Conversations Group:
Approaching division and communion through the
lens of the reality of life and the truth of faith
Thomas Pott, O.S.B.                                                                 I

## Part I
## The Background: Principles and Method

1  The Malines Conversations: Re-opening the path to unity              11
Nicholas Sagovsky

2  Revisiting Biblical narratives: How can Scripture inspire us
for work and life today?                                                           21
Cyrille Vael, O.S.B.

3  Learning lessons from Liturgical Theology                                       41
Joris Geldhof

*Interlude*:  Brian Farrell: *A focus on the whole Church
as a source of inspiration*                                                        49

## Part II
## The Journey:
## Reading the Signs of the Times

4  Ecclesial, social, and historical developments from
the Malines Conversations to today                                                 53
Maryana Hnyp

5 Taking stock of the present situation of our churches 69
Keith F. Pecklers, S.J.

6 Taking Stock of the present situation of our churches 2:
Overcoming the difficulties 85
Jeremy Morris

7 Humanity, Society and Church: Reading the Signs of the Times 101
Cyrille Vael, O.S.B.

*Interlude*: Gordon Lathrop: *Notes on Liturgy and
Ecumenism from a Lutheran* 115

## Part III
## The Horizon: Shared Sacramentality

8 'Unveiling Mysterion': Reanimating the sacrament
by rooting it back into its own soil 119
Thomas Pott, O.S.B.

9 Sanctification of memory and the disclosing of the Holy City 131
Michael Nai Chiu Poon

10 Ordination in the Church of England: Theology and practice
in the Common Worship Ordinal 141
David Stancliffe

11 The celebration of the Sacrament of Ordination
in the Roman Catholic Church
Joris Geldhof 153

*Interlude*: Simon Jones: *Not-nothingness: The reality of life and
Holy Order in the light of* Apostolicae Curae *and* Saepius Officio 163

## Part IV
## The First Step: Healing Memories

12 History and *Apostolicae curae*: The limitations of its
historical starting point
Thomas O'Loughlin 167

# Contents

13  Exploring *Sorores in Spe*: A hermeneutic of hope          187
    James Hawkey & Joris Geldhof

14  'Sisters in Hope of the Resurrection': A Fresh Response
    to the Condemnation of Anglican Orders (1896)            201

Epilogue: Rowan Williams                                     225

List of Contributors                                         229

List of Members of the Malines Conversations Group           233

# Preface

When Johann Adam Möhler came as a young lecturer at the Catholic faculty of the University of Tübingen in 1825, he wondered why there had been little discussion between its members and those of the larger and illustrious Protestant theology faculty on matters of common concern. The conversations he began led to his *Unity in the Church*, proposing principles for the reconciliation of Christianity in the body of one Church, not only as the insistent call of the Holy Spirit, but also as a more clearly faithful manifestation of Catholicism. He presented ever closer convergence in unity of spirit through prayer, unity of mind through doctrinal accord and, when perfect communion in the Church was achieved, unity of body. His book later came to the attention of Cardinal Wiseman in England, who showed it to St John Henry Newman. In succession it influenced Yves Congar, a *peritus* at the Second Vatican Council. Its themes are plain in *Lumen Gentium*, the Dogmatic Constitution on the Church, and *Unitatis Redintegratio*, the Decree on Ecumenism.

Thus at the root of ecumenical dialogue is not only the exchange of gifts and mutual learning, nor only the imperatives of mission and service at the call of Christ and the Holy Spirit, but also the encounter of individuals moved to engage with one another's different approaches to Christ in faith and discipleship. The essays from the Malines Conversation Group that follow stand in a long line of such personally committed theological dialogue and contact among Catholics and Anglicans. As far back as the 17th century, the dialogue begun by Bishop Lancelot Andrewes with St Robert Bellarmine in 1609 led to exchanges over the next three decades until the fall of Archbishop William Laud of Canterbury, that even included proposals for retaining an English liturgy, married clergy and a measure of distinct governance, in an Anglican Church re-united with the Catholic Church.

In the nineteenth century, too, Anglican contacts with Catholics were part of the renewal of spirituality, pastoral theology, parish life and liturgy in the Church of England. They even favoured initiatives, both from the Anglican leadership and at Rome, to establish embryonic octaves of prayer for unity.

In the later twentieth century, the Agreed Statements of the first official Anglican-Roman Catholic International Commission produced ecumenical milestones. Yet the same problems as in the 17th century for doctrinal and authoritative approval on both sides continue to delay the effect they would have had if they been implemented. Although the Anglican-Roman Catholic dialogue continues to make progress, the hope for visible unity keeps returning to the obstacle posed in 1896 by Pope Leo XIII's adverse decision on the validity of Anglican orders in *Apostolicæ Curæ*. So definitive are its terms in the view of the Group, that even the substantial agreement of ARCIC I fails to transcend them. The essays in this book make a strong plea for a fresh examination of whether steps towards visible and organic unity may now proceed further.

Two friends, the Anglican Viscount Halifax and the French Catholic Abbé Fernand Portal had sought a different resolution to the question in the 1890s; and the response of the Archbishops of Canterbury and York to Pope Leo, *Sæpius Officio*, so impressed Halifax that in 1897 he called for renewed prayer for the unity of Christians each Ascensiontide. By 1908, in the same spirit, Spencer Jones, an English vicar and Paul Wattson, a soon to be Catholic American friar, had established the Church Unity Octave. The Lambeth Conference later that year made its *Appeal to all Christian People* to move towards visible union for Anglicans with other Churches.

The Conversations of 1921-27 sponsored by Cardinal Mercier at Malines (Mechelen in Belgium) saw Portal and Halifax convene with others to examine differences in doctrine, law and discipline, and their possible resolution. The paper from Dom Lambert Beauduin on 'The Anglican Church, United not Absorbed' drew on his pastoral experience as a kind of industrial chaplain celebrating the sacraments in a fast changing and secularising world, commending the urgent need for unity in mission, and also as a chaplain with Belgian troops exiled in southern England. Here, furthermore, he came across the daily life and worship of the Church of England, as a liturgical church in which he recognised an affinity with his own Catholic Benedictine ethos.

Conversations among Anglican and Catholic contacts continued through the 1930s, illuminated above all by Abbé Paul Couturier, who also visited England, as he was recasting the Church Unity Octave as the Week of Universal Prayer for the Unity of Christians in the charity and truth of Christ that we know today. To his convictions, formed in his friendships across the churches, we owe the ideas of *émulation* and *parallélaboration*, which we nowadays recognise as the exchange of riches described by the Decree on Ecumenism and St John Paul II's 1995 encyclical on ecumenism, *Ut Unum Sint*, and in our mutual 'receptive ecumenical learning' as we are drawn on our way beside one another to union in Christ in his kingdom.

The prayer of Christ that his disciples be one is not only a petition but a promise. For prayer according to his mind manifests in fruit and effect. So, the new Malines Conversations Group asks what is to be the concrete outcome of a hundred years of these friendships and dialogue. How can the impasse of *Apostolicæ Curæ* be unblocked, if we are to advance to unity? Pope Benedict XVI, as Cardinal Jozef Ratzinger, Prefect of the Congregation for the Doctrine of the Faith, famously said that it was not possible to change what Pope Leo XIII had said; yet he observed that the reality of the Anglican ordained ministry is 'never nothing'. Furthermore, from 1931 Old Catholic bishops began to participate in Church of England episcopal consecrations and in 1964 the Second Vatican Council described the Anglican Communion as a beloved sister. Moreover, with the benefit of a fresh theological and historical assessment of the Catholic Church's own teaching, it declared that not a few of the sacred actions of those outside the visible Catholic Church truly engender a life of grace and provide access to the community of salvation. What if this scholarship available to the Fathers of Vatican II had been available to Leo XIII? Can it now provide for a reset of the conditions in which the Malines Conversations of 1921-27 took place?

I am grateful to the Malines Conversations Group for setting out their reasoning from such a range of deeply informed perspectives, to try and address a besetting impediment to Roman Catholic-Anglican unity from a century and a quarter ago. It puts me in mind of the late Metropolitan Kallistos Ware, who saw that when unity comes it will not be down to our efforts but God's miracle. In the meantime, he said, we must be assiduous in dismantling all the obstacles we human beings have established that stand in its way. The case set out by the Group does not encompass developments in the Anglican Communion that have arisen since the agreements of ARCIC I on Faith and Order, such as the ordination of women, different principles on the right to life from conception to death and, more recently, the spiritual care of homosexual couples. But the task that is being asked of us, if we are to expect the miracle of Christ's promise, is to bring, as both St John Paul and Pope Benedict proposed, a reconciliation of mind and memory, for there to be a healing and reconciliation of body too.

This will take into account not only fresh approaches, but comprehend with integrity the faith and doctrine of both our Communions across their living history and tradition. For at the heart of the solution stands the atonement of Christ on the Cross and the central importance to us both of the priesthood's purpose in the oblation of that sacrifice for our salvation in every celebration of the Mass, our Eucharist.

Answers to constant prayers for Anglican-Catholic unity and the absence of a comprehensive solution on this particular obstacle have eluded us for 125 years, despite much progress and ever closer friendship in keeping with those who have gone before us. I thank the Malines Conversations Group for bringing fresh light to bear upon an enduring difficulty and welcome this initiative of Anglican and Catholic friends to reset the terms of engagement in our Churches' dialogue, so that together we may be renewed in giving to the world 'a convincing account of the hope that lies within us.'

# Introduction

# The Malines Conversations Group: Approaching Division and Communion Through the Lens of the Reality of Life and the Truth of Faith

## THOMAS POTT, O.S.B.

At Ecumenical Vespers in the Basilica of Saint Paul Outside the Walls in Rome on January 25, 2014, Pope Francis said, 'Christian unity will not appear suddenly as a miracle but will be given to the followers of Christ step by step as they walk together and work together. To journey together is already to be making unity.' And Archbishop Justin Welby, at the second meeting of the Malines Conversations Group in London in March 2014, said, 'One of the inspirations in conversations involving ecumenical endeavour should be the idea of pilgrimage. In pilgrimage, we are not looking so much at each other, rather we look after each other, we look for the care of each other, but not *at* each other; our focus is on the person who leads us, on Christ himself.'

Walking together, working together, serving together, living together: all expressions of communion of life, of real *lived* life, notwithstanding the separations we may be suffering in the realm of faith, religion, and because of all sorts of historical and cultural circumstances. Pope Francis' and Archbishop Justin's words are at the same time encouraging and discomforting, words of hope and of disenchantment. Because if Christian unity is already in some way what we are living while 'walking together', what then may still be the value of our Eucharistic communion in the Body of Christ in which precisely and ironically we seem to celebrate our dividedness? Walking together but not sharing the Eucharist – at least for members of churches that share the same 'sacramental faith' about the Eucharist – what does that mean, firstly, for the way in which we understand 'unity in the Body of Christ' and, secondly, for the place we allow the truth of our faith to occupy in the reality of our lives? In other words, to what extent is what we celebrate in church relevant to what we experience in life? And to what extent does sacramentality go beyond the rites we perform in church, embracing, inspiring and animating our way of being in the world?

These questions become particularly discomforting when we think of the fact that, as 'divided Christians', we already 'walk' so much together, sharing all the important things of life. But when it comes to sharing the Eucharistic bread, the meal of the Lord which ought to be the source of our unity as the divine gift par excellence, we are thrown back into our comfortable, age-old divisions. Instead of expressing our unity within the One Body into which we are baptized by the force of the same Holy Spirit, our sharing of life uses a language other than our faith. Our Eucharist, hence, is reduced to being not much more than a pious exercise.

Sacramentality, in this broad sense of the reality of life and the truth of faith, has been one of the core drivers of the Malines Conversations Group from its beginning in 2013. It is interesting to note that the first meeting of the Group took place in the same week in which Pope Francis and Archbishop Justin Welby were installed in their respective sees.

Three particular events or ideas inspired the foundation of the Group.

1  At the celebration of the fiftieth anniversary of the Pontifical Council for Promoting Christian Unity, on 17 November 2010, Archbishop Rowan Williams urged the Roman Catholic Church to help the other churches reflect on why it is that in so many churches, the Eucharist is not experienced as the obvious centre of Christian life. This, of course, may be true for many Christian communities. But it applies most certainly to the Roman Catholic Church, for which the Eucharist has always remained central in its theological thinking, albeit much less in the life of the 'common faithful'. In a similar sense, the concept of communion is also often understood in a superficial way: we will think of 'my communion with Christ' rather than 'my communion with the others in Christ.' Nevertheless, this exactly is the meaning of communion – *communio sanctorum* – to which St Paul refers in his First Letter to the Corinthians, when he states: 'When you come

together to eat [the Supper of the Lord], wait for one another. ... About the other things I will give instructions when I come.'[1]

2  Another inspiration came from the Annual National Service for Seafarers at St Paul's Cathedral, London, where I happened to be on Wednesday 12 October 2011. I was struck by the texts of readings and hymns, in which the sea and its dangers were presented as symbols of human life, the life we essentially share with all other people. I wondered to what extent the Church is a celebration of this sharing of life, rather than the symbol of our divisions. And what does liturgy mean in all this? My thoughts – my *memory* – went to a small seafarers chapel on the Belgian coast in Knokke. The celebration at St Paul's Cathedral didn't seem so different from what is celebrated on a simple and daily basis in that chapel. Because, in essence, it is all about life, faith, hope and love, of which the sea, the water, the winds and our relationship to them, are a mighty common – indeed 'ecumenical' – symbol. Here we find ourselves essentially at the level of 'memory', the core dynamics of what constitutes liturgy.

3   The third inspiration came from the solemn celebration of the Feast of Ss Peter and Paul in St Peter's Basilica, Rome, on 29 June 2012. Following his visit to Westminster Abbey in 2010, Pope Benedict XVI invited the Choir of Westminster Abbey to sing alongside the Sistine Chapel Choir at the Papal Mass, the first such invitation to a non-Catholic choir. This type of ecumenical event seems to testify to the good relations between our churches, as they are the result of a sincere ecumenical commitment to walk, sing and pray together. But I couldn't help wondering what the participants in the original Malines Conversations (1921-1926) would have thought about this event, given that the prospective of restoring Eucharistic communion between our churches is not even on the table.

Together, these prompts led us to take up the inspiration of the Malines Conversations. Just as the first Conversations were founded on the genuine bonds of friendship between Lord Halifax, Abbé Portal and Cardinal Mercier, the Malines Conversations Group sees itself as a group of friends, bound together by the sincere conviction that unity is in our midst, if only we are

---

1   1 Cor 11: 33-34

capable of welcoming and deepening it. Can conversations about the real life of our churches and their members – and about all that binds them together in life, love, faith and hope – give us an indication of how to overcome the ecclesiological, canonical and theological impasse that our churches face on the road to unity among Christ's disciples?

# WORKING METHOD

Since 2013, the Malines Conversations Group has been gathering annually, always in spring, alternately at Anglican and Roman Catholic venues. During the pandemic of COVID-19 (2020 — 2021), physical gatherings were replaced by a couple of Zoom meetings which proved to be very productive. It was initially decided to have not more than fourteen members, seven on each side, in order to be able to sit around one table. Today, however, the group has eighteen members. Moreover, since 2015, a number of guests have been invited to each meeting. The meetings consist of presentations, by members or guests, and discussions, all of which are recorded and edited, so as not to lose track of the work done and to help further reflection.

Liturgy and sacramental theology have been a central focus of the Group since its beginning. This explains why the Group is made up of a larger number of liturgical theologians than might be expected from an ecumenical group dedicated to theological study. However, the presence of moral and biblical theologians, church historians, ecclesiologists and ecumenical theologians among its founding members shows that the members of the Group are convinced of the importance of multi-disciplinarity as a way to realistically move forward.

Since the outset, the Group has enjoyed the patronage of former Archbishop Rowan Williams and Cardinal Godfried Daneels (†2019), and at the encouragement of Cardinal Kurt Koch, Prefect of the Dicastery for Promoting Christian Unity, has sought to maintain close contact with the official dialogue commissions and our respective ecumenical institutions of both communions. Nevertheless, the Malines Conversation Group is independent of any official body or institution. Indeed, an essential element is its informality. Furthermore, the Group can decide its own agenda, and has thus discussed issues which can less easily be taken into consideration by the official dialogue commissions. One of these issues is what may be called the 'elephant in the room' of Anglican-Roman Catholic theological dialogue: the Roman Catholic non-recognition of the validity of Anglican orders as decreed in Leo XIII's bull *Apostolicæ Curæ*. In fact, with the encouragement of members of the official dialogues, the question of Anglican Orders has become a central component of our conversations approached from a variety of angles, including the change to the context of this question arising with the ordination of women.

# THEMATICAL EVOLUTION

At the first meeting (Chevetogne, Mechelen and Leuven, 2013), the discussions focused on cultural, social, religious and liturgical differences from the original Conversations in Malines to the present day. We also began to consider the question of the 'universal anthropological dimension' of the liturgy as a reality that goes beyond the practical ordo and the specific praying assembly. In Canterbury (2014), at the second meeting, the programme was structured around the idea of '*uni non absorbé*', the complexity of the concept of 'memory', and communion as a graded reality. This led to the third meeting in Boston (2015), devoted to exploring the concept of sacramentality as something in which the reality of life and the truth of faith embrace each other – *should* embrace each other – and which, in the real life of our Churches, is articulated in multiple ways. The Boston meeting resulted in the identification of four points of focus which have helped to determine the themes of future meetings: (1) a re-reading of the narrative of what happened in 1896, taking account of *Apostolicae Curae* in its own terms, and an awareness of the gap between the debate itself and its outcomes; (2) a re-reading of the narrative of the last fifty years which have seen an intensification of relations and significant theological dialogue (ARCIC) – particularly important as the theological and linguistic categories of *Apostolicae Curae* are ill-suited to deal with the present situation; (3) re-thinking apostolic succession from the perspective of liturgical practice and questioning the gap between sacramental practices, theological categories and reality; and (4) finding strategies to confine a document to history, assessing its *raison d'être* in historical contextuality, in relation to its relative canonical character. Thus, from the theme of sacramentality, the Group moved on to explore the narrative of the last fifty years of relations between the Anglican Communion and the Roman Catholic Church, with a special focus on the narrative of the persistent heritage of *Apostolicæ Curæ* (fourth meeting, Rome, 2016). Careful sacramentological analyses of the development of the rites of ordinations over the last century in both our churches, alongside rigorous biblical and patristic hermeneutical examinations were intended to find new ways of reading and understanding the reality of life and the truth of faith within this broad topic.

At our meeting in Rome, Cardinal Coccopalmerio underlined the importance of the exchange of gifts – for example, pectoral crosses given by the Pope to Anglican bishops – and the meaning these gifts disclose in a 'mysterious – and thus "sacramental" – way'. With this kind of gesture, the Catholic Church already intuits, recognizes 'a reality'. Interestingly, Cardinal Coccopalmerio preferred the word 'reality' to 'validity', which is a practical application of what we came to call under-tunnelling: when it is impossible to face a problem head-on or by going over it, one attempts to dig a passage underneath. The concept of 'validity' tends to enclose the event, the living account, in a 'sanctuary' of canon law and doctrine. The notion of 'reality', on the other hand, stimulates a living narrative which can begin to breathe organically and inhale the air of our times with living lungs. According to the Cardinal, liturgical research was needed to frame the concept of 'validity'. He recommended that the group do its homework in this area. This strongly guided the work of the subsequent meetings.

From the fifth (Cambridge, 2017), to the seventh meetings (York, 2018), several themes became central, all of which have been approached as much as possible from a soteriological-sacramentological perspective rather than from a canonical-ecclesiological point of view: questions of gender, the evolution of moral teaching form *Humanae Vitae* (1968) to *Amoris Laetitia* (2016), challenges regarding 'reform of mentality' and 'ministry and order' between canon law and sacramentality. In all these questions, there are profound wounds that must be healed, offended and violated memories that must be purified, and lots of mentalities that must be reformed.

During those years, the Group took on three concrete tasks: the publication of this book, *Malines: Continuing the Conversations*, intended to present the group's work and vision; preparation to mark the commemoration of the centenary of the start of the Malines conversations (1921-2021; postponed to 2025 because of the pandemic); and the drafting of a document on the theological, ecclesiological, pastoral and hermeneutical impasse resulting from the Catholic Church's clinging to Leo XIII's bull *Apostolicae Curae* as 'definitive teaching' on Anglican ordained ministry.[2]

With this book, the Malines Conversations Group intends to give an insight into the last ten years' work, albeit in a more evocative than recapitulative way. The first three parts reflect the threads of thought and attention that have

---

2 Congregation for the Doctrine of the Faith, 'Doctrinal Commentary on the Concluding Formula of the *Professio fidei*, n. 11.' https://www.vatican.va/roman_curia/congregations/cfaith/documents/rc_con_cfaith_doc_1998_professio-fidei_en.html

Part I

# THE BACKGROUND: PRINCIPLES AND METHOD

# Cardinal Godfried Danneels († 2019)

Real ecumenism requires a common faith experience. That experience is based primarily on common prayer. It is not simply gathering and being in some place together. It is a common search for the transcendent experience of God and the invisible world. It is a common 'experience' of God Incarnate in a world that puts its confidence primarily in empirical research, engineering, rationality, a world that glorifies the senses. The Churches are bearers of a faith perspective that sees much farther than the eyes of the body. The Churches are God's 'crown land', a place where one hears and heeds the call: 'Repent.' Create a place in the world where one turns away from evil and focuses on the good.

Cardinal Godfried Daneels (†2019)

MCG II, 18

# Chapter 1

# The Malines Conversations:
# Re-Opening the Path to Unity

## NICHOLAS SAGOVSKY

The Malines Conversations (1921-6) represented an extraordinary initiative that proved both prescient and, in the short term, unsuccessful. It was prescient because in four short meetings of 'friends' the key theological points at issue between Anglicans and Roman Catholics were identified and, in a preliminary way, addressed. It was, in the short term, unsuccessful because the mere fact that ten men from non-representative sub-groups within the two communions were meeting, with a measure of encouragement from their respective authorities, could only ever be a bridge-building exercise. Once it became public knowledge, it raised so much hostility, especially amongst English Catholics, that the conversations had to be brought to an end and church leaders on both sides quickly distanced themselves from what had taken place. Nevertheless, a channel of meeting and exchange had been established; the path to unity had been re-opened.

## THE FIRST CONVERSATION

The Malines Conversations began in the drawing room of Cardinal Mercier of Malines on December 6, 1921. The Roman Catholic group consisted of Cardinal Mercier, Abbé Portal and Mgr van Roey, Vicar General to Mercier. The Anglican group consisted of Lord Halifax, Armitage Robinson, Dean of Wells, and Walter Frere, Superior of the Community of the Resurrection at Mirfield. Twenty-five years earlier, Halifax and Portal, who were personal friends, had worked closely, but with a conspicuous lack of success, for the recognition of

Anglican orders.[1] Encouraged by Frere, who saw an opportunity in the Lambeth Declaration of 1920,[2] they were instrumental in bringing a wider group of 'friends' together with the much-respected Cardinal.

Halifax had prepared a memorandum as a basis for discussion.[3] Having been translated into French, it was read aloud by Cardinal Mercier. Halifax covered the necessity of baptism for membership of the Church, the possibility of interpreting the Thirty-Nine Articles in a way that did not conflict with the decrees of the Council of Trent (for which he quoted the commentary by Bishop Forbes of Brechin on the Thirty-Nine Articles[4]), and, with particular reference to the (first) Vatican Council, the conditions under which, in the Catholic Church, a truth is defined as an article of faith. Discussion then ranged over the sacraments, especially the eucharist, extreme unction and confession, the definition of dogma and the exercise of episcopal jurisdiction in the Catholic Church. On the second day, the Appeal of the Anglican Bishops at the Lambeth Conference of 1920 was read paragraph by paragraph and discussed.[5]

---

1   For the narrative, see Viscount Halifax, *Leo XIII and Anglican Orders* (London: Longmans, Green and Co. 1912); J. J. Hughes *Absolutely Null and Utterly Void* (London: Sheed and Ward 1968). See also G. H. Tavard's creative *A Review of Anglican Orders: The Problem and the Solution* (Collegeville: Liturgical Press 1990); R.W. Franklin ed., *Anglican Orders, Essays on the Centenary of* Apostolicae Curae (London: Mowbray 1996); Christopher Hill and Edward Yarnold SJ, *Anglican Orders, The Documents in the Debate* (Norwich: Canterbury Press 1997).

2   The Bishops of the Anglican Communion, gathered at the Lambeth Conference in 1920, issued an 'Appeal to all Christian People' in which they set out minimum conditions for Christian unity. They did not make episcopacy an absolute precondition for unity, saying only that, '[I]f the authorities of other Communions should so desire, we are persuaded that, terms of union having been otherwise satisfactorily adjusted, bishops and clergy of our Communion would willingly accept from these authorities a form of commission or recognition which would commend our ministry to their congregations, as having its place in the one family life.' (VIII) This was clearly not drafted with Anglican-Catholic reunion in mind, and certainly not as a means of overcoming the problem of the condemnation of Anglican Orders. Frere, in particular, however, saw its relevance for the Malines Conversations. In that context, the question of the 'form of commission or recognition' required of Anglican clergy to be once more in communion with the Church of Rome was raised sharply, together with that of the recognition of the fruitfulness of Anglican ministry.

3   The text of the Memorandum is in Lord Halifax ed, *The Conversations at Malines, 1921-1925* (London: Philip Allan 1930), pp. 71-78. 'Halifax' below refers to this collection. Walter Frere (*Recollections of Malines*, London: Centenary Press 1935) notes that what Halifax gives here is a draft of his memorandum which was subsequently modified. For corrected extracts from the modified text, see Frere, 14-19. Sources for the topics discussed in the first conversation include the '*Compte Rendu*' signed by the Secretaries, Portal and Frere (Halifax, pp. 9-26); 'The Conversations at Malines 1921-1925: The Anglican Statement (July 1927)' in A. Denaux and J. Dick eds, *From Malines to ARCIC, The Malines Conversations Commemorated*, Bibliotheca Ephemeridium Theologicarum Lovaniensium CXXX (Leuven: Leuven University Press 1997), pp. 47-64; also 'The Catholic Statement', which is to be found in Halifax, pp. 291-306 and in Denaux and Dick, pp. 65-74. Both Statements were first published in *The Conversations at Malines 1921-1925; Les Conversations de Malines 1921-1925* (London: Humphrey Milford 1928).

4   A.P. Forbes, *An Explanation of the Thirty-nine Articles; with an epistle dedicatory to the Rev. E. B. Pusey, D.D.*, 2 vols (Oxford: Parker 1867, 1868).

5   Significantly, the text of the Appeal to all Christian People forms Annexe 1 of Halifax, pp. 65-70.

This led to discussion of what, after the condemnation of Anglican Orders as 'absolutely null and utterly void' in 1896, might be a possible way forward towards corporate reconciliation. On the third day, the minutes (*Compte Rendu*) of the meeting were agreed. Writing to Cardinal Mercier after the meeting, Armitage Robinson again underlined the link between the Lambeth Appeal and this new venture: 'Our conversations with Your Eminence ... will I believe have done much to inform you as to the true position of those who seek an approach and an understanding on the basis of the Lambeth Appeal.'[6]

# THE SECOND CONVERSATION

The second conversation took place on March 14-15, 1923.[7] For this meeting, following the approach of the Lambeth Appeal, the Anglicans had prepared a short memorandum in which they requested that the conversation now be focused not so much on doctrinal issues but on practical questions which would arise if and when there was 'a reasonable measure of agreement on doctrinal matters'.[8] The nature and unity of the Anglican Communion was discussed, together with the jurisdiction of the Pope. Was it possible in principle to secure the right of the Pope to intervene in local dioceses but also to secure the freedom currently enjoyed by Anglican dioceses? At this point, the delicate issue of Anglican orders was discussed. Robinson argued forcibly that the question ought to be examined afresh. He maintained that the Catholic Church had done Anglicans 'a cruel wrong' in rejecting their orders, that 'they would have to repent of it', and that they should, 'at the least say that [Anglican orders] were only somewhat doubtful, not null and void.'[9] There was then a discussion of the 'form of commission or recognition' that would be required by the Roman Catholic authorities if Anglican clergy were to be recognized by Rome. When the Anglicans asserted that, were the Churches to be reconciled, certain aspects of Anglican practice – the use of the vernacular in English rite liturgies, communion in both kinds, and the right of the clergy to marry – must be retained, the Catholics responded that there was precedent for all three

---

6   Letter from Armitage Robinson to Cardinal Mercier, 17 December 1921, quoted from Archdiocese of Malines Archive by Bernard Barlow, *'A brother knocking at the door'*, *The Malines Conversations 1921-1925* (Norwich: Canterbury Press 1996), p. 72.

7   See *'Compte Rendu'*, Halifax, pp. 27-40.

8   See Halifax, pp. 79-82. The Lambeth Appeal had proposed that *'terms of union having been otherwise satisfactorily adjusted*, bishops and clergy of our Communion would willingly accept from [the authorities of other Christian communions] a form of commission or recognition which would commend our ministry to their congregations, as having its place in the one family life'.

9   See Barlow, p. 98 (based on Armitage Robinson Papers, Westminster Abbey [DAR/02/07/008]).

amongst the Uniate Churches of the East. However, the Cardinal thought that Rome, whilst likely to accept the marriage of those already ordained at the time of any reunion, was unlikely to accept the marriage of clergy ordained thereafter. At the conclusion of the meeting a statement was agreed which was in effect a first sketch of a plan for corporate reunion.[10] It was the germ of the paper prepared by Dom Lambert Beauduin and read by Cardinal Mercier at the fourth conversation.

# THE THIRD CONVERSATION

The third meeting, which took place on November 7-8, 1923, focused on the primacy of the Bishop of Rome.[11] Both groups were enlarged to include a further two distinguished scholars: amongst the Anglicans, Charles Gore, former Bishop of Oxford, and Dr Kidd, Warden of Keble College, Oxford, and amongst the Catholics, Mgr Batiffol, Canon of Notre-Dame, Paris and M. Hemmer of the Institut Catholique, Paris. A paper on 'The Position of Peter in the Primitive Church: A Summary of the New Testament Evidence' had been prepared by Robinson.[12] After discussion, Battifol presented a response.[13] It was then agreed that each group would present a short written statement. Robinson summarised his position by saying, 'There is, so far as I am able to judge the evidence, no trace in the New Testament of a jurisdiction of St. Peter over other Apostles, or over churches founded by them.'[14] For the Catholics, Hemmer appealed to the Vatican Council which 'defines as of the Catholic Faith the primacy of universal jurisdiction conferred on Peter, grounding itself on the two texts *Tu es Petrus* and *Pasce oves*'.[15] A paper by Kidd entitled, 'The Petrine Texts as Employed to AD 461' was also presented.[16] Battifol replied.[17] After this it was, according to the Anglican Statement, 'generally agreed' that

---

10 See Halifax, pp. 83-88 (French); Barlow, pp. 221-5 (English). The preamble of this statement makes clear the initial impetus given by the Lambeth Declaration: Halifax, in approaching Cardinal Mercier and asking whether he would be disposed to receive 'some of his friends, members of the Anglican Church like himself and desireous [*sic*] like he, to work for the coming together of the Anglican Church and the Roman Catholic Church', had said, 'The moment was appropriate ... because 250 Anglican bishops, meeting in conference at the palace of Lambeth, had expressed in a very clear and explicit way their lively desire to see realised the catholic unity of Christianity.'

11 See '*Compte Rendu*', Halifax, pp. 41-50.

12 See Halifax, pp. 89-102.

13 See Halifax, pp. 103-122.

14 Halifax, p. 100; Denaux and Dick, 'The Anglican Statement', p. 56.

15 'The Anglican Statement', p. 58.

16 See Halifax, pp. 123-33.

17 See Halifax, pp. 135-49.

Kidd's conclusion could be slightly modified to produce five basic points of agreement.[18] Kidd also gave a paper on, 'To what extent was the papal authority repudiated at the Reformation in England?' but this was little discussed.[19]

# THE FOURTH CONVERSATION

The fourth conversation took place on May 19-20, 1925.[20] It was intended to focus on the relation between episcopacy and the papacy. Mgr van Roey had written a paper on 'The Episcopacy and the Papacy from a theological viewpoint'.[21] This had been circulated before the meeting. It led to a thorough discussion which finished with a review of the conditions for the Pope making an infallible pronouncement. The afternoon was given to the reading of a lengthy paper by Hemmer on 'Relations between the Pope and the Bishops from an historical viewpoint'.[22] The following morning Mercier surprised the participants by reading the paper which he had commissioned from 'a canonist' on 'L'Eglise Anglicane Unie non Absorbée.'[23] The paper, in fact by Lambert Beaudu-in, sketched, without using the word, a possible 'uniate' status for Anglicans in a reunited Church, which would accord patriarchal dignity to the Archbishop of Canterbury by the symbolic gift of the *pallium* from the Pope and would allow to Anglicans their own corpus of canon law, together with their own rites and structures. The boldness of the proposals all but reduced the group to silence, apart from one comment by Gore to the effect that any proposal along these lines must apply to the whole Anglican Communion. In the af-

---

18 For the 'points of agreement' (in English), see the *Compte Rendu*, signed by Frere and Hemmer (Halifax, p. 47). They are also recorded *verbatim* in The Anglican Statement (Denaux and Dick, p. 58) and (in French) in slightly differing form in the Catholic Statement (Denaux and Dick, p. 72). The points (as recorded by the Anglicans) were: 1. That the Roman Church was founded and built by St. Peter and St. Paul, according to St. Irenaeus. 2. That the Roman See is the only historically known Apostolic See of the West. 3. That the Bishop of Rome is, as Augustine said of Pope Innocent I, president of the Western Church. 4. That he has primacy among all the Bishops of Christendom; so that, without communion with him, there is in fact no prospect of a reunited Christendom. 5. That to the Roman See the churches of the English owe their Christianity through 'Gregory our Father … who sent us baptism'. This sketch of a 'joint agreed statement' is the harbinger of many post-Vatican II joint agreed statements, both bi-lateral and multi-lateral, from The Anglican-Roman Catholic International Commission (ARCIC) and other similar bodies. Point 5 is not above dispute, owing to Northumbrian Christianity, which came to the northern Angles not as a result of Gregory's mission (597) but from Ireland, via Iona, with the arrival of Aidan (635).
19 See Halifax, pp. 151-58. In his Prefatory Note to *The Roman Primacy to AD 461* (London: SPCK 1936), Kidd wrote, 'We never got face to face with the question of a primacy of jurisdiction at Malines. But it has been constantly in my mind ever since.'
20 See '*Compte Rendu*', Halifax, pp. 51-63.
21 See Halifax, pp. 159-74. For Kidd's Memorandum in reply, see Halifax, pp. 175-85.
22 See Halifax, pp. 187-241.
23 French text, Halifax, pp. 241-61; English text, Denaux and Dick, pp. 35-46.

ternoon, Gore himself read a paper on unity and diversity entitled '*Concedit* [Cyprianus] *salvo iure communionis ... diversum sentire*' which turned on a distinction between 'fundamental doctrines' (essentially those of the Vincentian Canon: 'what has been believed everywhere, always, and by all') and those (such as transubstantiation, the Immaculate Conception and Papal Infallibility) which were the fruit of induction by the Church but were nevertheless taught as *de fide*.[24] Gore asked whether, as a precondition for corporate reconciliation with the Orthodox Communion and the Anglican Communion, Rome might require acceptance only of those articles embraced by the Vincentian Canon. He was answered by Batiffol, who deployed Newman's theory of the development of doctrine to reject Gore's use of the Vincentian Canon, saying that 'The Church has never considered definitions of faith as provisional, but as revealed truths, and obligatory.[25] The Holy See cannot accept that some dogmas be accepted while others are denied.'[26] In the afternoon, Batiffol concluded his presentation and in the evening the Anglicans presented a brief summary of the points concerning the relation of the Pope and the bishops with which they agreed.[27]

# THE FIFTH MEETING

A fifth and final meeting took place on 11-12 October 1926. Cardinal Mercier had died in January and Portal in June. Van Roey, who had been appointed Archbishop of Malines, presided. The aim was merely to agree on two reports of the previous four meetings, the Catholic report concentrating in particular on the points of agreement, the Anglican statement bringing out the con-

---

24 Gore's paper is not in 'Halifax', but is given as Addendum VII in Frere, *Recollections*, pp. 110-19. Gore says he wishes 'to put in a plea for the widest possible toleration of differences between churches, both in doctrine and practice, on the basis of agreement in the necessary articles of Catholic communion.' (p. 113) The '*Diversum sentire*' of Cyprian, as he expounds it, might well be translated as (the attaining of) 'differentiated consensus'. For Gore, who in this claims the authority of Cyprian, an element of diversity ('*diversum sentire*') is bound to underly any verbal agreement. Y. Congar takes up Gore's argument in his important article 'Agreement on "Fundamental Articles" or on the Positions of the Early Church' in *Diversity and Communion* (London: SCM 1984), pp. 107-25. With reference to Gore's use of Cyprian (challenged by Batiffol in Halifax, pp. 263-87), he writes: 'The very idea of diversities compatible with communion, or of the necessary but sufficient minimum of common doctrine to be held in common if unity is to be preserved, is in fact the object of all my research' (p. 118).

25 See Halifax, pp. 263-87.

26 Barlow, p. 155. What Batiffol denied outright was precisely what the Second Vatican Council addressed by speaking of a '*hierarchy* of truths'.

27 See Halifax pp. 289-90.

tinuing points of disagreement.[28] Halifax was desperate to see these reports published as soon as possible but there was nervousness on both sides: on the Anglican, because Archbishop Davidson was coping with virulent attacks on the proposed text of a revised *Book of Common Prayer* from those who would seize on any perceived concessions to Rome at Malines; on the Catholic because of continuing hostility from Cardinal Bourne and other like-minded English Catholics who advocated an approach to unity through individual conversion and who increasingly had the ear of the Pope Pius XI. Not until the proposed revision of the *Book of Common Prayer* had been rejected by Parliament, were the reports published – without consulting any of the participants or the church authorities – on the personal initiative of Halifax.[29]

# THE MALINES CONVERSATIONS: THE LEGACY

The Malines Conversations, which focused on corporate reunion not individual conversion, were extraordinarily prescient. The little group of 'friends' identified the key ecclesiological and doctrinal points that were at issue between their communions, laying the ground for the work of the Anglican-Roman Catholic International Commission (ARCIC) which has gone over much of the same ground with new, post-Vatican II resources, pointing ways forward, but not yet shifting the log-jam. The key doctrinal and ecclesiological issues are three:

1. The exercise of authority by the Bishop of Rome. The nub of this, as clearly identified at Malines, is the relation between the jurisdiction of the Bishop of Rome and the jurisdiction of all the bishops, both individually and collegially.
2. The identification of new doctrines as '*de fide*', to be held by all the faithful. Anglicans have been troubled in particular by the definitions of the Immaculate Conception of Mary (1854), Papal Infallibility (1870) and, after the Malines Conversations, the Bodily Assumption of Mary (1950).

---

28  See G.K.A. Bell, *Randall Davidson, Archbishop of Canterbury* (London: Oxford University Press 1952), p. 1300. Davidson had suggested to Cardinal Mercier that there be one, or perhaps two, statements (one Anglican, one Catholic), 'both as to the matters on which misunderstandings may have been removed, and as to the points which remain obdurately outstanding as unremoved obstructions' (*Davidson*, p. 1295). Mercier was doubtful about publishing 'negative conclusions' (hence, the emphasis of the Catholic report on points of agreement), but Davidson's approach can clearly be seen in the Statements of ARCIC, particularly those on Authority.

29  See Barlow, pp. 171-77. Halifax also published a brief booklet, *Notes on the Conversations at Malines, 1921-1925, Points of Agreement* (London: Mowbray 1928).

For the Orthodox, the definition of Transubstantiation (1215) presents a similar difficulty.

3 The condemnation of Anglican orders as 'absolutely null and utterly void' (1896).[30]

In addition, as perhaps the most creative legacy of the Malines Conversations, Lambert Beauduin anonymously re-imagined the path to unity by sketching a possible 'uniate' status for Anglicans, which has intrigued and captivated ecumenists ever since.

# CONCLUSION: THE MALINES CONVERSATIONS, THE MALINES CONVERSATIONS GROUP AND THE PATH TO UNITY

One aspect of the work of the Malines Conversations Group has been to try to understand better what took place in the Malines Conversations themselves. After nearly a hundred years, we see them as prescient if not immediately successful, because we look at them through the lens of Vatican II and the rich bilateral and multi-lateral ecumenical conversations of the last fifty years. We can see how the work of ARCIC is foreshadowed in the Malines Conversations of a previous generation. The Malines Conversations were an astonishing bridge-building exercise at a time when such bridges did not exist.

What is clearer to us, and was less clear to the participants in the Malines Conversations, is that agreed forms of words can be achieved in ecumenical conversations, but this is not the end of the ecumenical matter. Agreed forms of words have to be received and owned by the official and unofficial bodies of the communions to which the signatories belong: they have to be 'good enough' to be acceptable to both parties. The processes of reception demand something more like a continuing conversation than a once-for-all decision. That conversation will draw on all sorts of tacit factors which condition the ongoing interaction. It is not only in the field of explicit Christian doctrine that Anglicans and Catholics share a great deal, but also in the field of 'natural theology' or 'theological anthropology'. Together, we inhabit a world where the advance of secularization, the encounter with world religions, diverse understandings of morality, gender and sexuality, globalization, inequality, and

---

30 ARCIC has never formally considered this question, though, as George Tavard reports (*A Review of Anglican Orders*, p. 7), there was some informal discussion by ARCIC I.

environmental degradation, together with the aftermath of the global Covid-19 pandemic, present challenges which we face in common. Hopefully, as we uncover 'tacit' convergence in areas such as Christian anthropology, natural theology, and ethics we can together return to the issues identified in the original Malines Conversations, understanding them better, because we better understand the whole approach of the other party.

There are, of course, new challenges. Perhaps the most formidable is the ordination of women as deacons, priests, and bishops in the Anglican Communion. It is hard to see what kind of institutional unity will be possible while Canterbury and Rome take opposite lines on this question. However, as the years of ecumenical dialogue since Vatican II have shown, there is much that is shared in our understanding of what it is to be a deacon, a priest, or a bishop. The commissioning of nineteen pairs of bishops, Anglican and Roman Catholic, to walk and to work together, in the church of San Gregorio al Celio, Rome would not have been possible without a high degree of mutual trust at an institutional level.[31] A great deal of mutual learning about what it is to be Church has taken place – for instance, in the context of the current exploration of synodality within the Roman Catholic Church.[32]

One key lesson the Malines Conversations have to teach is that, in our debates on controversial doctrinal issues, we need not seek *identity of meaning* but rather *sufficient* mutual understanding to *imagine* in a new way the path towards unity. The participants in the Malines Conversations had high hopes of institutional reconciliation which, a hundred years later, seems hardly less challenging as a goal. In that sense, their conversations were unsuccessful. However, the mere fact that such conversations had taken place in such a positive spirit of friendship and mutual respect, and with such a strong vision of unity, was an extraordinary achievement. After nearly four hundred years of institutional separation, the participants in the Malines Conversations had done nothing less than to re-open the path to unity – along which the members of the Malines Conversations Group, together with many other Anglicans and Catholics, continue to travel as sisters and brothers in Christ.

---

31 The Commissioning by Pope Francis and Archbishop Justin Welby took place at a Solemn Vespers celebrating the fiftieth anniversary of the meeting of Pope Paul VI and Archbishop Michael Ramsey (1966), shortly after the closure of the Second Vatican Council, which led to the creation of the Anglican-Roman Catholic International Commission (ARCIC, 1970) and the International Anglican-Roman Catholic Commission for Unity and Mission (IARCCUM, 2001).

32 There is a wealth of information available about Synod 2021–2024 (the three-year 'Synod about Synodality') at https://www.synod.va/. For the ecumenical dimension, see especially the joint letter of 28 October 2021, sent out by Cardinal Kurt Koch, President of the Pontifical Council for Promoting Christian Unity, and Cardinal Mario Grech, General Secretary of the Synod of Bishops, in which they stressed that, 'as ecumenism can be understood as an "exchange of gifts", one of the gifts Catholics can receive from the other Christians is precisely their experience and understanding of synodality'. The participants in the Malines Conversations would have been astonished and delighted!

# Clare Watkins

There is a basic difficulty in this mismatch of experience and dogma, symptomatic of our inability to practice and articulate discernment in relation to present experience. Yet, as we know from Pope Francis: 'Realities are more important than ideas' (*Evangelii Gaudium*, 233), as ideas are at the service of praxis (Ibid., 232). What we need, I suggest, is a way of understanding the experiences of ministry which allows memory to exercise its task of discerning the realities – experienced as well as conceptual – of which our theology tries to speak.

Clare Watkins
MCG IV, 264

A pneumatological perspective can also alert us to that expansivity of grace, the radical freedom and worldliness of the action of the Spirit, which is so much a renewing feature of Vatican II's ecclesiology. Such an unbounded notion of grace, which resists too defined and structured containment of our subject, draws our Churches into conversations of discernment rather than quasi-legalistic judgement. Potentially this liberates our ecumenical conversations from a preoccupation with archaeological type approaches to our stories, where our history is told and re-told in hope of seeing the old statements in a new light (important as this has been and can still be); and brings us into a properly theological encounter with experience, and its demand for careful discernment.

Clare Watkins
MCG IV, 269

# Chapter 2

# Revisiting Biblical Narratives: How can Scripture Inspire Us for Work and Life Today?

CYRILLE VAEL, O.S.B.

## 'IN TRANSFER': HENCEFORTH OUR NEW LIFE CONDITION

Change, transformation and evolution are dynamics that are not only inherent to life, but which even constitute life. But their impact on the contemporary scene of everyday life takes such intense forms that it is essential to acknowledge the deconstruction of the static patterns and structures of the culture inherited from our societies. This means the collapse of any certainty about the nature of society itself and its institutions.[1] Many studies and analyses have already been dedicated to this question, but most of them are limited to a descriptive study of the changes and come to reductive conclusions and judgments predominantly devoid of realistic interesting future perspectives. Alternatively, their prospects are merely constructed with the same cultural parameters that necessitated precisely this global cultural shift.

We could label our current culture as 'Being in Transfer: Our New Life Condition.'[2] But shouldn't we start focusing on the nature of the concepts and the changes? What are the mechanisms that lead to that transformation, and why are they being anxiously criticised by many established institutions? By what means can they be rightly understood, integrated or accomplished? What role

---

1   Cf. Ayesh Perera, *Postmodernity in Sociology. Characteristics and Examples in 2023.* (https://simplyso-ciology.com/postmodernism.html)

2   Title of an exhibition on *Contemporary Culture, Art and Science,* by Ars Electronica in Luxembourg, 3 September — 27 November 2022.

can the sciences and the arts play in this process of cultural transformation, and, above all, what role could the age-old tradition of our religions play, particularly in the field of existential and anthropological problems that are urging us to transform ourselves as a society, and that urgently need to be integrated into our consciousness and daily existence.

All media and an infinite range of studies and publications inform us daily about the immense complexity of current human existence. Besides disorienting legitimization crises, the global decline of Western hegemony, the proliferation of intellectual and economic marketplaces, and exponential processes of deconstruction, humanity suddenly appeared to have been plunged into the crippling, isolating pandemic of COVID-19, with the threat that this would not necessarily be a one-off. Indeed, we witness all kinds of cruel wars, increasingly alarming climate change, questions of new kinds of minorities struggling for recognition, the ever-sharpening problem of the issue of energy resources and distribution, the emergence of new economic dynamics and systems, and so on. But the gigantic challenges posed by the unprecedented development of the sciences – which offer humanity a panoply of infinite new possibilities, thanks to the convergence of scientific disciplines such as nanotechnology, biotechnology, information technology and artificial intelligence – and the place of culture and religion in this exponentially growing digital world, are urgent and vital questions. Because, slowly but surely, a fundamentally different anthropological image is emerging that is driving our humanity forward into this transformation. The urgent need not only for serious reflection but also for integration and action inherent in all these new realities, as well as the vital and existential dimension of these changes, oblige us to reconsider our attitude to them, and to reorient our way of 'being present' in the world, which now makes openness, courage, dialogue and collaboration indispensable.

The established institutions that have been the bearers of our political, economic, and diverse cultural systems for hundreds of years do not have strongly supported adequate structures, nor the designated mindset, to process, shape, and integrate into their own evolution the new emerging consciousness, the new insights, the new dynamics that are being born in an ever-increasing number of individuals all over the world. The lack of, or difficulty in, opening up to this transformation, gives birth to the seemingly ever-increasing series of tensions we are currently witnessing between institutions and groups of individuals, and reveals growing polarization. The question is how can we understand these changes not as a provocation, not as a personal or collective violation, nor as a compromise, but rather as a challenge, a quality, a vital force, that drives humanity forward? For we should not forget that the ultimate goal of efforts to overcome innate limitations is human flourishing, and this mission carried out by these changes is based on the deepest and most ancient aspirations of humanity, including Christianity. Can our religions play a role in this transformation process? Certainly not in terms of responsibility or accountability, nor by reductional criticism referring to outgrown anthropological references.

# THE TOPICALITY OF NARRATIVES

What a delightfully unsettling question the European Literature House *Passa Porta in Brussels posed on the occasion of the European Literature Festival:*[3] 'Why is it so important, precisely now, today, to reflect on the necessity of literature and story-telling? … The addition in this question "precisely now" seems to imply a necessity. But which one?'[4] 'Precisely now', which can be understood as 'more than ever', is a familiar way to spice up an assertion with a sense of urgency. This surely points towards society's awareness of the profound global change that is taking place. Such 'urgency' reflects the fundamental question of how to interpret the basic reality of life and the existential need for behaviours and intellectual dispositions which integrate rather than separate. Due to the rapidly accelerating, irreversible changes in our living environment, people are finding it increasingly difficult to deal with 'objective truths'. But does not that 'precisely now' also imply the idea that we can steer those changes in a certain direction as if we would lose something if we did not?[5] But what would we lose?

Taking some time to pore over statistics of some of the most successful movies, one will notice undoubtedly a trend: most of the movies on that list that came out in the last two decades are rooted in the 'fiction genre',[6] where the role of imagination is particularly central. Contemporary people are strongly drawn to literature in which the magical world intersects with everyday reality. It illustrates how individuals today approach the so-called magical and how they appear to seek deeper meaning in life. In modern society, which is governed by rationality, science, and efficiency, individuals appear to transition

---

3  *Creative Writing in Europe.* (https://www.passaporta.be/en/projects/passa-porta-festival).

4  Guy Bourgeois, 'Zin van literatuur,' *Azerty Factor*, 25 February 2016. (https://azertyfactor.be/tekst-lezen/zinvanliteratuur).

5  Cf. ibid.

6  See Gary Smailes, 'Which Book Genre is the Most Popular?', *Bubble Cow*, 10 February 2023. (https://bubblecow.com/blog/popular-book-genre).

comfortably into fictional worlds where all kinds of supernatural, irrational, and peculiar depictions are connected and displayed. In contrast, traditional religions are often passed down and labelled as outdated, backward or unscientific by those considered to have enlightened minds.

Many rather 'conservative' religious tendencies and certain classical psychoanalytic schools point out the danger that imagination leads to infantile wish-fulfilment that keeps people immature, inducing escapism from real life, denying facts, inciting to unlimited imagination, introducing superheroes, legitimizing subcultures, and so on. This view is obviously reinforced by the postmodern awareness that contemporary society is no longer at all clear about what is real and objective.[7] And besides, people today can often become caught up in an obsolete dichotomy of what is subjectivity and what is objectivity, what is imagination and what is reality. However, it is easy to overlook that the monumental scope of these worlds, created around characters and stories, forms a story of their own. Is fiction or storytelling erroneous and misleading by definition? 'Fiction is the lie through which we tell the truth,' remarked Albert Camus, the man who asked us to imagine Sisyphus happy with his fate. Such an arbitration today could result in severe cognitive dissonance. In a culture enchanted with the self, the burden of such responsibility is rarely entertained.[8] However, aren't we all somewhat modern-day Sisyphus, punished by Zeus for our hubris? Yet this might hint at the most useful role of fiction in our age: notably a resurrection of the lost art of reading myths, and listening to storytelling and narratives. Through them, we can contextualize and reflect on our current anxieties and problems, we can gain different perspectives to see truths, challenges and possibilities that we don't notice when we are blinded by too much one-dimensional reality, too much news, too many facts, and too much controversy in our daily real world.[9]

We are all constantly influenced by our own images and by images from our wider environment and culture. It is not just that we think in terms of narrative arcs, but people themselves are made of stories: our lives, our identity (individual or collective paradigms), as well as our professional careers, and even the 24 hour world news, are made of narrative arcs. 'Reality and history make a story not only because they need to be told as stories, but because they contain

---

7   Cf. Hetty Zock, 'Harry Potter en de transitionele ruimte' in Birgit Verstappen (ed.), *Vreemde verhalen, goed nieuws?* (Tilburg: Valkhofpers 2003), pp. 36-53.

8   Cf. Derek Beres, 'This is why reading fiction is as important now as it ever was.' *Education, Skills and Learning. World Economic Forum.* 2018. (https://www.weforum.org/agenda/2018/12)

9   See Henri Philibert-Caillat, L'étranger d'Albert Camus. 2020. (https://libresavoir.org/index.php?title=L'Etranger_d%27Albert_Camus).

events required for the proper understanding of what is happening.'[10] In history, formed by patterns and matters of inevitability, narratives are links in the cause-and-effect chain which connect the premise with the conclusion. If the human need for narratives is not restricted to dramatic conventions but originates from our very sense of self, then the question arises as to whether we should enrol ourselves in them in performance, or should we extricate ourselves from them.[11]

Narratives have the characteristic that they support the function of the human imagination, which lies at the intersection of intuitive and rational thought and action, in what we might think of as the 'research process' of knowledge generation. Our concept of the imagination refers, at least in part, to the ability of individuals to handle images. Thinking in images releases us from the horizontal rational reasoning which tends to dominate our intellectual processes. When we think rationally, solutions come from the thought that comes first in the order of thinking. Through imagination, one can generate new ideas from small information, conceptualise images, designs or abstractions and gain insight into the past or the future. Imagination thus allows us to think creatively towards future. Indeed, 'imagination is the driving force behind human thought, and human civilisation is created by the operation and exercise of the imagination. Current developments in scientific technologies are the best examples of the process leading from the concretisation of human imagination to the demonstration of creativity.'[12] Contemporary sciences investigate the inherent connection between imagination and sense-making by emphasizing the function of imagination in individuals' philosophical development.[13] New disciplines in neuroscienc even point to the necessity of the imagination for humans to creatively engage with reality and experience meaning.[14] They explore how the same part of the human brain that is able to recognise the self is also in charge of imagining the future,[15] through perceiving and inventing narratives.

---

10  Alexandru Panoiu, 'What is 'narrative necessity', and does it apply to worldbuilding?' (https://world-building.meta.stackexchange.com/questions/7281).

11  See Deborah Person, 'The Necessity of Narrative?' in *Exeunt*. 2011. (https://exeuntmagazine.com/features).

12  See Hsiao-Chi Ho, Chia-Chi Wang and Ying-Yao Cheng, 'Analysis of Scientific Imagination Process' *Thinking Skills and Creativity*, 10 (2013), pp. 68-78. (https://doi.org/10.1016/j.tsc.2013.04.003)

13  See Stephen T. Asma, 'The Power of Religious Imagination' *Oxford University Press's Academic Insights for the Thinking World*, 2018 https://blog.oup.com/2018/06/why-we-need-religion-excerpt/

14  Cf. the excellent study of Stephen T. Asma, 'Imagination: A New Foundation for the Science of Mind' *Biological Theory* 17, (2022), pp. 243-249. (https://doi.org/10.1007/s13752-022-00410-4)

15  The prefrontal cortex and its subdivisions including the hippocampus. See Robert Martone, 'How Our Brain Preserves Our Sense of Self' Mind and Brain, *Scientific American* (2021) (https://www.scientificamerican.com/article/How-our-brain-preserves-our-sense-of-self).

Narratives are open to multiple interpretations, and although we all perceive the same characters, events, and actions, our individual understanding can vary significantly. In today's culture, where our minds often shift between fact and 'fiction', we typically need some form of information, either within the text or in a 'paratext', to give us clues as how to interpret the narrative at any given moment. Inspiration can be drawn from the paratexts passed on by others, including philosophers, heroes, politicians, and religious traditions.

Most of our knowledge is stored in our minds and expressed in the form of narratives. Human imagination combines previous experiences in a distinct way to generate thoughts that have new meanings, potentially leading to creative thinking. From everyday life, with all its complex facts, contradictions, problems, and conflicts, humans can design a rich and intelligible discourse based on a transparent set of presuppositions coming from or suggested by transmitted narratives to create a flexible basis through imaginative discourse.[16] This approach considers all relevant aspects and combines them into a coherent, original and new narrative. This results in an opportunity to engage with one's own discourse, as inspired by transmitted narratives, which one may choose to partially or entirely join, or withdraw from. One of the most meaningful features of a narrative is that it prompts humans to think, without prescribing their thoughts.

Moreover, narratives never stand on their own, and it is the prerogative of individuals to determine whether or not to realize them. Thus, narratives always respect human freedom. Consequently, real narratives withhold conclusive judgments or a definitive meaning from the reader or audience, leaving things unresolved and seeking closure. However, this represents a sort of ethical and aesthetic decision as the creators of the narrative have chosen not to offer closure. Imagination is an essential element of the human creative process and recognizing it as such entails acknowledging ourselves as responsible agents and creators. Imagination enables us to envision not only images but also new worlds and futures. Through narratives, one is invited to enter not only the space of the *mundus imaginalis*, but also the hidden world of one's own potentiality as a creator. The implication is that we are responsible for the narrative we present to the world because it goes beyond the mere story. Historical facts inherently have certain interpretations. They never give answers, but they do provide clarification. Being mindful of this necessitates a thorough consideration of the entire narrative.

---

16 See Wolfgang Jonas, 'Design Research Thinking - A Narrative' in *Communication Knowledge. Proceedings of the colloquium 'Communicating (by) Design'* (Brussels: Hogeschool voor Wetenschap en Kunst Brussels & Chalmers University of Technology 2009) p. 66.

Thus, fiction – as referred to by Albert Camus – and narratives should not be considered as inherently 'untrue'. Instead, its accuracy is determined by its intended meaning, rather than by factual accuracy. Moreover, true events and facts require a narrative to become part of history; they cannot be considered stories unless an 'author' shapes them accordingly. Narratives utilize 'reality effects' to incorporate intricate details into their stories, attempting to persuade readers of the authenticity of the events by making them more vivid, concise, credible, and impactful. Facts never 'speak for themselves' but become elements in one's story.[17]

# DISCOVERING TRANSITIONAL SPACE

To return to our question 'How can our religion function in the contemporary culture of "in transfer"?', it is precisely creative thinking, boosted by the cultural and spiritual values expressed and mediated in narratives, that can become a resource for personal belief systems and meaningful cognitive frameworks at the individual level. Having a new potential to assume personal responsibility 'enables the ethical and spiritual regeneration of the wider world, where the ability to relate meaningfully to life and to others remains an ever-present and enduring reality.'[18]

It is from this perspective that the Christian tradition can offer an intermediate space, not a neutral or alternative space, but rather a space in which individuals can experience the complexity and contradictions of the fundamental changes taking place in contemporary culture. The Christian tradition can conceive, through its rituals and sacred scriptures a space for our society as a sort of existential laboratory where various aspects of reality, past, and future can intersect, be experienced, and act together. This would be an existential space that allows individuals, as well as groups, to approach and influence these fundamental changes: a space where traditions, arts, technologies,

---

17  Throughout history, it has been ubiquitously argued that imagination, as the realm of the imaginary, always needs a critical approach in order to replace the imaginations of 'earlier and more ignorant' ages with the truths uncovered by modern science. However, this argument, being reductionist, equates religious imagination with being antithetical to scientific thought and therefore inferior. Such a view is outdated and flawed by contemporary scientific research. Both the scientific and the religious (as part of the humanities) share the use of the imagination in its function of constructing the world and shaping the future. The difference between them is not in their different capacities, but in their different uses of the same capacity. For further analysis of this topic we refer to Jonah A. Koetke, 'The Role of the Imagination in Religion and Science' *Symposium on Undergraduate Research and Creative Expression (SOURCE)* (2018) 754. (https://scholar.valpo.edu/cus/754)

18  See Laura Praglin, 'The Nature of the "In-Between" in D.W. Winnicott's Concept of Transitional Space and in Martin Buber's *das Zwischenmenschliche*', *UNIversitas: Journal of Research, Scholarship and Creative Activity.* 2 no. 6 (2006) (https://scholarworks.uni.edu/universitas/vol2/iss2/6/)

sciences, and so on, meet at the level of transformation, so that people today can open themselves up to new perspectives that could help them to articulate the real questions and make clear choices. This intermediate space could aptly be designated as a 'transitional space'.

This 'in between' space offers the possibility of thinking beyond any number of troublesome binaries inherent to our existential condition: external life and inner reality, the subjective and the objective, social and personal, positioning and agency, reflection and action, construction and reality. Or more eloquently, 'a space where boundaries soften, allowing us to stand at the threshold and prepare to step beyond the confines of "who we were" into "who we are becoming."'[19] Empirical research indicates that reading and listening to narratives creates a transitional space for the human mind, with the capacity to transport the reader from real life to imagination and back to real life, helping the individual in an ongoing process of self-transformation, dealing with mental representations of the person you think you are and the person you want to become. Reading and listening to narratives occurs within this intermediate realm of experience, because when individuals engage in reading or listening to narratives, they belong neither to the world of imagination – evoked by the narrative – nor to the world of shared reality, but rather to a transitional space of experience that takes on characteristics of both worlds. In essence, transitional space emerges from the generation of a 'transitory realm of new possibilities - a fusion of person and message, the product of which is greater than the sum of its parts and which forms the basis of future raising awareness, deeper knowledge, new identity or adequate action.'[20]

The transitional space offers tools to individuals and groups enabling them to transcend the given conditions of daily life by constructing cognitively unique and new creations of normative frameworks. Narratives suggest innovative understandings, new values, wiser focuses that can transcend the classical binary reasoning of many of our inherited religious and paradigmatic power structures, move beyond unfruitful polarisation and open up to renewed, fertile, ways of nurturing meaning.

---

19  See Thomas Axelson, 'Narration, Visualization and Mind. Movies in everyday life as a resource for utopian self-reflection'. *Conference: CMRC, The 7th International Conference on Media, Religion & Culture, Toronto, Canada, 9-13 August 2010.* (https://www.researchgate.net/publication/279489088_Narration_Visualization_and_Mind_Movies_in_everyday_life_as_a_resource_for_utopian_self-reflection) For more interesting analysis, see Thomas Axelson, 'Movies and the Enchanted Mind: Emotional Comprehension and Spiritual Meaning Making among Young Adults in Contemporary Sweden', *Young 25 no. 1 (2017), pp. 8-25.* (https://journals.sagepub.com/doi/epdf/10.1177/1103308816668920).

20  See Alexander Skandalis, 'Transitional space and new forms of value co-creation in online brand communities', *Journal of Business Research, 155A (2023)* (https://www.sciencedirect.com/science/article/pii/S0148296322008578)

# BIBLICAL REASONING: OPENING NEW HORIZONS

From the perspective of Roman Catholic doctrine, it is generally affirmed that a final solution to the recognition of Anglican orders can only be found in the wider context of full communion in faith, sacramental life and shared apostolic vision. Indeed, strategically, ecclesiological arguments certainly surround the issue. But resourcing our theological thinking in biblical narratives is the best way to approach the issue, in a way the members of the Malines Conversation Group have begun to call 'undertunneling.' Biblical reasoning is one way out of theological and ecclesiological dead ends. But the biblical reasoning needed in our context is not meant as an ornamental, pious or meditative exercise, or even as a historical exegesis, but as a discernment of deeper realities and dynamics at work in the vital structures of creation, to which we bind all our logic.

The life experience of many people, as well as the complexity of the surrounding world and culture, show us that our ecclesiological and theological resources have become highly dysfunctional. In this sense, our churches, in their teaching and preaching, have reduced the biblical content to stories. The Bible, however, is not a basket of stories, regardless of how constitutional or useful they may be, but rather a basket of narratives. We must become increasingly aware of this.

Stories have two fundamental attributes: the first is that a story is self-contained, it has a beginning, an evolution and an end, during which a certain reality is solved. The second is that a story is about the storyteller, or about a person, a people, a nation, but they are not about us today; in the best case we are invited to use our imagination to figure out what we might do if we would find ourselves in that context. On the contrary, a narrative is always open-ended; there is always some kind of opportunity on the horizon yet to be achieved, but it is not clear whether it will be achieved at all. Therefore, the resolution of a narrative hinges upon us; it hinges on the solutions we take; how we realize that narrative. A story surely can be inspiring; it can be invitation to imitation. But a narrative is a huge dynamic which is ever-continuing, ever-transforming.

The Bible is one of the most powerful narratives in history. It tells us how we are created, how we fall in sin, how we cut short the passages of life, how throughout the dynamics of revelation a stream of salvation is given to us, even a Saviour. But it is not guaranteed; it is up to us, to the choices we make, to the actions we undertake. Each of our churches itself is one narrative within that narrative. It is the instrument, the channel that catches, bundles, transmits the transforming forces of creation given through that biblical revelation which is still going on. We need to come together, to pray, to study. It requires struggle to realize this opportunity, individually and institutionally. We ought not forget that throughout history, millions of people have given their lives for that narrative. They reveal the power of this narrative to us: the ultimate sacrifice. Hence, our biblical approach is not one of following stories and references about how things should be, how we should reason, a self-justification; but it is a constant call to action, asking us to become aware, to take responsibility and to act now.

The rediscovery of the Bible as a narrative is essential because, in the context of the increasing pressure to perform in people's lives today, the global unmasking of the objective truths of knowledge and the parameters of justification we thought we had about truth and reality are no longer tied to objective structures but have become a linguistic event. We are witnessing a worldwide collapse of the credibility of our classical channels of transmission, characterised by a reduced knowledge and shrinking memory of the deeper senses of the Christian faith. This context, as it were the dark side of a mentality created by the fragmentation of the knowledge we pretend to have of our Christian faith, constitutes a certain cognitive 'obesity' that is becoming increasingly dysfunctional for bringing about the 'eu-angelion'. Rediscovering the Bible as a narrative offers us the opportunity to shift our natural psychological, ecclesiological and theological impasses, both personally and institutionally. Instead of closing ourselves off by increasing our perception of risks and threats and denying our perception of the power of our message, of our mission, the rediscovery of the Bible as a true narrative, functioning as an authentic 'transitional space', opens up ever new possibilities for the development of our true identity, our true memory, which is the transmission of transfiguring forces. This means transmitting life, the true tradition: shifting the focus from the past to the future.

Of course, there are risks involved because the future is unknown, unpredictable and full of challenges. But change and challenge are the inevitable consequence of life. Isn't that what the Bible teaches all the time, that the future is worth fighting for? The Bible teaches us that God's people are always on the move, always committed to the future. This is one of the main characteristics of the Bible: the fact that it is a narrative. We should therefore ask ourselves whether we accept the challenge to purify our memories, which have become 'obese stories,' whether we are able to read the signs of the times and whether we are willing to go beyond the safety of acquired knowledge. The result will also be a widening of our temporal horizons because the focus on the future creates new possibilities for the Church to become a true community with an essential eschatological dimension: for this Christ died and rose again 'according to the Scriptures.' Indeed, the power of the prophetic vision and the presence of the eschatological reality are both utterly necessary in any ecumenical research.

# THREE EXAMPLES OF BIBLICAL NARRATIVES

In what follows, I would like to present a few biblical narratives on the theme of the 'sacramentality of life' – one of the core mandalas of the work of the Malines Conversations Group – highlighting how they can be the transitional space in which contemporary meaning may emerge. These three biblical episodes provide a panorama or a perspective for reflection, while exploring how the Bible itself portrays the Mystery – 'Sacrament' – of Life.

## Creation[21]

To create means to give shape, to bring to life, to give form, which means 'irruption': irruption of different and opposite forms. But forms always contain in themselves the principle of the opposite: every form even receives its own identity through what is perceived as being its opposite. Different and opposite forms not only disturb pretended achieved systems of harmony and unity, but they are needed in the process of a deeper self-identification, in the growth through successive new integrations. This is the unique dynamic of life.

If God – the source of life – creates by shaping forms through the principle of separation, this also means that there is no life without separation. *In principio* God creates everything in one act; but when God creates humanity – in his own image (this means 'image of the source of Life') – God realizes this in several steps, which shows us that 'being human', 'being the image of God' is a continuous becoming, a dynamic, an evolution. The final step is when God blows his own *Ruah* or *Havel* into man, which brings him to life. This continuous blowing is the *Ur-Sakrament,* as Hans Urs von Balthasar stated. It means that life is a sort of existential umbilical cord to God. Without this *Ur-Sakrament* of life, no other sacraments are possible, no knowledge at all is possible, no religion, nothing. This 'umbilical cord' means that in the structures of Creation, humanity is from all eternity the hidden face of God, and that God

---

21  Gen 1-3

is from all eternity the hidden face of human beings. So, life is a gift – and we are not the source of it.

Once human beings are created as a dynamic image of the Source, God withdraws in himself (*Tsimtsum* in Hebrew). By this act the principle of freedom was given. But, as I have already proposed, according to the structural logic of the Creation, nothing can exist without its opposite: freedom is only possible by setting up a prohibition, by issuing a law – 'you may not "consume" the fruits of knowledge, or you will die.' The famous original sin – the path that leads to death – is nothing else than the existential gap between the principle of life and the knowledge we pretend to have in this life. After the birth of freedom, God bestows on humanity its deepest vocation: humanity has to fulfil creation. But how? If humanity is the image of God, then humanity in turn must further create by bringing together, by integrating what the dynamics of life and creation bring up as different and disturbing forms. In God, who is the source of life, all things are one; by integrating the differences in life, humanity becomes the co-creator and bearer of unity – though never the source – and fulfils its vocation as the image of God. By eating the seductive fruit, humanity says 'no' to that unification dynamics, 'no' to the dynamics of the *Kenosis,* which is the only way of gaining real knowledge of Life.

In this sinful act, humanity considers itself to be the source of life. In doing so humanity condemns itself to a lifelong battle defending this pretence at fully-achieved knowledge, this pretended achieved unity or pretended full memory, and consequently all experiences perceived as disturbing or adversarial become threats of existential danger instead of being invitations to fulfil human identity as co-creator. This sacramentality of life, in the awareness that life is a divine gift, clearly shows us that original sin is an existential concept and not a moral one. The ethical aspect comes only after this, the inherent consequence of the original sin. In fact, the prohibition doesn't concern the ethical distinction humanity will make between good and bad, but consists in the verb 'eat': the destruction of a reality in order to satisfy its own pretended identity, comfort and power. This alienation will be experienced in the field of alterity, inter-personality and labour.

The 'GPS' to stay on the road of life, to stay embedded in that *Ur-Sakrament,* is one of integrating differences in order to find one's own real identity, becoming a real image, an 'icon' of the source of life. It is God's soteriological concern that man is driven out of Paradise, so that he is obliged to walk the kenotic way of integrating evolution and of incarnating God's Word so that he may become a blessing for Creation.

# Cain and Abel[22]

It is very important[23] to realize that immediately after the narrative of the Creation and the Original Sin, Genesis confronts us with the first murder. This first drama, the 'Original Drama,' gives us the opportunity to expose a number of mechanisms that lie deep in the religious soul of human beings, because the context of this narrative is a cult event. The narrative shows us how the cult event, the ritual, which is the prototype of every initiation act, can result in a crime – here in murder – when by its mere external, blind, self-centred motivations it increases the gap between life itself and the knowledge we think we have about life. The issue here is about the gap between life itself and knowledge of the spiritual, the religious act.

Cain the firstborn, the man whose vocation is to be 'one', to dedicate himself to unity and harmony, the man who owns and works the land, the man who has the knowledge of the secrets of the earth (in Aramaic: *'strong blacksmith'*): he is the 'initiated one', who knows how the material world is linked with the spiritual. He opens the way that leads from earth to heaven, he knows the 'sacred' in creation and protects it. He represents the intelligence of the art of sacred action.

Abel the second born, the man whose vocation is to be 'two', to be the person who reveals the duality of life by 'being the other', to be different, the shepherd who wanders and guides the flock, the man who knows the variability of the wind and the sky (in Aramaic: *Havel, 'vulnerable breath'*): he is rather the 'illuminated one', who knows how evolution is linked with reality. He opens the way that leads from heaven to earth, he knows his flock because he lives with it and changes continually its course in function of all sorts of concrete needs. He represents the intelligence of the art of sacred viewing.

In the figure of Cain, the firstborn, human beings can recognize their being initiated, their priestly dimension: their being responsible for the spiritualization and the sacralization of matter; hence he directs his eyes towards the earth. In the figure of Abel, the second born, they can recognize their being illuminated, their prophetic dimension: their being responsible for the materialization of what is hidden. Abel integrates himself into the incarnation-process – a process that God himself will experience when the Word becomes Flesh – as the shepherd of God's Word; hence he directs his eyes towards the heavens.

---

22  Gen 4: 1-16

23  For this paragraph, I owe a great deal of inspiration to my confrere P. Maxime Gimenez; cf. idem, *La Paix - La joie sans mélange d'être en vérité*, (Paris: Cerf 2011).

It is interesting to note that both enter into a 'religious' context, one of cult and rite, each bringing his offerings. These two different ways of offering are interesting because they stand for complementary kinds of theological logic. For the time being, however, all we need to notice is that Cain and Abel are themselves the fruits of knowledge between man and woman – the 'first' human couple, the human couple *in principio* – driven away from the Tree of Life because they had eaten too early from the Tree of Knowledge. In this sense, Cain and Abel can been seen as the fruits of the incomplete union, in as far as this union is characterized by the original drama of the disharmony between life and knowledge of life. But in this ritual scene of Cain and Abel, a second chance is given, where everything can be played again. The condition of this second chance is that the two brothers accept to grow and look beyond the obstacle of the visible separation, of the external division that necessarily emerges between them. We must be aware of the fact that unity between life and knowledge is rooted in the mystery of the primordial unity between God and humanity: there, where the Adam and Eve in ourselves have failed.

Abel does not effectuate anything by his offering, in contrast with Cain, whose offering is the fruit of an 'initiated knowing' which exhibits the features of his own knowledge, with the danger of appealing to his own justification. Cain did not see that God asks to be recognized in the image of a shepherd, the 'illuminated', and of the 'slaughtered lamb'. Abel and his lamb are the symbol of life that can only be given away freely. This is not an offering but a gift (it is curious to observe that in the text Abel's offering is called a 'gift', *dora*, Cain's offering instead is called a 'sacrifice', *thusia,* when we might expect the reverse). Life comes first, it is the condition that makes possible any offering, any ritual. If the gift of life does not come first, no consequent knowledge is possible at all, no theology, no liturgy, and nothing can reach the level of 'sacred': no offering and no prayer in the whole world could have the value and the efficiency of a 'blessing' (remember Christ's words: 'What can someone give in exchange for their life?'[24]). Abel offers, but he does not effect the offering. The only source for the sanctity of offering (hence also of prayers and of liturgy) is in God himself, being pure gift and pure grace. An offering only becomes truly sacred when a human being recognizes that the source of all gifts is situated in the eternal outpouring of Divine Life. When the human being is able to recognize that the source of the sacredness of their offerings, of their gifts is far beyond themselves, only then offering and ritual can get their true value and efficiency: not the value or efficiency that they think they are

---

24  See Mark 8:37

themselves, nor the value they give to things by all sorts of theological structures ('knowledge'), as well-intended they may be. Only then can the human being realize their deepest vocation, namely becoming a co-creator, transmitting Divine Life, being Divine Blessing.

Therefore, Cain needs to learn how to read the visible realities of life differently. He needs to learn how to recognize that his younger brother, the disturbing one – the one who came later and reveals himself as being 'two' – is not at all the principle and the cause of his rejection by God (cf. Jean-Paul Sartre: 'hell is other people'), but exactly the one who will give him the opportunity and the grace of being the firstborn in the Creation, of being the one who knows how to edify a new unity. Abel, in his turn, needs to recognize that it is his older brother who will give him the grace of being blessing for the world. Each one does not only need to be mutually recognized in his alterity, but also in his being necessary in order to realize himself, through the other. Of course, in Cain we all commit the terrible mistake of thinking that God chooses *a priori*. Like Cain, furthermore we accomplish this mistake in our heart. It is not God who judges, but Cain. It is not the source of life that judges, but knowledge. Therefore, Abel's murder has taken place in Cain's heart before it was accomplished with his hands. When the intelligence of the eyes is lost, the intelligence of the hands will be lost as well.

The fact that God looks upon Abel's offering, means that God recognizes this offering as a divine principle, the most appropriate one, in order to initiate humanity into what God gives us: life. God invites Cain to understand, above all visible logic, that God's 'acceptance' of Abel's offering contains a message for Cain. The fact that God looked upon Abel's offering was an invitation, a sign for Cain, to enter through the ordeal of non-judgment in the mystery of being the first-born: integrating Abel's blessing in order to edify a new knowledge, a new unity, a new life, so that Cain becomes in his turn real image of God, source of Life. Abel's offering expresses the reality that God gives his own life to humanity through blood, rather than that Abel should offer blood to God. The offering of Abel attests that the mystery of life that freely gives itself away as the abundant diffusion of the Divine Spirit, results in nothing else but a perfect incarnation of the divine in human beings. The intention is to initiate us into a new knowledge of God, situated at the level of the principle of life itself, and not at the level of the knowledge of life or its exercise of power, be that religious or otherwise.

Looking upon Cain's dismay, God warns him: *'isychason'*, ('remain with yourself' or 'stay in your inner');[25] in other words: do not let yourself be carried away by the illusion that your knowledge contains the full science into the dividing chains of causal thinking, which makes you blind for any dynamic reading of reality. It implies that the 'Way', 'Truth', and 'Life' are based on soteriological, pastoral realities, and not in the first place on theological and ecclesiological static structures. All this is at the image of Christ, who revealed himself as the incarnated Word through healing, blessing, teaching, and rising from the dead.

It is of course impossible here to analyse how the rest of the text continues to teach us about life in its relation to knowledge and to the concept of unity. In an ecumenical perspective it would be a very interesting issue to analyse what sort of concept of unity is emerging from the narrative of Cain and Abel. By killing the principle of his being different, Cain kills all the possibilities within himself to become what he has to be, i.e., the first born, whose responsibility it was to assure that all stayed linked with the stream of life. And this results in a second expulsion, again out of soteriological concern, but differentiated from the first expulsion because eight curses are being implied, each of which has a specific impact on Life and unity. The whole Old Testament is an anticipation of Christ, in whom Cain and Abel, priest and prophet, will be unified, whereas the eight curses will be transfigured into the eight Beatitudes, reconnecting knowledge again with the stream of life: this is the existential foundation of sacramentality.

## Job

When Satan asks God for permission to put Job to the test, it is amazing to see how God permits Satan to touch Job in everything, except the command: 'Do not touch his life.'[26] Without entering into the interesting issue of the book Job – which is a profound elaboration of the problem of suffering, justice and life' I only will highlight the young Elihu's remarkable discourse in chapter 32 where he denounces two attitudes:

1  the superficiality of the three apologetic theologies of Job's friends;

---

25  Gen 4:7
26  Job 1:12

2 the fact that Job puts God on trial with an attitude of auto-justification based on the knowledge Job pretends to have of the secrets at work in Creation and Life.

Elihu indicates further that Job's suffering – in losing everything life has granted him: wealth, health, knowledge, structures, culture, family, religion, etc., thereby exposing himself to his own naked life, has brought out the hidden sin of the blinding pride of that pretended knowledge, opening Job's ear to the imperfection of every remaining knowledge. That is why God, on his turn, puts Job on trial and asks him: 'Who is this that darkens counsel by words without real knowledge?'[27] Then, in two chapters, God severely rebukes Job concerning those secrets at work in creation and life, after which God pauses in silence for Job's response. His response will be one of not giving an answer. Because, being stripped of everything, even of his skin (his identity according to the language and imagery of Genesis), facing his naked life, he slowly discovers that he does not know, and he keeps silent. So, God speaks again and comes to the point of teaching Job that no creature has enough wisdom to run creation and not enough knowledge concerning its processes of life, which means that no creature has any right to judge him who is the source of life as well as of the power of its dynamics at work in the evolution of Creation.

An interesting detail is that Tradition made Job the example of the Just One, although he is from Uz, which is not in Palestine. We only know that he was a 'God Fearer', a person who worships the Hebrew God but without being circumcised into the family of God's covenant. Nonetheless, in the judgment reserved for the apologetic theology of the three friends, God calls Job four times 'his servant'. Of course, this is in echo with the ironic provocation of Satan in the opening act of the narrative, when Satan wanted Job to curse God and to curse life, so that Job would die forever after meaningless pains. Here emerges the deeper aim of the game, which is the soteriological essence of the whole scenery. Besides, the Septuagint mentions that God will resurrect Job, thereby inscribing him in the vein of the Messianic stream that runs throughout the story of redemption. We see in Job, being not Hebrew, being the 'not-alike-us', how the stone which the builders (the specialists in knowledge) rejected, one who has become the cornerstone.

---

27  Job 38: 2

# CONCLUSION

These three short texts – indeed, the entire Old Testament – seek to make us conscious of the fact that, because of the sacramentality of life – life as *Ur-Sakrament* – all sanctification comes from God who is the source of life, and not from any knowledge humanity might pretend to have of life, even religious knowledge; knowledge that would enable people to judge how God's work of sanctification is taking place. This requires of course that humanity should learn to perceive the whole creation and its evolution in a different manner than simply trusting in exterior events and proceeding towards judgment by way of causal thinking, deciding alone what is good or bad according to that achieved or accumulated knowledge. Above all in religious matters – and let us not overlook here today's obvious challenges of sacramental theology and ecclesiology – God's logic is not human logic.

## Cardinal Francesco Coccopalmerio

I am convinced that, within ourselves, we must make clearer that there are diversities which create differences between the Churches and diversities which create divisions between the Churches. The diversities that create differences but not divisions are numerous and the most important. The diversities that cause division only regard matters of faith, the fundamental truths of faith. For example, if I would have a diversity in faith, like concerning the divinity of Christ, believing that Christ is or is not God, that creates division. But differences concerning the truths of faith that create division are actually very few. Today's ecumenism acknowledges a hierarchy of truths. Only when I have a difference regarding the faith in fundamental truths I can say that I am a divided Church. But if I have a difference in things which don't concern fundamental truths of faith, I cannot say that I am divided; then I only have differences, even very positive and good ones.

Cardinal Francesco Coccopalmerio
MCG IV, 16

# David Richardson

Friendships do not themselves create unity but without them the cause will be lost. Writing of the fourth of the Malines Conversations, the Anglican W.H. Frere noted that when the ten participants from the Third Conversation returned to Malines they gathered in Cardinal Mercier's house in 'the added warmth of pure friendship'. Further friendships emerge as key to the ecumenical journey. The strands of friendship continue to link together people, at all levels, with a passion for unity. From international ecumenical structures to the microcosm of Christian life, the local parish, people of divergent backgrounds come to know each other and work together, finding common cause in this elusive search for what is so central to the Christian message.

The present Malines Conversations Group, exploring as it does some difficult questions still blocking the path to unity between Anglicans and Roman Catholics, meets in the awareness that though friendships do not themselves create unity, the commitment to one another that friendships bespeak often opens unexpected doors through which the Spirit of unity may enter.

# Chapter 3
# Learning Lessons from Liturgical Theology

## JORIS GELDHOF

That there is an immense ecumenical potential in liturgy boils down to stating the evident. No serious theologian or church leader would radically disagree with that, at least openly. However, when it comes down to making this insight more concrete, it turns out that it is not so evident anymore. Old discussions around the indispensable value of theory over against practice, around ministry and authority, and about Scripture and Tradition immediately arise from the horizon of an uneasy past, often resulting only in the confirmation of noted ecclesial dividing lines and classical doctrinal disagreement. Therefore, the simple proposal of the present essay is to have a careful look at the model of 'liturgical theology' as represented, among others, by Aidan Kavanagh,[1] and to see what it can offer for fostering and strengthening the ecumenical relationships between Anglicans and Catholics today. I think that there are three areas which are particularly apt to learn from: (1) the presentation of an encompassing vision for ecumenism, (2) an integrative method or hermeneutic to live up to that vision, and (3) a sharp and steadfast focus on the goal to be achieved.

## THE VISION: EUCHARISTIC AND INCLUSIVE

The inspiration of liturgical theology, understood as *prima theologia*, is

---

1 The choice for Aidan Kavanagh (°1929–†2006) is of course not an absolute but at the very least a useful and instructive one. As connoisseurs know, his highly original work gives a special twist to what is commonly understood by 'liturgical theology'. A monk of the Abbey of St Meinrad and professor at Yale Divinity School, Kavanagh was one of the most talented scholars and teachers in liturgy of an entire generation. In addition to groundbreaking work in the field of Christian initiation, one of his major accomplishments was that he enthusiastically received and made widely known Alexander Schmemann's thought in Catholic theology and far beyond. One of Kavanagh's pupils was David W. Fagerberg, at present emeritus professor of liturgy at the University of Notre Dame, who sets forth this line of thinking energetically.

instrumental to keep alive a vision for ecumenical interaction and exchange. It provides a centre which is not and cannot be recuperated by theories, declarations and scholarly discussions but instead represents the very life of the Church.[2] While the discourse on the difference between primary and secondary theology is not unproblematic for all kinds of reasons, there is nothing wrong with a consistent focus on liturgy itself, i.e., the actual celebrations of the Eucharist, the Liturgy of the Hours, the sacraments, and sacramentals, as generative of the theological imagination and constitutive of theological thinking.

Liturgy has an independence which never coincides with any normative idea about it, let alone with an alleged objective description of it. It is a reality of its own to live from rather than to control or manipulate for purposes foreign to it. The liturgy offers an immense amount of fresh fruits but it testifies of little respect to only grab them and disregard the long process that yields them their original taste and shape. Aidan Kavanagh time and again emphasized this in an idiosyncratic but convincing rhetoric. 'Liturgical theology', he says, 'as distinct from other sorts of theology which may be about the liturgy, is obliged to begin and end with an accurate perception of what liturgy is in itself, and of how a liturgy functions with the larger context of what I have called rite. Fundamental to this perception is that liturgy is *worship of God corporately as church*.'[3] Two elements from this quotation require some comment.

First, Kavanagh rightfully underscores the intrinsic connection between doxology and ecclesiology as the fundamental characteristic of Christian liturgy. Liturgy is permeated in all the elements of which it is composed by a God-centered and community-forming direction. God is the one who is addressed as well as the one who establishes the entire environment within which liturgical gatherings and liturgical actions take place. Liturgy helps to keep one's orientation towards God and his redemptive love for people; it provides ritual structures, prayer texts and patterns of behavior – an *'ordo'* – to realize and interiorize the absoluteness of this focus.[4] Liturgy is the primary place where God meets his people and where his people meets him – a truly

---

2  Lambert Beauduin, *Liturgy the Life of the Church*, trans. Virgil Michel (Farnborough: Saint Michael's Press, 2002).

3  Kavanagh, *On Liturgical Theology* (Collegeville: Liturgical Press 1992), pp. 135–6 (emphasis added).

4  It was pioneer Alexander Schmemann who put the study of the 'ordo' on the agenda of liturgical theology: 'Thus the word Ordo, taken in its basic and general sense, is defined by what we have called the shape or structure of worship. For this reason the elucidation of the content of the Ordo and its place in the liturgical tradition of the Church constitutes the primary task of liturgical theology.' Alexander Schmemann, *Introduction to Liturgical Theology*, trans. Asheleigh E. Moorehouse (Crestwood: St Vladimir's Seminary Press 2003), p. 33.

mysterious reality. Kavanagh clarifies: 'Christians have traditionally under-stood their liturgical efforts to be somehow enacting the mystery itself, lock-ing together its divine and human agents in a graced commerce, the effective symbol of which is that communion between God and our race rooted in the union of divine and human natures in Christ Jesus.'[5]

This mention of Jesus Christ is by no means accidental. Through its con-nection with the category of 'mystery', it reveals how important the image of the Body of Christ is. Liturgy is all about *receiving* and *becoming* the Body of Christ, whereby the sacramental and ecclesial meanings and implications of the metaphor mutually reinforce one another.[6] The Body of Christ is the real-ization of all liturgical efforts; though situated beyond the reach of the senses, the intellect, the passions and the emotions, it constantly offers and creates op-portunities to join and does so in a tangible way. The Body of Christ is the em-bodiment of the liturgical vision of Christians: 'The Liturgy is nothing more nor less than the Body corporate of Christ Jesus, suffused with his Spirit and assembled in time and space, doing its best by doing the world as the world is-sues constantly from God's creating and redeeming hand.'[7]

Second, Kavanagh puts a noteworthy emphasis on the concept of 'rite'. When reflecting on the deepest nature of Christian liturgy, he comes to the conclusion that 'prayer' is insufficient to capture its essence; 'rite' is the more adequate alternative. Kavanagh explains: 'Not every prayer is liturgical, but rite always includes prayer without being reducible to this form of discourse alone.' He clearly operates with a substantially broad understanding of ritu-al: 'Rite means more than liturgical custom. It could be called a whole style of Christian life, which is to be found in the myriad particularities of wor-ship, in canonical law, in ascetical and monastic structures, in evangelical and catechetical endeavors, and in particular ways of theological reflection. The liturgy specifies all of these, and in doing so makes them accessible to the community which assembles within a particular style of Christian life.'[8] This intertwinement of 'style' and 'rite' is particularly intriguing for through them the grand liturgical vision of Christianity is both upheld (*ad intra*) and com-municated (*ad extra*) unceasingly.

---

5   Kavanagh, *On Liturgical Theology*, p. 120.

6   At this point is appropriate to insert a reference to Saint Augustine of Hippo, and in particular to his renowned sermons on the Eucharist (notably no. 272 and no. 227). Cf. also Henri de Lubac, *Corpus mysticum: The Eucharist and the Church in the Middle Ages*, trans. Gemma Simmonds (London: SCM Press 2006).

7   Kavanagh, *On Liturgical Theology*, p. 176.

8   Aidan Kavanagh, *Elements of Rite: A Handbook of Liturgical Style* (Collegeville: Liturgical Press 1990), p. 44.

Liturgical theology invites everyone who is concerned with the future of faith and Church and in particular with the unity among Christians, to always embrace and never loosen the vision which combines God, Church and world. Liturgical theology moreover makes one realize that the liturgy 'does not merely reflect or express its repertoire of faith. It transacts the Church's faith in God under the condition of God's real presence in both Church and world.'[9] In other words, liturgy can never be something external to ecumenical initiatives, and inasmuch as it is (and kept as such deliberately), it can be argued that attempts of such initiatives, no matter how well intended, will fail. For liturgy as a common celebration in actual remembrance of and profound gratitude for God's love and the liberation from what hampers that love, is not merely a sign but itself a moment and component of the history and economy of salvation. Liturgy does more than simply, or noncommittally, refer to God's grace and salvation; it offers the real means to enter into the encompassing mystery qualified by them and can therefore be said to be soteriological from A to Z. As a corollary, the vision propelled by liturgical theology is always and cannot but be Eucharistic and inclusive: the whole world and the whole Church and all the peoples are invited at the Lord's table.

# THE METHOD:
# SYNTHETIC AND HOLISTIC

If this is true, it follows that ecumenical initiatives such as our Malines Conversations, have to adopt an overall synthetic and holistic method. To be sure, there is nothing wrong either with analysis or with scholarly specialization. To the contrary, a lot is to be learnt from meticulous investigations of the exact meaning of concepts and formulations, of authoritative texts and of historical details. But such enterprises can neither be the central occupation of our endeavors nor the end or our journey. We must put together many such things, reckoning with the fact that we may neglect or overlook much additional and even pertinent input. And we must keep an eye on the vision and move forward with a view to eventually mobilizing the whole, not individual sections, of the one, holy, catholic, and apostolic Church.[10]

---

9  Kavanagh, *On Liturgical Theology*, p. 8.

10  Kavanagh has intriguing things to say about the Church's catholicity. He defines 'catholic' as 'Citywide and Worldwide in its nature and ends,' and continues to say: 'Catholicity is a quality endowed upon Church by City and World. [...] The Church and sectarianism are thus antithetical realities, and that the Church Catholic is one denomination among others, a sort of religious boutique in the suburbs, is an unthinkable proposition. When the Church fails at being catholic, it begins to fail at being one, holy, and apostolic as well.' *On Liturgical Theology*, p. 43.

This means, first and foremost, that a real connection with liturgy is always preserved, or, more adequately put, that this connection is always and spontaneously cherished. When one says 'preserved', the implication is that there is an anxiety that it can be easily lost and, thus, that it is necessary to take protection measures – which sooner or later gives rise to rigidity and conservatism. However, when one says 'cherished', it is clear that one assumes a free bond which nonetheless cannot be made undone: a *sacramental* connection, like God's covenant with his people. Clearly, sacraments are always liturgical and liturgy is always sacramental.[11]

Moreover, the connection with liturgy must always be constitutive instead of merely illustrative or corrective. While it is true of course that the liturgical practices of the Churches can be meaningfully used as an inexhaustible resource for examples, references or quotations, the liturgy is drastically reduced if it only serves in a functionalist or instrumentalist way. Rather, the liturgy is instrumental and instrument in a deeper sense. It is the living 'organ' through which God seeks contact with his creation to redeem it.[12] It is the heart of an encounter in love and trust permeated by an immeasurable transcendent reality. Liturgy is in-formed in-formation: the infinite and invisible God leaves concrete marks and traces of his saving presence in the very shape of the liturgy in time and space, in its multiple forms and in its fundamental order. It therefore capacitates, facilitates, and instructs in much deeper ways than any pedagogical or, for that matter, ideological strategy can possibly achieve. Kavanagh straightforwardly asserts: 'Being, like a feast, an end in itself, the liturgy inevitably forms its participants, but does not educate them in the modern, didactic sense of the word.'[13]

Clearly, the liturgy constitutes a reality the contours and boundaries of which are unknown and unknowable. It is mystery in the most proper sense of the word. Liturgy is the establishment of God's mystery for Church and world.[14] Therefore, when sacraments and sacramentality are discussed in the context of ecumenical conversations, there cannot be a restriction to two or seven or any other delineated number of ceremonies which have traditionally acquired a privileged status. While always keeping an intrinsic connection with baptism and Eucharist, it is much more fruitful to think and speak and

---

11  David W. Fagerberg, 'Liturgy, Signs, and Sacraments' in Hans Boersma and Matthew Levering (eds), *The Oxford Handbook of Sacramental Theology* (Oxford: Oxford University Press 2015), p. 455–65.

12  The Latin word *instrumentum* renders the Greek *organon*.

13  Kavanagh, *Elements of Rite*, p. 28.

14  For some theological background, see Joris Geldhof (ed.), *Mediating Mysteries, Understanding Liturgies: On Bridging the Gap between Liturgy and Systematic Theology* (Leuven: Peeters 2015).

do research in terms of sacramental – i.e. *mysterial* (for not mystic or mysterious) – density and intensity. As mystery, liturgy cannot be captured in binary schemes of thought, logic, and language; it is situated both beyond and between sacred and profane, private and public, time and space, the natural and the supernatural, the personal and the collective, etc.

Another consequence is that, from this mystery-induced holistic methodology, firm connections are to made with the different *munera* of the Church. These 'offices' are the priestly, royal and teaching roles, which it shares with and receives from Christ and which can probably be best understood as a kind of vocations (for they are never once and for all achieved and continue to inspire and orient one's actions). It is, in the end, Christ who prays, celebrates, rules, comforts, supports, gathers, worships, preaches and announces. He is, and through him the liturgy should be, in the middle of any activity which the Church employs to serve the poor and the needy, to bring the Good News to everyone and to assemble in communities anywhere in the world. Works for justice, peace and reconciliation have to take a start in the liturgical encounter with the Lord, and they have to imagine their end also there. Otherwise, the wise and beautiful words of the Second Vatican Council, namely that the liturgy is 'source and summit' of the Church's life of faith,[15] end up being hollow and mere speech.

From the same center a renewed pact is also to be sought with the arts. Without any doubt, many existing connections between Christian faith and culture can be maintained or strengthened. But when the focus more concretely becomes ecumenical progress, liturgy, broadly understood as above, is likely to modify a great deal. Liturgy, it can be argued, is the matrix of the sacramental imagination of Christians, and, when taken seriously, this insight can have a tremendous impact on ecumenical dialogue. The use of images, pictures, icons, and other visual symbols, not to mention the whole auditive world of chant, music, and silence, as well as creations which touch on the other senses, can not only fertilize the exchange, but also become part of the interaction itself. Definitely, here lies a field for further explorations and engagement. Inasmuch as liturgical theology's integrative and holistic method teaches that the sacramental and liturgical necessarily go through the sensory realm, ecumenical conversations would benefit greatly from more intensive interactions with the arts, for in addition to truth and goodness, God is also beauty.

---

15 *Sacrosanctum concilium*, no. 10.

# THE GOAL: PARTICIPATION IN TRANSFORMATION

The multiple method sketched above and the vision from which it emerges, allow us to keep attentive to the ultimate goal of ecumenical strivings. This goal often risks being concealed amidst the many occupations, tasks, and agendas. Sometimes it is even completely buried under the pressure of the powers that be. Or it evaporates because of the heat of untenable tensions between different commissions, influential characters, lobby groups, opposing interests, or belligerent ideologies. Those are the moments when liturgical theologians should take their responsibility, remind anyone involved of the fundamental sacramental-mysterial outline of Christian faith and Church, and explain that the goal of ecumenical dialogue is none other than the *raison-d'être* of liturgy.

The universal existential cause of liturgy is to make the whole creation participate in the transformation of the world brought about by the pascal mystery, which encapsulates the history of salvation and centers it around life, words, death, resurrection and ascension of Jesus Christ. Or, in the words of David Fagerberg: 'To fully comprehend the ritual liturgy we must appreciate the saving economy that it epiphanizes, and eschatology can thicken our understanding of liturgy. The liturgy celebrates the Paschal mystery, and that mystery stands at the center of a timeline between the protological alpha and the eschatological omega. Everything leads up to it, and everything flows out of it,' including ecumenism. Fagerberg adds: 'By its anamnetic and epicletic link to the Paschal mystery, liturgy brings heavenly activity to earth,'[16] and it is this double link, I would argue, rooted in soteriology and doxology, that ecumenical initiatives must never forget, if they do not want to deteriorate into sterile discussions and bureaucratic declarations.

What this encompassing transformation moreover means is aptly exemplified by the significance of the Eighth Day, 'the span of time following the completion of creation in redemption accomplished by the Messiah.'[17] The deep symbolism of Sunday, the Eighth Day of the week as well as Day of the Lord, flows forth from of its entanglement with the structure of the week and in particular its beginning and its end. The Eighth Day does not alter chronology, but by permeating the course of time itself, it re-signifies its totality.[18] It

---

16 David W. Fagerberg, *Consecrating the World: On Mundane Liturgical Theology* (Kettering: Angelico Press 2016), pp. 33–4.

17 Kavanagh, *On Liturgical Theology*, p. 56.

18 Gordon W. Lathrop, *Holy Things: A Liturgical Theology* (Minneapolis: Fortress Press 1998), pp. 36-43.

profoundly transforms it by weaving it into the sacramental tapestry of the divine economy.[19]

Participation in this comprehensive transformation touching the life of the soul and the body, the fabric of society, the culture of peoples and the organization of nations within and among themselves, is what liturgy is all about and, more importantly, what liturgy is *for*. It is a never-ending series of opportunities to enter into, to deepen, to broaden and to widen God's love so that it enlightens all darkness. In spite of the many cultural and linguistic difficulties it is often confronted with, liturgy offers a surplus of transparency against any opacity or obscurity. It represents an abundant fullness which cannot be made undone by any lack or shortcoming.

Ecumenical conversations are invited to align themselves with this sheer positivity. They must substantially and positively contribute to and, ontologically speaking, share in the attempts to realize the goal as described above. No matter which issue they deal with, and whomever is involved in them in whichever capacity, the liturgical-sacramental proximity of God towards his people must be served to the best of our capacities. A deep awareness must always prevail that, of its very nature, liturgy cannot be divisive; it is instead that what unites par excellence. Perhaps, in all its simplicity, that is the most profound lesson to be learnt from liturgical theology.

---

19 For a profound exploration of the notion of a 'sacramental tapestry', see Hans Boersma, *Heavenly Participation: The Weaving of a Sacramental Tapestry* (Grand Rapids: William B. Eerdmans 2011).

# Interlude

# A Focus on the Whole Church as a Source of Inspiration

## BRIAN FARRELL

Looking at the question of what the Malines Conversations Group can do, I really have no specific plan to offer. However, there is one thing that I would be happy to see, and that is as you take up and discuss some of the traditional questions that still remain, you will also be aware and be conscious of the fact that the future of Christian unity has to do with the movement of the *whole* Church. Therefore, it is wrong to keep thinking that the only thing we have is theological dialogue. Ecumenism has to be much more complex and different, much more difficult, but also a much more active 'grassroots' effort. If we are not sufficiently aware of this, it will probably in many places become what Kasper used to call 'savage ecumenism'. In other words, if you just do anything you like, that will be the end of it. So, if we are not part of this wider, *practical* ecumenism, without losing sight of the importance of the theological, then it is going to escape from reality, and we end up with chaos. And our churches will certainly suffer from that.

It's interesting that at the beginning of this century, about twenty years ago, the World Council of Churches set up a group called 'Ecumenism in the Twenty-First Century', and one of the things that came out in their report was that the Churches had entered the new millennium more concerned than before about their identity, and that the ecumenical movement had moved from the prophetic edge to the comfortable center. I always use this thought as a stimulus because I do think that in many of our dialogues, this is exactly what we are seeing.

In the Catholic Church we have fourteen bilateral dialogues and in many of them, we work hard and try to illustrate the various themes and questions that we present to ourselves. But there does not seem to be the kind of enthusiasm, or even the hope that our predecessors surely had, because they left us a huge heritage of marvelous conversations and events. Most of us, if we had to write about what we are doing today, we wouldn't have the same idealism. So,

49

it is true that our dialogues have taken on a routine, and they need to find *inspiration*. This is something that perhaps you can seek to germinate and give, especially to the dialogue with the Anglican Communion.

If we think about how relations between Christians are being fostered and carried out today, one could say that at the local level and at the level of practical cooperation, it's plain sailing! Everything can be done, people gather together, they pray together, and they work together, they support each other, etc. The real question is at the institutional level, at the universal level: what is holding us back?

Well of course, a huge part of what is holding us back is that we haven't overcome the controversial questions of the past. We are all under stress – pastoral stress – and it is very difficult to keep the ecumenical ideal in the forefront of our pastoral programs. All the churches are facing new questions. There is no such thing as a monolith, either in doctrine or in practice anymore, and I am the first to admit that we have huge tensions within our own Catholic Church.

In many different ways, including the question of the Eucharist, one of the compelling issues that really bothers me is the fact that our Church no longer knows how to transmit the faith. One of the things that is very difficult – and I am talking perhaps at the diocesan level throughout the world – for our priests and bishops, is to actually think and believe that they should, that they can, that there is a way for them to cooperate with the other Christians, because each one is stuck in the traditional, pastoral methods that we have always followed and used. Here we have a huge task of ecumenical education!

Finally, we talk so much about overcoming the European centeredness of our ecumenism, but in a sense Europeans in themselves are incapable of doing that because they are shaped by their history. I think we have to look with great expectation to the younger Churches in the rest of the world. I am sure that is going to be a huge transformation of the Churches and of Ecumenism. *How* that is going to happen is one of those things that, more than planning it, you just let happen. In that sense, we just have to confess we are too self-centered here in our European club.

Part II

# THE JOURNEY: REeading The SIGNS OF THE TIMES

# Chapter 4

# Ecclesial, Social, and Historical Developments from the Malines Conversations to Today

MARYANA HNYP

I prefer a Church, which is bruised, hurting and dirty because it has been out on the streets, rather than a Church, which is unhealthy from being confined and from clinging to its own security.

More than by fear of going astray, my hope is that we will be moved by the fear of remaining shut up within structures which give us a false sense of security, within rules which make us harsh judges, within habits which make us feel safe.[1]

In the history of Christianity, the twentieth century has often been called the century of ecumenism. Numerous events constructively contributed to this development, such as the 1910 World Missionary Conference in Edinburgh, the 1925 Universal Christian Conference on Life and Work at Stockholm, the first World Conference on Faith and Order at Lausanne in Switzerland in 1927, and the first Assembly of the World Council of Churches at Amsterdam in 1948.[2] Of a remarkable importance also became a series of informal ecumenical discussions between English representatives of the Anglican Church and Continental European representatives of the Roman Catholic Church from 1921 to 1927 – what we refer today to as 'the Malines Conversations', which marked the first time after the sixteenth century that Anglican and Roman Catholic theologians had gathered around the same table. The Conversations

---

1   Pope Francis, Apostolic Exhortation *Evangelii Gaudium* (*The Joy of the Gospel*), §49.
2   Cf. J. Rodano, *Celebrating a Century of Ecumenism* (Grand Rapids, MI: Wm. B. Eerdmans Publishing Co 2012; S. Kobia, 'Ecumenism in the 21st Century', *The Ecumenical Review* 70 no. 1 (2018), pp. 21-29.

were seen as 'a dramatic breakthrough in the history of the ecumenical movement,'[3] proving that such ecumenical dialogue was possible. Yet, in the recorded history of the Roman Catholic Church they tend to remain rather a historical footnote in the Church's account of the ecumenical relations.

Today, almost ten decades after the conclusion of the Conversations, we can credit them with two major accomplishments: firstly, in the development of the Roman Catholic ecumenical movement and secondly in the development of a post-modernist Roman Catholic theology of Eucharist. While aiming at taking the acknowledgment of the Conversations beyond a mere recollection of a past significant event, which at times is also perceived as an ambiguous legacy, but rather to acknowledge it as an inspiration for a deeper understanding of an authentic unity, in this contribution I offer some of my reflections on these two major accomplishments of the Roman Catholic Church since the Conversations. In doing so, a methodological attempt is made to reflect upon the changes in the Roman Catholic Church's perception of ecumenical relations, in particular with the Anglican Communion, by the means of sketching the changes in the Roman Church's self-understanding, while making some methodological observations and outlining some further challenges for ecumenical theology.

# ECUMENICAL PROJECT AND THE SHIFT IN THE ROMAN CATHOLIC CHURCH'S SELF-UNDERSTANDING

Characterised with their spirit of openness and respect to the other, the Conversations drafted a model for ecumenical dialogue. This project, noble, necessary, and challenging in its essence, maps the Roman Catholic Church's journey towards a deeper self-conception as well as a better understanding of other Christian ecclesial communities in order to recognise and embrace an authentic unity. And although ecumenical openness has become a rather normative way of contemporary ecclesial living together, it is yet important to point out, that despite many accomplishments so far, this project is still far from being complete.

---

3   A. Denaux, J. Dick, *From Malines to ARCIC: The Malines Conversations Commemorated* (Leuven: Leuven University Press – Peeters 1997), p. viii. In his *The Malines Conversations Revisited* John A. Dick recovers the story of the Conversations behind the historical fact and offers a tale of intrigues and deliberate misinterpretations in particular from the side of certain Roman Catholic oppositionists; cf. J.A. Dick, *The Malines Conversations Revisited* (Leuven: Leuven University Press – Peeters 1989).

On 21 October 2009, Pope Benedict XVI announced the decision to establish 'personal ordinariates' for Anglicans wishing to enter into full communion with Rome. This generated various reactions, including the BBC's provoking headline 'Rome goes fishing in Anglican pond.'[4] While clarifying the Vatican's action, Cardinal Levada stated that it was an effort to honour the legitimate liturgical, spiritual, and pastoral traditions of Anglicans who themselves have sought full communion with the Catholic Church on precisely those terms. In other words, as Russel Murray noted, the Roman Catholic Church designed an answer to the knock at its door with pastoral sensitivity.[5]

The issue, however, could be approached from another perspective. By means of such personal ordinariates, subsequently established by the apostolic constitution *Anglicanorum Coetibus*,[6] the Vatican has essentially changed the way the Catholic Church receives Anglican faithful into full communion. It left theologians wondering whether this change signalled a shift in the Catholic Church's methodology for ecumenical engagement, and, as a possible consequence of this shift, whether the Catholic Church will eventually alter the very goal of this engagement.

The dynamic element that moved the Roman Catholic Church into ecumenical dialogue was the Second Vatican Council's renewed understanding of the Church's nature as *communion*. While the precise interpretations of the Church's identity still remain under discussion in Catholic social discourse, the Catholic Church moved irreversibly into the path of constructive dialogue with other Christian communities with an aim of finding full visible union. In its *Decree on Ecumenism* (*Unitatis Redintegratio*), the Council departed from the pre-conciliar attitude of 'Come home to Rome', declaring that all who believe in Christ, and have been truly baptised, are already in communion with the Catholic Church.[7] While recognising the differences, sometimes so serious that are considered the obstacles to full visible union, the Catholic Church committed itself to defining its relationship with other Christian communities not as a matter of black-and-white full unity or no communion, but as a distinction between full and incomplete communion.

---

4  R. Pigott, 'Rome goes fishing in Anglican pond', *BBC News* 21 October 2009, available at http://news.bbc. co.uk/2/hi/uk_news/8318663.stm (accessed on 18 October 2023).

5  R. Murray, 'A New Ecumenism: is Rome's Anglican Outreach a Step Backward?' *Commonweal*, 29 January 2010, p. 8.

6  Apostolic Constitution *Anglicanorum Coetibus* (4 November 2009), http://www.vatican.va/holy_father/ benedict_xvi/apost_constitutions/documents/hf_ben-xvi_apc_20091104_anglicanorum-coetibus_ en.html (accessed on 18 October 2023).

7  Decree on Ecumenism *Unitatis Redintegratio* (21 November 1964), §3, available in English at http://www. vatican.va/archive/hist_councils/ii_vatican_council/documents/vat-ii_decree_19641121_unitatis-red-integratio_en.html (accessed on 18 October 2023)

This sense of communion flows from the conciliar understanding of the relationship between the Roman Catholic Church and the Church of Christ; *subsistence*. As it is stipulated in *Lumen Gentium*, 'this one Church of Christ ... *subsists in* the Catholic Church; ... although *many elements of sanctification and truth* can be found outside its visible structure. These elements, as gifts belonging to the Church of Christ, are forces impelling toward catholic unity.'[8] Through this document, the Church admitted that there are genuine ecclesial elements of sanctification and truth outside the Catholic Church. In fact, it is the existence of these elements in other Churches that propels them toward Catholic unity.

Such perception of the nature of the Catholic Church in relation to other Christian communities was a major departure from Pius XI's 1928 encyclical *Mortalium Animos*. The encyclical dramatically extinguished, in particular, the plausible attempt to seek visible union between the Christian Churches of Rome and Canterbury launched during the Conversations, and set the Catholic Church's general approach to ecumenical work in an eclipsed state until the eve of Vatican II. The fear and/or unwillingness to engage into an equal and just ecumenical encounter was arguably due to the Roman Catholic Church's centuries-long conviction that it, and it alone, was the true Church.[9] This teaching was sanctioned by the supreme teaching authority of the Roman Catholic Church[10] and it was found in the Catechism and popular expositions of doctrine used everywhere.[11]

Arguably, the temptation of centralism within the Church has arisen as a reflection of the prevailing centralism of the larger civic society. Conditioned mainly with an overemphasis on the task of securing the orthodoxy of her doctrinal teaching, the forms of ecclesial leadership that match with the power centralisation of the secular sphere has resulted in far-reaching consequences that range from persecution to internal divisions within the Church. Centralised decision-making within the Roman Catholic Christian community primarily based on its vigorous self-confidence and a lack of trust that the Spirit of God wishes to work in and through everyone, continuously endangers

---

8   Dogmatic Constitution on the Church, *Lumen Gentium* (21 November 1964) §8, available in English at http://www.vatican.va/archive/hist_councils/ii_vatican_council/documents/vat-ii_const_19641121_lumen-gentium_en.html (accessed on 18 October 2023).

9   The history of use of the marks of the Church in apologetics and theology is well argued by Yves Congar in his *L'Eglise une, sainte, catholique et apostolique* (Paris: Cerf 1970).

10  See H. Denzinger, H. Hoping, and P. Hünermann, *Enchiridion symbolorum definitionum et declarationum de rebus fidei et morum* (Freiburg: Herder 2014), para. 802, 870, 3303.

11  See the classic *Catechism of the Council of Trent for Parish Priests,* trans. John McHugh and Charles Callan, (New York: Wagner 1934), pp. 101-109.

healthy and healing relationships and structures both within the same Church and with other ecclesial communities. It is precisely such a peculiar self-belief of the Roman Catholic Church as an eternal, complete and unchangeable body of knowledge that has transformed the process of Gospel enculturation into rather a mission of cultural infiltration, resulting in the eventual marginalisation of the main goal – sharing the biblical joy of salvation. The concept of unity with other Christian Churches, consequently, was employed to a mere enforcement of conformity. As Yves Congar argues, the Roman Catholic Church seemed to perceive 'Latin' and 'centralisation' as the chief guarantees of unity, whereas they appeared to be the causes of alienation and estrangement.[12] The history of ecclesiology unveils the layers of the Roman Catholic Church's triumphalism and the desire for control manifested through the harsh imposition of the Latin rite, Roman canon law and the European mode of theological reflection, which has stifled the religious dynamism of communities in many countries.

How exactly the shift in the Roman Catholic Church's understanding of being the only true Church to acknowledging the saving elements in other Christian Churches emerged, is an interesting matter, yet it is not possible to address this particular case here. What is essential here though, is the Church's emerging realisation of the priority of being the Body of Christ over an institutionalised form of community.[13]

Since the Council, the Catholic Church's ecumenical methodology consisted in dialogue, guided by the concept of communion and founded on the principle of subsistence. Yet, with the establishment of the Personal Ordinariates, it is questionable whether this methodology is intact. Does this paternalistic action signal a new form of *uniatism* adopted in the form of a re-establishment

---

12 Cf. Y. Congar, *L'Eglise une, sainte, catholique et apostolique.*

13 The significance of the Church's self-perception in the communal terms in moral discourse, among many, is argued for by Karl Rahner who developed his insights on the Church as the historical relational subject of its own self-realisation; cf. Id., The Shape of the Church to Come, trans. and introd. by E. Quinn, (New York: The Seabury Press 1974); Id., Hearer of the Word: Laying the Foundation for a Philosophy of Religion (New York: Continuum 1994); Id., 'Notes on the Lay Apostolate' in his Theological Investigations, vol. 2, (Baltimore: Helicon 1963), pp. 319-52. For a review of Rahner's ecclesiology, see: Leo O'Donovan, 'A Changing Ecclesiology: A Symposium' *Theological Studies* 38 (1977), pp. 736-62. Yves Congar, who reflected in depth on the image of the Church as people of God, as the multitude through which God reigns and related to his people; cf. Id., At the Heart of Christian Worship: Liturgical Essays of Yves Congar (Collegeville, MN: Liturgical Press 2010); Id., Diversity and Communion (Mystic, CT: Twenty-Third Publications 1985). For a review of Congar's ecclesiology see Jean-Pierre Jossua, Yves Congar: Theology in the Service of God's People (Chicago, IL: Priority 1968), and Timothy I. Macdonald, The Ecclesiology of Yves Congar: Foundational Themes (Lanham, MD: University Press of America 1984); and Bernard Lonergan, who although without the use of the specific term 'moral' viewed the Church as communal fully conscious process of self-constitution (Selbstvollzug) with the implications on the Church's 'Christian witness'; cf. Method in Theology (Toronto: University of Toronto Press 2003), pp. 361-367.

of a full unity? While benevolent in itself, paternalism proves to be one of the most controversial formative principles of the ecclesial community: although aiming primarily at a striving for the good of the people, it yet signifies a general asymmetry bordering with discriminatory attitudes in relationships, though manifested in a rather subtle way. Historically, in the period of the Church's adaptation to patriarchal-imperialistic society, the Church failed to fully implement the New Testament morality of inclusiveness and equality. Inversely, the Church seems to have gradually transformed into an exclusivist patriarchal society with an overemphasis on the values of submission and obedience, as the fundamental structural principles of the Church's functionality. More specifically, this ecclesial paternalistic neurosis, is revealed in two major pathologies: sexism and xenophobia, both revealed in forms that are concerned with the perception of other traditional modes of theological thinking as a threat to doctrinal orthodoxy.

Clearly, behind official Roman Catholic ecumenical activity and warm mutual agreement on a few dogmatic matters, there remains an 'ecumenism of the return'. It might be well argued that the methodology of *Anglicanorum Coetibus* falls back on the track of the ecclesiology of *Mortalium Animos* rather than *Unitatis Redintegratio*. Did the officials of the Roman Catholic Church change their perception of ecumenical unity from the noble pursuit of a 'common quest' to the patronising move of bringing all the others into the Roman Catholic Church's embrace? The answer to this question has not yet emerged. It remains to be seen whether the establishment of the Personal Ordinariates, for instance, would create a precedent for other Christian communities that are seeking similar re-union with the Roman Catholic Church, the Lutherans for instance?

# A FEW METHODOLOGICAL CONSIDERATIONS ON THE ETHICS OF ECUMENISM

Concurrently, contemporary Catholic theologians seem to develop a more inclusive, more complex and more attuned to human historical context view on ecumenical relations. Many seem to agree that only by means of dialogue, combining discernment and mature conviction, reciprocal forgiveness, cooperation and integration, ecumenical unity can be attempted to be achieved. Limiting ecumenical dialogue only to the dogmatic or juridical issues is a step backwards, as ecumenism is not merely an intellectual matter, but ultimately a moral issue – the just and loving treatment of the neighbour as the image of Christ. It brings the issue of ecumenical unity to the most fundamental level of personal and social ethics, recognising the desire and commitment to Christian unity as part of the person's fundamental disposition towards good. The desire of being one in Christ is an inevitable consequence of the genuine conversion to God and to each other, a matter of the reintegration of all parts of Christianity into one Lord and into each other. Yet, by no means should ecumenism be perceived as merely a return of the separate parts of Christianity to the Roman Catholic Church, not only in terms of juridical belonging and dogmatic convictions, but equally in terms of the adaptation of moral and practical theological concepts.

It is in this context, that the critical assessment of the conclusions of the Malines Conversations offers us a lesson. As the men at Malines dreamed, the constructive dialogue between the Churches of Rome and Canterbury should be characterised by 'fresh eyes...open minds... and changed hearts... a renewed spirit of civility, dialogue, generosity and broad and serious consultation' (Cardinal Bernardin).[14] The fear and polarisation that inhibits the discussion, however, anchors the desire of leadership rather than faithful unity. Sadly enough, despite the theoretical framework promoting inter-relational mode of the ecclesial unity, in practice there often seems to be an overemphasis on the institutionalisation within the Catholic Church, an establishment as a goal in itself. Contemporary secularisation as a reaction against the Church's misuse of power is a call for the Church to rethink her structures, especially with regard to the forms and style of authority. Unless the Church's structures are characterised by institutional flexibility complemented by depth of discernment and prophetic courage, the Church will not succeed in an efficient and effective working as a whole. Equally, without the willingness to renew herself on the institutional level the Church will not be able to live up to her genuine vision of being the sign and the sacrament of God's grace.

Ecumenical dialogue in the context of theological ethics is arguably one of the most significant steps in the Roman Catholic Church's history. The Second Vatican Council clearly showed that the age of sterile, disputatious theology is past. As people are living in fruitful learning communities, amid reconciled diversity and astonishing relatedness, the Churches need to renew their teachings on moral matters to contribute to such a living Christian solidarity and unity in diversity.

In contrast to the doctrinal issues related to Christian unity, which seem to

---

14  Quoted from J. Dick, 'Unfinished Agenda' in A. Denaux and J. Dick, *From Malines to ARCIC*, p. 76.

be productively discussed, the ethical, moral, and practical issues in the field of ecumenical dialogue seem to be rather delicate and often causing serious tensions. A few elements of the so called 'unfinished agenda of the Malines Conversations' include, not only the burning questions such as the ordination of women, and the understanding of human sexuality, but also the issues of a married clergy, remarriage after divorce and the Eucharistic sharing in mixed marriages. Some bridge-building and healing is certainly needed in both Roman Catholic and Anglican Churches, if the authentic unity is sought.

The fear of modernism and virtually everything that belongs to the secular sphere, which has haunted also the Malines Conversations, seems to have contributed greatly to the development of the Catholic Church's defensive attitude toward the society. Particularly now, when the Church's prophetic presence is so needed, the Church becomes more and more peripheral. By proposing seductively simple answers to the complex moral and pastoral issues, the Church risks falling into inadequate fundamentalist Christianity, and increasing even more the seemingly insuperable gap between the Catholic Church leaders on one side and the theologians and large groups of believers on the other.

Yet, the Church is an inseparable part of the human environment, that is called to a continuous rediscovery of its nature as a multidimensional and inter-relational community of the *people of God* in a concrete historical context while being the *sign and the sacrament of God's grace*. This is ultimately bound up with the renewal of the Church's mission and consequently her structural transformation. While pursuing its mission of helping people to better recognise God, it should and must involve itself in social transformation by its prophetic presence, remaining vigilant to the signs of the times, witnessing the good and criticising the evil; by teaching God's word, and more importantly by learning its manifestation from people within and around it. And yet, the sound transformation of the Church's theological reflection and its structural relationships requires not only its own re-conceptualisation, but also the Catholic Church's willingness for reconciliation with other ecclesial communities on the grounds of equality.

Contemporary Catholic Church stands in urgent need for a collaborative, dialogue-shaped, and inclusive ministry. To be a faithful, non-competitive ecumenical partner means taking the other party seriously, in particular, by believing in the authentic faith experience and the tradition of the other. Only those blinded by historical ignorance and fear of loosing control refuse to acknowledge this. Particular cultural and ecclesial traditions cannot be denied nor ignored today. Moreover, the encounters with the others' differences challenge own views and ethical convictions. If the Anglican – Roman Catholic common project is to revive and succeed, both sides need to commit to the open and faithful appreciation of the other party. It is a commitment to grow in awareness together with the concrete historical human community.

# SEARCH FOR A DEEPER UNITY: ECUMENICAL OPENNESS TOWARDS EUCHARISTIC HOSPITALITY

The growing recognition of contextual approaches to theology and the importance of popular religion and inculturation raised the awareness that not only the tradition and the texts of the Church, but equally that her practice has to be taken into serious consideration.[15] The awareness of the increased gap between ultimate union of the Catholic Church's theory and praxis, manifested itself through the methodological shift from the comparative ecclesiocentric theology approach to a Christocentric (or rather Eucharist-centric) methodology with a strong emphasis on what I came to call a positive ascending anthropology.[16] This particular methodology, for instance, is vividly used in the agreed texts of the World Council of Churches Commission on Faith and Order, as well as in the texts of the bilateral conversations.[17]

Christian liturgical ethics is ethics of the Great Supper, as it is in the Eucharistic assembly – not in private prayer or contemplation – that judgment, repentance, reconciliation and God's love are experienced in their full Kingdom signification. The shape of pedagogy, which is required for an authentic Christian ethic, which challenges the world with the standards of the Kingdom, is nothing other than the shape of the liturgy. As such, liturgy is a continuous reality that celebrates human existence in God's presence and so transforms the social community. (Good) liturgy that culminates at the table of the Lord, which liberates the participants from the slavery of sin, dead traditions, and distorted images of God, never stops; it continues from the altar to the daily table, becoming the true liturgy of the world.

In the last decades of the twentieth century Catholic theological discourse

---

15  Cf. L. Vischer, 'The Convergence Texts on Baptism, Eucharist and Ministry' *The Ecumenical Review* 54 (2002) p. 434.

16  M. Hnyp, 'Re-examining Second Marriage in Catholic Moral and Pastoral Theology: In Search of an Alternative Avenue through the Eastern Practice of Oikonomia' *INTAMS Review* 17 no. 1 (2011), pp. 25-36; M. Hnyp, 'De migratiecrisis: een crisis in ons hart? Antropologische en ethische reflecties over migratie en multiculturele relaties in Europa' *Tijdschrift voor Geestelijk Leven* 3 (2016) pp. 69-79.

17  For more info on the Commission on Faith and Order, see https://www.oikoumene.org/en/what-we-do/faith-and-order (accessed on 18 October 2023).

seemed to grow more into the direction of uniting the focal aspects of the Church as moral community around the Eucharist, testifying the Church's self-perception through the union between sacraments, liturgy and morality.[18] Although the Second Vatican Council made a plausible attempt to revive the essential connection between these dimensions, it yet left many unresolved matters in the systematic expression of this union. Besides presenting a broader understanding of the sacraments through referring to Christ and the Church as sacraments and consequently the recognition of the ecclesial reality of other Christian communities,[19] the acceptance of religious liberty,[20] the recapturing of a unitive understanding of God's revelation, enhanced collegiality and the role of the laity, as well as the biblical and liturgical renewal, the Council did not seem to succeed in rising up the perception of the liturgical dimension of human existence, neither did it succeed in the amplification of the significance of this understanding to the Latin theological tradition.

As the principal and the central act of worship of the Christian Church, the Eucharist has been the integral part of its identity since the very beginning. There are many aspects of the Eucharist that seems to fuel interesting discourse within the contemporary theology of the Eucharist; yet, one aspect seems to stand out unquestionable: the Eucharist is a meal. As a meal, it evokes the most basic and practical components for the sustainability of a person's life – it connects with human hunger. Paradoxically, in the Eucharist, the utterly ordinary draws an extraordinary attention.

Being built on the Eucharist that is essentially the redemptive self-gift of Christ in the form of his body given with love for the others, the Church, as

---

18 Cf. H.-M. de Lubac, *Corpus Mysticum: L'Eucharistie et l'Eglise au Moyen Age* (Paris: Aubier-Montaigne 1944); in English translation: *Corpus Mysticum: The Eucharist and the Church in the Middle Ages* (Notre Dame, IN: University of Notre Dame Press 2007); Id., *Paradoxe et Mystère de l'Église* (Paris: Aubier-Montaigne 1967); J. Ratzinger, *Das Neue Volk Gottes: Entwürfe zur Ekklesiologie* (Düsseldorf: Patmos [1969] 1977); Id., *Eucharistie, Mitte der Kirche* (München: Wewel 1978); Id., *Kirche, Ökumene und Politik: Neue Versuche zur Ekklesiologie*, Robert Spaemann zum 60. Geburtstag zugeeignet, (Einsiedeln: Johannes 1987); Id., *Gott ist uns nah. Eucharistie: Mitte des Lebens* (Augsburg: Sankt Ulrich 2006). Also the analysis of Ratzinger's position see: Miroslav Volf, *After Our Likeness: The Church as the Image of the Trinity* (Grand Rapids, MI: Wm. B. Eerdmans 1998); Among many contributions by Paul McPartlan, see *Sacrament of Salvation: An Introduction to Eucharistic Ecclesiology* (Edinburgh: T&T Clark [1995], 2000); Id., 'Ut Unum Sint: Eucharist and Ecumenism' in J. McEvoy, M. Hogan (eds), *The Mystery of Faith. Reflections on the Encyclical Ecclesia de Eucharistia* (Dublin: Columba Press 2005), pp. 341-355; Id., 'Liturgy, Church and Society' *Studia Liturgica* 34 (2004), pp. 147-164; Id., 'IARCCUM: Growing Together in Unity and Mission' *Ecumenical Trends* 36 (2007), pp. 17-21; for a comparative study of Henri de Lubac and John Zizioulas on a subject, see also Id., *The Eucharist Makes the Church: Henri de Lubac and John Zizioulas in Dialogue* (London: T&T Clark, 1993).

19 *Lumen Gentium*, §8.

20 See J. Gros, 'Dignitatis Humanae and Ecumenism: A Foundation and a Promise' in J. Ford (ed.), *Religious Liberty: Paul VI and Dignitatis Humanae*, (Brescia: Istituto Paolo VI; Washington: Catholic University of America 1995), pp. 117–148.

the Eucharistic community, implies that Christ's followers are to be gifts for the nourishment of the others. When the practice of the Eucharist is central in the life of the Church, the breaking and sharing of bread is a critique of the present organisation of the hungry social body. The divine reality breaks into human history in the ways in which the members of the Christ's body conceive the meaning of the nourishment and their own identity in relation to the hunger of the others. 'The church is the church', Dietrich Bonhoeffer writes, 'only when it exists for others.'[21] Like the Eucharist itself, the bodies of church members are food for the nourishment of the world, to be broken, shared, and consumed. Such an understanding of the Church as the Eucharistic community, which also lays at the heart of liberation theology, marks according to James Nickoloff an 'ecclesial shift' from 'moral exhortation to solidarity'.[22]

In the Eucharistic meal, eating is a radically public, communal act. The economic and political boundaries,[23] normally restricted to the family are extended in Eucharist to the widow, stranger, orphan, alien and the hungry. William T. Cavanaugh, Henri de Lubac, and Michael de Certeau,[24] among others, have documented how a dramatic inversion came about in Eucharistic theology. Patristic and early-medieval tradition, using the Pauline images of the body of Christ, spoke of the sacramental body of the Eucharist as *corpus mysticum,* or the mystical body of Christ, and the Church as *corpus verum,* or the true body of Christ.[25] Around the twelfth century, however, there was an inversion of meaning. In following centuries, the sacramental body of the Eucharist was increasingly seen as Christ's *corpus verum,* and the Church, his *corpus mysticum.*[26] And thus as *corpus verum,* the Eucharistic host became the object of reverence, rather than the centre of a communal performance. A shift was in progress in which the emphasis was increasingly placed upon the miracle of transubstantiation in the priest's blessing of the bread and wine, making the Eucharist more an object rather than an action that transformed of the

---

21  D. Bonhoeffer, *Letters and Papers from Prison*, edited by E. Bethge (New York: Simon and Schuster 1997), p. 382.

22  J. B. Nickoloff, 'The Church of the Poor: The Ecclesiology of Gustavo Gutiérrez' *Theological Studies* 54 no. 3 (1993), p. 512.

23  Here I use the words 'economic' and 'political' in their original meaning, in sense of a norm of household, and whatever constitutes the philosophical or theological discourse on the 'polis', on the dynamism of life in society.

24  See W.T. Cavanaugh, *Torture and Eucharist* (Oxford: Blackwell 1998); H. de Lubac, *Corpus Mysticum: L'Eucharisie et L'Église au Moyen Age* (Paris: Aubier 1949); M. de Certeau, *The Mystic Fable* (Chicago: University of Chicago Press 1992).

25  Cavanaugh, *Torture and Eucharist*, p. 212.

26  De Lubac, *Corpus Mysticum*, pp. 34-39.

community itself.[27] Adoration replaced sharing. Controversies have raged over what happens to the bread and wine when the priest blesses it, the issue, which the Anglican and Roman Catholic theologians were struggling about during the Malines Conversations as well.

Yet, the Eucharist is a gift, invoking an interpersonal encounter. In *God without Being*, Jean Luc Marion argues that the Eucharist as gift is governed by the charity of God's free gift of love, which sustains each moment of the present. In order to receive the Eucharist properly, one does not explain the gift, but is assimilated into its movement in the performance of companionship and compassion. Thus, our failure to recognise the gift, which is love, lies precisely in our failure to love.[28] Full personal presence involves the response of the other. Presence in the deepest sense is mutual, interpersonal one. It is not enough for one to offer; the other must reciprocate by accepting the offer and offering him or herself. And it is right here at the core of our Christian belief that religious fundamentalism becomes most vivid: full (or I rather prefer 'complete') Eucharistic communion between various Christian denominations is still *practically* impossible.[29] Our liturgy, so beautifully defined as a celebration of union between God and human beings, becomes a real test to ecumenical unity. The Eucharistic meal, as such, serves as a critique of the status quo for the individualistic and relativistic tendencies in both secular and ecclesial societies. It is a challenging invitation for the concretisation of mutuality and interconnectivity.

---

27  Jean Luc Marion notes this tendency to regard the Eucharistic host in a way which 'fixes' and 'freezes' Christ 'in an available, permanent, handy, and delimited thing' in *God without Being: Hors-Texte*, trans. Thomas A. Carlson (Chicago: University of Chicago Press 1991), p. 164. Accompanying these changes in Eucharistic theology, the Church itself began to acquire the identity of the mystical body of Christ. The Eucharist became, in de Certeau's words, 'the visible indicator of the proliferation of secret effects (of grace, of salvation) that make up the real life of the church'. The Church was not becoming the embodiment in history of the true social body of Christ, but rather, more 'opaque' (De Certeau, *The Mystic Fable*, pp. 84, 86).

28  Marion, *God without Being*, p. 178.

29  Cf. Congregation for the Doctrine of the Faith, *Letter to the Bishops of the Catholic Church on Some Aspects of the Church Understood as Communion*, available at http://www.vatican.va/roman_curia/ congregations/cfaith/documents/rc_con_cfaith_doc_28051992_communionis-notio_en.html (accessed on 18 October 2023); J. Meyendorff, 'Notes on the Orthodox Understanding of the Eucharist' *Concilium* 24 (1967) pp. 29-30; A. Denaux and J. Dick (eds.), *From Malines to ARCIC: The Malines Converstaions Commemorated* (Leuven: Leuven University Press – Peeters 1997). The theme of Eucharistic intercommunion is particularly relevant to the issue of Eucharistic communion in mixed marriages. For a few reflections on this matter see: Jan (Cardinal) Willebrands, 'Mixed Marriages and Eucharistic Communion' *Origins* 10 no. 19 (1980), pp. 289-292; Bishop Barnabas Halem'Imana of Kabale (Uganda), 'Mixed Marriages: Practical Ecumenical Problem' *Origins* 10 no. 20 (1980), pp. 311-313; M. G. Lawler, *Ecumenical Marriage and Remarriage: Gifts and Challenges to the Churches* (Mystic, CT: Twenty-Third Publications 1990), esp. pp. 14-19; 86-92; M. G. Lawler, 'Interchurch Marriages: Theological and Pastoral Reflections' in C.E. Curran, J.H. Rubio (eds), *Marriage: Readings in Moral Theology* (New York-Mahwah, NJ: Paulist Press 2009), pp. 253-276.

Such a perception of the Church as communion in the narrower sense, and the Church as a Eucharistic community in its wider meaning, with the distinctive Eucharistic morality flowing from it, offers the firm theological ground for furthering ecumenical unity on the basis of Eucharistic ecclesiology. The growing attention to the ecumenical dialogue grounded principally on the understanding of the Church as Eucharistic communion became prominent in the so-called 'Lima text' by the World Council of Churches, *Baptism, Eucharist and Ministry* (1982).[30] The document emphasised that it is in the Eucharist that the Church's unity, both on the local and on the universal level, is fully manifested. Although without explicit elaboration of the subject, the document hinted at the possibility of building the practice of intercommunion between Christian Churches as the manifestation of mutual recognition of one another as part of one Mystical Body of Christ. The 1987 response of the Holy See to the Lima Document suggested that it was 'perhaps the most significant result of the [ecumenical] movement so far.'[31] Nonetheless, the complex question whether complete Eucharistic communion between Christian Churches can be fully accepted and recognised, and if so, then how, still seems to remain unresolved.

While paying his visit to the Westminster Abbey in September 2010, Pope Benedict XVI with a gracious tone and in strong affirmation called Anglicans and Catholics to 'full communion.'[32] Though thoughtful upon the first sight, this appeal to the Church of England was, in fact, unrealistic, as it indirectly reminded them that the same Eucharistic meal yet couldn't be shared at the same table.

By the realisation of herself as the Eucharistic community founded to serve Christ through serving humanity, seeking union with other Christian

---

30 World Council of Churches, *Baptism, Eucharist and Ministry*, Faith and Order Papers No. 111, (Geneva: Oikoumene 1982) (also available at https://www.oikoumene.org/sites/default/files/Document/FO1982_111_en.pdf (accessed on 18 October 2023)), esp. section II. D., p. 14. On the brief analysis of the document in the context of the ecumenical discussion on the significance of the Church as communion, see: Gary D. Badcock, *The House Where God Lives: The Doctrine of the Church* (Grand Rapids, MI: Wm. B. Eerdmans 2009), pp. 66-101. Official responses to BEM text are gathered by Max Thurian in *Churches Respond to BEM: Official Responses to the "Baptism, Eucharist and Ministry" text*, vols. 1-2, Faith and Order Papers nos. 129; 132; 135; vols. 3-4, Faith and Order Papers nos. 137; 143; 149, vols. 5-6, Faith and Order Papers nos. 144, (Geneva: Oikoumene 1986-1988). See also collection of reactions edited by Thomas F. Best and Tamara Grdzelidze, *BEM at 25: Critical Insights into a Continuing Legacy*, Faith and Order Papers no. 205, (Geneva: Oikoumene 2007).

31 'Roman Catholic Church,' *Churches Respond to BEM: Official Responses to the "Baptism, Eucharist and Ministry" Text*, ed Max Thurian, vol. VI (Geneva: World Council of Churches 1988), pp. 1-40, at p. 2.

32 Jonathan Wynne Jones, 'Pope to call for "full communion" between Anglicans and Catholics' *The Telegraph*, 18 September 2010, available at https://www.telegraph.co.uk/news/worldnews/the-pope/8011464/Pope-to-call-for-full-communion-between-Anglicans-and-Catholics.html (accessed on 18 October 2023).

Churches while building the Kingdom of God, the Catholic Church is called to continuously renew her teaching and reinvigorate her self-understanding. As the men of the Malines Conversations believed, striving for full visible union applies not to eliminating the striking differences; neither to seeking an alternative way of convergence, but rather to seeking the common ground on which common action and contemplation can effectively take place. Why not to seek it to sharing together the common Eucharistic supper?

# CONCLUSIONS
# OR, TO BE CONTINUED...?

Globalisation has diminished the significance of geography and has enabled the possibility of fruitful learning communities, reconciled diversity and astonishing relatedness. It also generates turbulence at the crossroads between national security and human insecurity, between (supra-)national sovereign rights and human fundamental rights, between overwhelming wealth and increasing poverty, between citizenship and discipleship. It is in this context that the Church needs to be recognised as an embodiment and realisation of reconciliation and God's mercy. In the history of Catholic theology there were too many hasty answers given too easily, whereas there was more time needed for reflection and deeper questions. Maybe it is time to turn our answers back to questions and dwell with them in silence for a while.

It is rarely possible to solve new concerns with old methodologies. Today we need to find new approaches that combine a better understanding of ourselves and of our foundations with a deep and profound interest in the other. Perhaps, it is time to reconsider fundamentally the major methodology of the Church: to rethink it from below, from the position of a vulnerable, often broken human person in close inter-relation with others, often *different* others, in the particular historical and cultural context. Contemporary ecclesiology seems to lack a positive ascending anthropology, where not an abstract ideal dictates the patterns of ecclesial life, but rather the serious appreciation and the most sincere concern for a genuine well-being of a person in connection with the other human beings oriented toward God becomes the focal point of the Church's existence and teaching.

Today, when faced with serious social concerns such as migration, the refugee crisis and poverty, we need to learn to be a gift to the other and to accept the other as a gift; to let this be a witness against contemporary materialism, in full liturgical sense. This gift is what we, as human beings most need from each other. If the incarnation – God's ultimate gift to us so solemnly celebrated in our Liturgies – is about crossing over the divine-human divide, our role as believers should be in incarnating the cross over the human-human divide. It is ultimately a mission of living out our Liturgy, of reconciliation and building a civilisation of love; not as a mere activism, but as a genuine testimony to God's undivided, unrestricted and universal love to humankind – a passionate concern for the good of all.

# Archbishop David Moxon

One has to keep the dialogue open, which is what the Anglican communion is actually trying to do.

This is very difficult, but it's Anglican. It's Anglican and we ought to be used to that and my view is that we ought to be comfortable with that. Because we always have been on a good day, we work things out slowly over time and I don't think that's a bad thing. And usually it's the most reliable thing to do in the long run in the apophatic sense and also in the Hegelian sense. I would say that Anglican ecclesial and ethical decision-making is essentially 'Gamalielian' in its spirit, and that is to say: if it's of God, something will thrive ultimately, if it's not of God, it will ultimately wither. We ought to have the patience to wait on God and keep our minds and our hearts and our prayers and our hermeneutics open and in compensation, until a new consensus emerges.

Archbishop David Moxon
MCG II, 123-4

# Paul Murray

One of the core pathologies of Catholicism since the Council has been our tendency to transmute legitimate and necessary internal diversity – of theology, spirituality, liturgical preference, and ecclesial disposition – into a fractious factionalism and mutually disregarding, even mutually denouncing, interior tribalism. The deleterious effects of this are multiple. It diminishes and distorts the Catholic witness to the world of what it means, with *Lumen Gentium*, to be 'sacrament of intimate union with God and of the unity of the whole human race.' Similarly it diminishes and distorts the confidence given to ecumenical partners of what it might mean for Catholicism to be a communion of communions. Most immediately, however, it serves to diminish and distort the very catholicity – the living and thinking *kath' holou*, according to the whole – of Catholicism. By so doing it alienates the members of the Catholic Church from the full range of riches, values, dispositions, sensibilities, practices, and ways of understanding that together comprise the Catholic constellation. It lets the whole be diminished by allowing some of its constituent parts to be lost from view.

Paul Murray
MCG II, 134-5

# Chapter 5
# Taking Stock of the Present Situation of our Churches

## KEITH F. PECKLERS, S.J.

In many respects, Archbishop of Canterbury Geoffrey Fisher's visit to Pope John XXIII on 2 December 1960, was as spontaneous and unexpected as the Pope's calling of the Second Vatican Council only months earlier. Both actions were reflective of how very far our communions had come, and whether directly or indirectly, articulated the hopes and aspirations of both Anglicans and Roman Catholics alike. Despite the spontaneity of those actions, however, they represented the fruit of the movements for ecclesial renewal which had emerged in the twentieth century: the biblical, ecclesiological, ecumenical, liturgical, and patristic movements which were woven together in the *ressourcement* of the 1940s: a return to the sources that would lead to a thorough renewal of pastoral and liturgical life especially in Europe, North America and Oceania.[1]

In the Roman Catholic Church, Belgium held a privileged place as a centre for the promotion of such ecclesial renewal. It was there that the liturgical movement was born in 1909, thanks to the impetus and socially-minded, ecumenical vision of Benedictine Lambert Beauduin (+1960), a monk of the Abbey of Mont César. Significantly, it was that same founder of the liturgical movement who was the secret architect of the Malines Conversations (1921-1925) hosted by Cardinal Desiré Mercier, Archbishop of Malines-Bruxelles to revisit the question of Anglican orders and their validity or invalidity. Beauduin's mantra which ran through the Conversations from start to finish was *'L'Église Anglicane Unie non Absorbée.'* ('United, not Absorbed.'). In the very year those Conversations concluded, Beauduin founded the Monastery of Amay-Chevetogne as a monastic community specifically dedicated to

---

1   See Gabriel Flynn and Paul D. Murray (eds), *Ressourcement: A Movement for Renewal in Twentieth-Century Catholic Theology* (Oxford: Oxford University Press 2012).

Christian unity with special concern on the reunification with the Anglicans and Orthodox.[2]

Behind these twentieth century movements, a discreet and informal sharing of information and ideas had already taken place in nineteenth century Europe. In the 1820s, the newly appointed Professor of Ecclesiology at the Catholic Theological Faculty of Tübingen Johann Adam Möhler (+1838), prepared for his lectures by spending several months at various Lutheran and Reformed Theological Faculties in northern Germany, listening to the lectures of distinguished theologians like Friedrich Schleiermacher (+1834) and others. It was there where he first learned of the recovered Theology of the Mystical Body of Christ, which had been lost for centuries in the Roman Catholic Church – so lost that it was actually considered subversive. In fact, when Möhler introduced the Mystical Body Theology through the publication of his 1825 text *Die Einheit in der Kirche*, it was considered too Protestant, and he published another book seven years later in 1832, *Symbolik*, where he attempted to moderate his position and assure his critics that he had indeed remained Catholic in his theological inquiry.[3]

Möhler is also significant for having served as an ecumenical bridge between Anglicans and Roman Catholics in that pre-ecumenical age. He spent his summer holidays in Baden Baden and came to know a number of Anglican priests from the Church of England who were there on holiday at the same time. It was, in fact, only six days after John Keble's Assize Sermon which began the Oxford Movement, that Möhler first encountered Anglicans there in the Black Forest. He later said that the most remarkable thing he experienced at Baden Baden was the Anglican liturgy celebrated each Sunday at the Spital church. That experience opened his eyes to all that Anglicans and Roman Catholics held in common. Those Anglican priests in turn, came to discover the Mystical Body theology thanks to their discussions with Möhler. In it they recognized that language as a potential influence for rediscovering the Catholic foundations of the Church of England and meshed well with the emerging Oxford Movement.[4]

In the twentieth century, A. Gabriel Hebert, an Anglican priest who was a member of the Society of the Sacred Mission, was a regular visitor at the

---

2   See Raymond Loonbeek et Jacques Mortiau, *Un Pionnier Dom Lambert Beauduin (1873-1960): Liturgie et Unité des chrétiens*, 2 vols, (Louvain-la-Neuve: Collège Érasme ed Éditions de Chevetogne 2001); see also John A. Dick, *The Malines Conversations Revisited* (Leuven: Uitgeverij Peeters 1989),

3   See Michael J. Himes, 'Introduction to the 1997 Edition' in Johann Adam Möhler, *Symbolism* (New York: Crossroad Herder 1997), pp. xi-xvii.

4   See R. W. Franklin, *Nineteenth Century Churches: The History of a New Catholicism in Württemberg, England, and France* (New York and London: Garland Publishing Inc. 1987), pp. 138-139.

Catholic Benedictine Monastery of Maria Laach, in the Rhineland near Trier. Each year as he made his annual retreat there at Maria Laach, he experienced first-hand the Roman Catholic liturgical movement as it grew in Germany. There he came to know the great protagonist of the German liturgical movement Odo Casel, O.S.B.; Abbot Ildefons Herwegen, an unsung hero of the movement who encouraged young monks in his charge to pursue and promote the movement; the Italian-German diocesan priest Romano Guardini who was another frequent visitor at the monastery; and the Augustinian Canon of Klosterneuburg in Austria, Pius Parsch, who founded the Roman Catholic liturgical movement in that country. In 1935, Hebert launched the liturgical movement in the Church of England with his text *Liturgy and Society*,[5] in which he stated that he owed a great debt to the Monks of Maria Laach for having opened to him the richness of the liturgy and its potential for renewal as a catalyst for an over-arching ecclesial renewal within the wider Church. As the years progressed, Anglican and Roman Catholic scholars in various theological disciplines grew in their scientific collaboration, discovering the same biblical and patristic foundations in their research leading to greater ecumenical collaboration.

# THE SECOND VATICAN COUNCIL: A WATERSHED EXPERIENCE

All this came to full stature in the Second Vatican Council. Indeed, it was only because of the various ecumenical developments mentioned above that the Council's strong ecumenical impetus took shape as it did. In this sense, Vatican II was as much a point of ecumenical arrival as it was a point of departure for the very significant growth in Anglican-Roman Catholic relations that would follow.[6]

One of the greatest gifts of the Council was the understanding that by its very nature, the Church is always on pilgrimage. This is well articulated in the Dogmatic Constitution on the Church, *Lumen Gentium*, 48. Such a recognition opens the door for the sharing of gifts – which in turn would develop into the method of 'Receptive Ecumenism' where no one Church has all the answers, but rather is interdependent on the others for its own growth. Indeed, the pilgrim path is one of slow, patient conversion rather than rapid

---

5   Gabriel Hebert, *Liturgy and Society: The Function of the Church in the Modern World* (London: Faber and Faber Limited 1935).

6   See Bernard C. Pawley (ed.), *The Second Vatican Council: Studies by eight Anglican Observers* (London: Oxford University Press 1967).

convergence. The Council's Decree on Ecumenism, *Unitatis Redintegratio*, with an astounding vote of 2137 bishops in favour and only eleven opposed, develops this notion even further in speaking of the riches within our common Christian legacy. We read at number four:

> Catholics must gladly acknowledge and esteem the truly Christian endowments from our common heritage which are to be found among those separated from us. It is right and salutary to recognize the riches of Christ and virtuous works in the lives of others who are bearing witness to Christ, sometimes even to the shedding of their own blood.[7]

In 1962 prior to the opening of the Council, Bishop Johannes Willebrands, Secretary of the Secretariat for the Promotion of Christian Unity which had been founded two years prior on 5th June 1960, made a visit to Archbishop of Canterbury Michael Ramsey, to personally invite Anglican observers at attend the Council. Predictably, Ramsey's response was both immediate and extremely positive.[8] He appointed The Bishop of Ripon, The Right Reverend John Richard Moorman to lead the Delegation. He was accompanied by The Reverend Dr. Frederick C. Grant, retired Professor of Union Theological Seminary in New York representing the Episcopal Church, and The Reverend Dr. Charles Harold de Sousa, Archdeacon of Colombo, Sri Lanka. Canon Bernard C. Pawley, the first Representative of the Archbishops of Canterbury and York in Rome (1960-65) was personally appointed by the Secretariat for Christian Unity, succeeded by Canon John Findlow who began his service as Representative in January, 1965. During the three-year Council several Anglican theologians served as substitutes in various sessions, among them The Reverend Dr. Howard Root of the University of Southampton, and The Reverend Dr. Massey H. Shepherd, Jr., of The Church Divinity School of the Pacific in Berkeley, California.[9]

During the course of the Council, a close and fraternal relationship grew between the Anglican and other ecumenical observers, and the Vatican's Secretariat for Christian Unity. Indeed, a spirit of ecumenical hospitality and

7  See Keith F. Pecklers, 'What Roman Catholics Have to Learn from Anglicans' in Paul D. Murray (ed.), *Receptive Ecumenism and the Call to Catholic Learning: Exploring a Way for Contemporary Ecumenism* (Oxford: Oxford University Press 2008), pp. 107-108.

8  Willebrands first visited Constantinople and Athens to extend an invitation in February; then to Lambeth Palace and the Evangelical Church of Germany in March; then to Geneva and a meeting of secretaries of world communions in April; and lastly to the Oriental Churches in May and June. Once positive responses came back, Cardinal Bea then sent out formal invitations to attend the Council.

9  Frederick Bliss, S.M., *Anglicans in Rome: A History* (Norwich: Canterbury Press 2006), pp. 61-63.

welcome pervaded the atmosphere from the beginning. When Pope John XX-III learned just before the opening of the Council that ecumenical observers were to be seated far from the altar, he insisted that they be moved to the front of the Basilica. And in the very early days of the Council, Cardinal Augustin Bea, S.J., President of the Secretariat, hosted a social for ecumenical observers and spouses. The sort of ecumenical friendship that we now take for granted in the twenty-first century was already operative in those early weeks of Vatican II. As Anglican Representative in Rome, Bernard Pawley took the lead in suggesting that ecumenical observers organize themselves as a group and they began meeting regularly. They met first for prayer – on Mondays and Fridays at the Ponte Sant'Angelo Methodist Church, and then on Tuesdays with officials of the Secretariat for Christian Unity to discuss items debated in the *aula* and debrief. Those meetings were initially held in the Hotel Columbus in *Via della Conciliazione,* just down the street from *Piazza San Pietro*, but the gatherings became so popular that they moved to *Foyer Unitas* (now the *Centro Pro Unione*) in Piazza Navona.[10]

The warmth and friendship between Archbishop Geoffrey Fischer and Pope John XXIII grew even stronger with their respective successors; Archbishop Michael Ramsey and Pope Paul VI. On 22nd March 1966, the Archbishop visited Rome to inaugurate the new Diocese of Gibraltar for Anglicans in continental Europe, and to dedicate the new Anglican Centre in space which the Doria Pamphili family had offered within its Palazzo in the *Via del Corso* (now in *Piazza del Collegio Romano*). Bernard Pawley had already proposed the idea of an Anglican Centre to Archbishop Ramsey in September 1963; now that dream had become a reality.

On 23 March, the Archbishop of Canterbury met with Pope Paul VI in the Sistine Chapel, and on the following day, the two prayed together at the Basilica of Saint Paul's Outside the Walls after they signed the *Common Declaration.* The text proposed 'to inaugurate between the Roman Catholic Church and the Anglican Communion a serious dialogue which, founded on the Gospels and on the ancient common traditions, may lead to that unity in truth for which Christ prayed.'[11]

It was after that prayer as they bade farewell to one another, that the Pope removed his episcopal ring and placed it on the finger of the Archbishop who proceeded to fall into the Pope's arms weeping, according to the late Canon

---

10 Bliss, *Anglicans in Rome*, pp. 63-64.
11 Quoted in Mary Reath, *Rome and Canterbury: The Elusive Search for Unity* (Lanham: Rowman and Littlefield Publishers Inc. 2007), p. 46.

John Andrew who served as Ramsey's Chaplain at the time and witnessed the event. On the evening before that audience Canon Andrew received a telephone call from the Pope's private Secretary, Monsignor Pasquale Macchi, who informed Andrew that the Pope intended to offer the gift of the ring to the Archbishop the following day. Macchi asked whether this should be kept as a surprise, or whether it would be more appropriate to inform the Archbishop beforehand. The Archbishop's Chaplain decided to keep it a surprise which made the moment all the more dramatic. Paul VI was known for his gift-giving in private audiences, so when he presented the Archbishop with his ring, the Pope gave John Andrew his personal leather-bound copy of the New Testament which the Pope had received and used during the Second Vatican Council. At the opening of the Council each participating bishop received a copy with the words *"Concilium Oecumenicum Vaticanum II"* engraved in a gold circle on the back of the text.[12] That ring presented to Archbishop Ramsey continues to be worn to this very day by Archbishops of Canterbury on their official visits to Rome.[13]

While the Pope's gift to the Archbishop was a magnanimous expression of friendship and an implicit recognition of the validity of the Archbishop's orders despite what was written in Pope Leo XXIII's Apostolic Letter *Apostolicae curae* (13 September 1896), it was a gesture consistent with the Pope's own openness in general and his appreciation of Anglicans in particular. Already in 1956 as Archbishop of Milan, Giovanni Battista Montini invited a group of Anglican priests for ten days together of prayer and conversation so that they could learn more about one another's traditions.[14] Nor was it the first time that a Roman Catholic bishop gave his ring to an Anglican. In January 1926, as Cardinal Mercier, host of the Malines Conversations, lay dying, he gave his episcopal ring to Lord Halifax as one final gesture of his deep desire for unity between Anglicans and Roman Catholics.[15]

# FROM ARCIC TO IARCCUM

In their *Common Declaration* issued at the end of Archbishop Michael Ramsey's historic visit to Pope Paul VI in 1966, the Pope and Archbishop spoke of 'a new atmosphere of Christian fellowship between the Roman Catholic Church

---

12  Canon John Andrew in a private conversation with Keith Pecklers. Church of Saint Thomas Fifth Avenue, New York, N.Y. 26 February 2007.

13  Bliss, *Anglicans in Rome*, pp. 93-95.

14  Reath, *Rome and Canterbury*, p. 43.

15  Loonbeek and Mortiau, *Un pionnier Dom Lambert Beauduin* (vol. 1), p. 504.

and the Churches of the Anglican Communion... a new stage in the development of fraternal relations, based on Christian charity, and of sincere efforts to remove the causes of conflict and to re-establish unity.'[16] Thus, in January, 1967, a first meeting of the Preliminary Anglican-Roman Catholic Commission met in Gazzada. A second meeting of the Preliminary Commission met in September of that year in Huntercombe, and finally a third meeting at the end of the year in Malta. What followed was the 'Malta Report' on 2 January 1968 agreed upon by the Preliminary Commission and sent to Pope Paul VI and the Archbishop of Canterbury. The text laid out a program which paved the way for what would become the Anglican-Roman Catholic International Commission (ARCIC). That report made it clear that agreed statements in the area of theology and doctrine had to be balanced with the lived reality of ecumenical progress at its various levels.[17]

The Anglican-Roman Catholic International Commission continues its work today in ARCIC III. There were nine Anglican and nine Roman Catholic members of ARCIC I whose work went from 1970 until 1981. The group did important work in the area of Eucharist, ministry, and authority, issuing four agreed statements in that period with its Final Report issued at Windsor in 1981.[18]

Pope John Paul II made a historic visit to Canterbury in May 1982, as a guest of Archbishop of Canterbury Robert Runcie, and that led to the launching of ARCIC II which made its own significant contribution, producing the widely recognized texts *Salvation and the Church* (1987); *The Church as Communion* (1990); *Life in Christ* (1994); *The Gift of Authority* (1999); and *Mary: Grace and Hope in Christ* (2004). ARCIC III has recently published an Agreed Statement *Walking Together on the Way. Learning to Be the Church – Local, Regional, Universal,* basing its work on the principles of "Receptive Ecumenism" (2018).

In 1995, Pope John Paul II published his ground-breaking encyclical letter *Ut unum Sint "On Commitment to Ecumenism"* in light of preparations for the great jubilee year of 2000 he wrote: 'The courageous witness of so many martyrs of our century, including members of Churches and Ecclesial Communities not in full communion with the Catholic Church, gives new vigour to the Council's call and reminds us of our duty to listen to and put into practice

---

16 See 'The Common Declaration' in Alan C. Clark and Colin Davey (eds), *Anglican-Roman Catholic Dialogue: The Work of the Preparatory Commission* (Oxford: Oxford University Press 1974), pp. 1-2.

17 See Part II of the 'Malta Report' and particularly paragraphs 8-16. See also Mary Tanner, 'From Vatican II to Misswissauga – Lessons in Receptive Ecumenical Learning from the Anglican-Roman Catholic Bilateral Process' in Murray (ed.), *Receptive Ecumenism,* pp. 259-260.

18 Reath, *Rome and* Canterubry, pp. 50-51.

its exhortation.'[19] Reading that encyclical together as Anglicans and Roman Catholics, we must honestly admit and indeed celebrate the fact that we hold much more in common than that which divides us, and that there is much that we have to learn from one another's traditions. But that learning must be experienced at a far deeper level than a mere cognitive theological exchange. In the words of Pope John Paul II, 'Dialogue is not simply an exchange of ideas. In some way it is always an exchange of gifts.'[20] The Encyclical received attention in ecumenical circles also because of the Pope's invitation to other Churches and ecclesial communion to assist him in discerning how best to exercise his ministry of papal primacy at the service of Christian unity.[21]

The following year, in December, 1996, during a visit of Archbishop of Canterbury George Carey to Pope John Paul II, the two signed a common declaration. The text stated that 'it may be opportune at this stage in our journey to consult further about how the relationship between the Anglican Communion and the Catholic Church is to progress.'[22] In that period there had been significant developments within the Anglican Communion regarding the ordination of women to the presbyterate and the episcopate, thus this common declaration sought to find a way forward amidst such obstacles, given the fact that there was a real possibility of our ecumenical relations being "interrupted or downgraded."[23]

This led to a meeting in May 2000, in which Archbishop Carey and Cardinal Edward Cassidy, then President of the Pontifical Council for the Promotion of Christian Unity, invited a group of Anglican and Roman Catholic bishops to come together in Mississauga, Canada, to find a way forward in our ecumenical relationship. At the end of the meeting, the bishops determined that a new body should be formed to 'translate our manifest agreement in faith into common life and mission.' This commission would have a different function from ARCIC: it would be a commission of paired bishops: one Anglican and one Roman Catholic per province or episcopal conference – seeking to concretize the theological vision articulated in acts of common mission and witness. Thus, in 2001, the International Anglican-Roman Catholic Commission on Unity and Mission (IARCCUM) was established. Six years

---

19  *Ut Unum Sint*, 1.

20  *Ut Unum Sint*, 28. See also *Lumen Gentium*, 13.

21  *Ut Unum Sint*, 88-96.

22  'The Common Declaration of 5 December 1996' *Information Service,* 94 (1976), 20-1, available at http://www.vatican.va.

23  Donald Bolen, 'Receptive Ecumenism and Recent Initiatives in the Catholic Church's Dialogues with the Anglican Communion and the World Methodist Council' In Murray (ed.), *Receptive Ecumenism*, p. 274.

later in 2007, the Commission published an important text with concrete suggestions about how that ecumenical vision might be lived out at the local level.[24] Among other suggestions offered in Part Two of the text, the bishops recommended that local parishes regularly make the profession of faith together with the possibility of renewing baptismal promises each year at Pentecost; attendance at one another's Eucharists while respecting the disciplines of our Churches; more frequent non-Eucharistic worship together; and praying for the bishop of the other Church in addition to one's own bishop in the bidding prayers during Anglican and Roman Catholic Eucharists.[25]

# THE 'EXCHANGE OF GIFTS' AND THE ECCLESIOLOGY OF SYMBOLS

In the years since the inception of ARCIC and then IARCCUM, the image of our ecumenical relations as a true 'exchange of gifts' and not simply 'an exchange of ideas' as Pope John Paul had suggested in *Ut Unum Sint*, has continued to take shape. As the giving of the ring from Paul VI to Michael Ramsey set us on ecumenical path from which we cannot turn back, popes in more recent years have given archbishops of Canterbury other gifts rich in ecclesiological symbolism, that have laid bare a certain inconsistency between what remains in print regarding Anglican orders and their invalidity, and the lived reality of relations between the Bishop of Rome and the Archbishop of Canterbury.

During Carey's 1996 visit, Pope John Paul gave the Archbishop a gold pectoral cross – the same gift that he gave to Roman Catholic Metropolitan Archbishops during an *Ad Limina* visits to the Pope every five years. And he gave the other Anglican bishops in the Delegation a silver pectoral cross – the same gift that he gave to suffragan Roman Catholic bishops during an *Ad Limina* visit. Of course this gesture begs the question: if the Archbishop of Canterbury isn't really a bishop, then why would the Pope have given him an episcopal cross? A similar episcopal cross was sent by Pope John Paul II to Archbishop Rowan Williams at his enthronement as Archbishop of Canterbury in 2003. Pope Francis offered the same gift to Archbishop Justin Welby at his enthronement in 2013, within a week of the Pope's own inauguration of his Petrine ministry. Most astonishingly, in October 2016 on occasion of the celebration of

---

24 'Growing Together in Unity and Mission: Building on 40 years of Anglican-Roman Catholic Dialogue – An Agreed Statement of the International Anglican-Roman Catholic Commission for Unity and Mission,' pp. 3-4.

25 'Growing Together in Unity and Mission,' nos. 100-103.

fifty years of Anglican-Roman Catholic relations at the church of San Gregorio al Celio, Pope Francis presented Archbishop Welby with a crosier – a pastoral staff, modelled on that of Pope Saint Gregory the Great. These gifts are much more than coincidental and are rich in ecclesiological symbolism.

On the Anglican side, there have also been important gifts offered to Roman Catholics. It is significant that one of the statues on the façade of Westminster Abbey is that of Oscar Romero, the martyred Roman Catholic Archbishop of San Salvador who was canonized by Pope Francis on 14th October 2018 along with Pope Paul VI and several others. Lord Williams of Oystermouth (former Archbishop of Canterbury) who chairs the Romero Trust in the U.K. led the delegation of six Anglican bishops – the largest delegation of Anglican bishops to attend such an event. It is also significant that on the Church of England's liturgical calendar, one finds post-Reformation Catholic saints listed such as Ignatius of Loyola, Francis Xavier, Teresa of Avila, John of the Cross, Francis de Sales, Vincent de Paul and others, whose feasts are all kept on the same day as found on the Roman Catholic liturgical calendar. This would have been unthinkable sixty or seventy years ago, but is a sign of just how far we have come on our ecumenical journey.

# WALKING TOGETHER: ANGLICANS AND ROMAN CATHOLICS FINDING A COMMON VOICE IN FACING FUTURE CHALLENGES

Happily, our communions are finding a common voice in speaking out against social problems and taking action together. In most places where Anglicans are found in significant numbers – firstly in the Western world and secondly in Africa – they live in the same cultural, indeed, multicultural and multiracial world as their Roman Catholic counterparts. One implication of this is that even where real differences keep us apart, Anglicans and Roman Catholics generally find it easy to work together, to cooperate on social questions, to pray together.

In his homily at the Oratory of Saint Francis Xavier 'del Caravita' in Rome on 26th October 2017 during the Installation of Archbishop Bernard Ntahoturi as Representative of the Archbishop of Canterbury to the Holy See and Director of the Anglican Centre in Rome, Archbishop Paul Gallagher, the Vatican's Secretary for Relations with States, stated this clearly:

You do not need me to tell you, that our world faces today an unprecedented number of challenges on every front, no continent is excluded and safe havens are in short supply. Some may have tended to see ecumenical endeavour as a question of the Church, almost an internal Christian affair, in which our unity will be the motor for the growth or even survival of Christ's Church. Given all we face today, given the urgency and precariousness of our situation, I would argue rather that ecumenical engagement is a moral imperative for all of us who are baptised in the name of the Blessed Trinity. We must proceed together as the one Body of Christ, not because it will be nice or cosy to do so, but because we have to in response to the pressing needs of humanity.[26]

In their conversations, Pope Francis and the Archbishop of Canterbury Justin Welby have spoken often about the need to walk together. In his address to Archbishop Justin during his visit to the Vatican on Monday 16 June 2014 the Pope addressed the issue of human trafficking where Anglicans and Roman Catholics have been walking together side by side:

At our first meeting, Your Grace and I discussed our shared concerns and our pain before a number of grace evils afflicting our human family. In particular, we shared our horror in the face of the scourge of human trafficking and forms of modern-day slavery. I thank you for the leadership you have shown in opposing these intolerable crimes against human dignity. In attempting to respond to this urgent need, notable collaborative efforts have been initiated on the ecumenical level and in cooperation with civil authorities and international organizations... Let us persevere in our commitment to combat new forms of enslavement, in the hope that we can help provide relief to victims and oppose this deplorable trade. I thank God that, as disciples sent to heal a broken world,

we stand together, with perseverance and determination, in opposing this grave evil... We must walk together.[27]

Two years later in 2016, during another visit of the Archbishop of Canterbury to Rome on occasion of the fiftieth anniversary of the founding of the Angli-

---

26 Archbishop Paul R. Gallagher, 'Ecumenism: A moral imperative for All who are baptised: The homily for the Inauguration of Archbishop Bernard Ntahoturi' in *Centro* 23/2 (Advent, 2017), 7.

27 'Address of Pope Francis to His Grace Justin Welby, Archbishop of Canterbury and his Entourage' (Monday 16 June 2014) https://www.vatican.va

can Centre and of the Anglican-Roman Catholic International Commission, Archbishop Welby made his own important declaration on the need to walk together:

> As we look around the world we continue to see enormous dangers to human dignity, and great suffering. The dangers faced are ones that many acknowledge, but to which few have a response. Into this mix of war, migration and climate change, economic deprivation, inequality and corruption, we see added the growth of extremist groups advocating religiously motivated violence, affecting most, probably even all, of the great world faiths. The internet enables their poison to spread around the world with lightning speed, catching the naïve and lost, and leading them into paths of destruction. Secular values disregard the unborn, especially those with disabilities, and disregard the aged. Family life is marginalised in the cause of economic necessity... Your Holiness, I ask that, as we have seen in these two days, despite those things that divide, we may be publicly determined to press forward where we may, together with all Christians... Let us walk closer together so the world sees new life and energy in the Church's worship, mission and witness. Above all so that the world sees Christ shining ever more brightly.[28]

On the occasion of that visit, Pope Francis and the Archbishop of Canterbury commissioned nineteen pairs of Anglican and Roman Catholic bishops paired from various countries around the globe at the conclusion of their weeklong IARCCUM-sponsored ecumenical pilgrimage begun in Canterbury. They were commissioned during Solemn Vespers at the church of San Gregorio in Celio – the very place from which Augustine of Canterbury had been sent on mission by Gregory the Great in the year 597 – to return to their home countries and implement this vision of 'walking together' through a practical and

lived ecumenism at the local level. In their Joint Declaration affirmed during the Vespers, the Pope and the Archbishop stated:

> The world must see us witnessing to this common faith in Jesus by acting together. We can, and must, work together to protect and preserve our common home... We can, and must, be united in a common cause to

---

28 'Archbishop Justin's address to Pope Francis' (6 October 2016) https://www.archbishopofcanterbury. org

uphold and defend the dignity of all people… As disciples of Christ we hold human persons to be sacred, and as apostles of Christ we must be their advocates.[29]

At the end of that historic IARCCUM pilgrimage, the bishops published a document entitled *Walking Together: Common Service to the World and Witness to the Gospel.* Their statement ended with these powerful words: 'We go forth now motivated by our commission to continue our pilgrimage in unity and mission, developing plans of action, spreading the vision we have shared among our episcopal counterparts, our clergy, and our lay faithful. We go forward together summoned to extend the mercy and peace of God to a world in need.'

One of those IARCCUM bishops on that pilgrimage was The Right Reverend Dennis Drainville, the 12th Anglican Bishop of Quebec. To mark his retirement as Bishop in 2016, he established a second, matching *cathedra* or episcopal throne in the Anglican Cathedral of the Holy Trinity for the Roman Catholic Archbishop of Quebec. As part of his retirement celebration Bishop Drainville blessed and dedicated the new *cathedra* together with Cardinal Gerald Lacroix, Archbishop of Quebec. Then, when Drainville's successor arrived, Bishop Bruce Myers, and his residence was not yet available, Myers moved into the Episcopal Palace in May 2016, and lived with the Cardinal for over a year where he shared in daily prayer, meals, and social life. The 'experiment' was so successful, that at the Cardinal's invitation, Bishop Myers seriously considered a permanent move back to the Episcopal palace.[30]

Inspired by that IARCCUM vision of walking together, Canadian Anglicans resident in Rome, Ken and Fawn White, founded the London-based 'Walking Together' Foundation in 2017 as a concrete realization of this vision. The first project of the Walking Together Foundation was an Anglican-Roman Catholic project in southern Malawi inaugurated in September 2017: the St. Timothy Scholarship Programme – a project co-sponsored by the Anglican Diocese of Upper Shire and the Roman Catholic Diocese of Mangochi with the full support and engagement of both bishops. It supports the education of forty of the poorest children in southern Malawi: twenty boys and twenty girls, half Anglican and half Roman Catholic with several Muslim students included in the mix, divided among four residential schools: two Anglican and two

---

29 'Common Declaration by Pope Francis and Archbishop of Canterbury' (5 October 2016) https:www.episcopalnewsservice.org

30 Cardinal Gerald C. Lacroix in a private conversation with Keith Pecklers. Residence of the Canadian Ambassador to the Holy See, Tuesday 23 October 2018.

Roman Catholic. A Rome-based Anglican-Roman Catholic Delegation made a formal visit in May 2018, carrying letters from the Pontifical Council for the Promotion of Christian Unity and Lambeth Palace commending this initiative. More recently, 'Walking Together' has launched an Anglican-Roman Catholic project in service of the poor in New Brunswick, Canada, and discussions are now underway with Anglican and Roman Catholic bishops in the Dominican Republic about a possible project there.

# CONCLUSION

One hundred years after those historic Malines Conversations, and more than fifty years after the Second Vatican Council and that historic encounter between Paul VI and Michael Ramsey, Anglicans and Roman Catholics continue their 'walking together on the way' on a common path toward God's reign of justice and peace that is more intentional than ever. The bonds of affection between our Churches are ever more deliberate and obvious to those who observe from the outside. Despite our various obstacles and theological debates, we remain committed to search for the unity that Christ desires for his Church, 'that all may be one.' What we can do together, we must do together, giving our lives over to our common mission: instruments in the service of unity, as Christ would have us do.

# Archbishop Donald Bolen

Ecumenical friendship; mutual accountability; covenant on a diocesan level; shared facilities; joint ministry on campuses in prisons and in hospitals; the practice of having ecumenical observers; martyrdom and the ecumenism of blood; the pursuit of holiness; common religious charisms; the work of reconciliation jointly and shared guilt; carrying one another's burdens; conciliarity and primacy and the way those are lived out at present. We haven't lived those well, but there's a horizon of possibility open for us by virtue of being in real but incomplete communion. It has not only been helpful, it has been incredibly fruitful ecumenically. And it leads, I think, to what seems to be a very honest description of the relationship between us: we receive gifts from each other and we recognize the integrity of the other. The communion may not be full, but it is real and genuine and profound.

Archbishop Donald Bolen
MCG VI, 149-50

# Bishop Catherine Waynick

No one 'member' of Christ's body has gained all the truth for all time. None has remained completely unchanged over its own history, and without the willingness to encounter and learn from each other, the various parts of Christ's fractured body will continue to claim they are being 'Spirit led' into truths which remain incomprehensible to our brothers and sisters in Christ. So when we ponder the sacramentality of the Church, we Anglicans, Roman Catholics, and Orthodox may need to broaden our definitions of both 'sacrament' and 'Church', and how our definitions and assumptions inform our relationship to the world around us. In my mind and heart the divine initiative of the Incarnation, the communal event of loving, the reshaping of relationships into new realities – all of this is the work of the *whole* body of Christ.

Bishop Catherine Waynick
MCG III, 62-3

## Chapter 6

# Taking Stock of the Present Situation of our Churches 2: Overcoming the Difficulties

### JEREMY MORRIS

The history of Anglican-Roman Catholic relations surveyed by Keith Pecklers in the previous chapter is a remarkable story of growth in mutual understanding and warmth between both communions, a story all the more extraordinary when seen against the background of the conflict and suspicion of the previous four hundred years. But it has not been without setbacks and failures, and without new obstacles being raised at almost every turn. The Malines conversations were a bold, even reckless, initiative right at the beginning of that story. But in order to understand just why a fresh look at what they set out to achieve seemed appropriate in the twenty-first century, it is also necessary to appreciate the history of the continuing differences and difficulties between the two communions. Addressing the World Council of Churches in Geneva in February 2018, the present Archbishop of Canterbury, Justin Welby, warned against the temptation to regard ecumenical dialogue as the centrepiece of ecumenical relations: 'Bi- and multilateral theological dialogue over the course of the twentieth century bore much fruit but at times it could appear to be akin to diplomatic renegotiation of borders: the barriers to communion still exist but not where we thought they did.' What was needed alongside theological discussion, he argued, was an 'ecumenism of action'.[1] By the same token, the history of relations between Churches cannot simply be assessed with reference to theological texts and contacts between church leaders: it depended on a welter of complicated social, political, national and local factors.

What I propose to do in this chapter is to fill out Keith Pecklers's account by

---

1 https://www.archbishopofcanterbury.org/speaking-and-writing/speeches/ecumenical-spring-arch-bishop-justins-speech-world-council-churches, accessed January 2019.

examining the changing historical context of ecumenism in the ninety years between the original Malines conversations and the convening of the 'Malines Conversations Group'. It would be impossible to do justice to all the relevant dimensions of the question in a short contribution, and so I shall concentrate on three: the contrasting contexts of the ecumenical movement in the 1920s and in the early twenty-first century; the transformation under way in the global context of European Christianity throughout the period; and finally developments in Anglicanism which have interrupted and complicated relations between the two communions.

# CHANGE AND CONTINUITY IN THE 'ECUMENICAL CENTURY'

The Malines conversations were an embryonic attempt at something like formal ecumenical dialogue between Anglicans and Catholics. But they were not without precedent and context. They came after a number of significant developments in the early history of the ecumenical movement, and reflected an anxiety and a deep hope (shared particularly by Anglo-Catholics) that Apostolic order should be at the centre of ecumenical endeavour. If their moving inspiration, from the Anglican side at least, was the frustration Lord Halifax felt at the way his overtures to the Vatican in the 1890s had backfired with the condemnation of Anglican orders in *Apostolicae Curae* (1896), their favourable moment was the momentum generated by the great World Missionary Conference in Edinburgh in 1910 (sometimes misleadingly called the start of the ecumenical movement), and the 'Appeal to all Christian People', a call to church unity issued by the Lambeth Conference of 1920.[2] In the conversations explicit reference was made to the Lambeth Appeal's plea for reception of each other's authorized ministries.[3] But the 1920s in general were a decade of ecumenical advance, epitomized by the two main streams of ecumenical relationship that

---

2   Viscount Halifax, *Leo XIII and Anglican Orders* (London: Longmans, Green & Co 1912); on Edinburgh 1910 and the ecumenical movement, see J. Morris, 'Edinburgh1910-2010: A Retrospective Assessment', *Ecclesiology*, 7 (2011), pp. 297-316, and also B. Stanley (ed.), *The World Missionary Conference, Edinburgh 1910* (Grand Rapids, Mich.: Eerdmans 2009); and for the Lambeth Appeal, C. Methuen, 'Lambeth 1920: The Appeal To All Christian People', in M. Barber, G. Sewell & S. Taylor (eds), *From the Reformation to the Permissive Society: A Miscellany in Celebration of the 400th Anniversary of Lambeth Palace Library* (Woodbridge: Boydell & Brewer 2010), pp. 521-64.

3   See Lord Halifax (ed.), *The Conversations at Malines 1921-1925. Original Documents* (London: Philip Allan 1930), p.10: Lord Halifax 'signale en particulier l'Appel des évêques en communion avec l'Archevêque de Cantorbéry [sic] réunis à Londres, en juillet 1920.' The Anglican report to Randall Davidson emphasized the importance of the Appeal in prompting Halifax to approach Mercier: see Lord Halifax *et alia*, *The Conversations at Malines 1921-1925* ((London: Oxford University Press & Humphrey Milford 1927), p. 6.

were eventually to issue in the World Council of Churches after the Second World War – the 'Life and Work' movement organized around conferences that began at Stockholm in 1925, and its parallel, 'Faith and Order', initiated formally by a conference at Lausanne in 1927. These were Protestant initiatives, it is true, and Pius XI condemned the nascent ecumenical movement in the encyclical *Mortalium Animos* of 1928, a condemnation usually assumed to include the Malines conversations.[4]

But, as R.J. Lahey showed in an article on the Church diplomatic background to the Malines conversations many years ago, the picture was actually more complex.[5] Cardinal Mercier repeatedly sought Papal approval for what he was attempting, and secured it. By the third meeting these were to all intents and purposes, from the Roman side, officially approved conversations.[6] It was really the Anglican authorities who were more cautious. Although Lahey appears to imply the Anglicans also viewed the conversations as official, Archbishop Randall Davidson's very carefully constructed letters and speeches on the question give a different perspective. Davidson was insistent there should be matching expressions of approval from both sides, but a letter he sent to the archbishops and metropolitans of the Anglican Communion in December 1923 denied the participants were in any sense representative: they had gone with his 'full encouragement', but they were 'in no sense delegates or representatives of the Church as a whole'.[7] Then, as now, the exercise of authority in the Church of England operated differently from the Catholic Church. For the Archbishop of Canterbury to lend his acknowledgement and personal support was not much more than a statement of personal opinion with no official implications; for Anglicans there was no means in place by which properly 'official' approval could be given.

That in turn indicates how the way in which churches think about these issues today changed dramatically in the course of the twentieth century. At the beginning of the century there was little Church of England bureaucracy to speak of, and virtually no central organization; Church House in Westminster was built not long before the First World War, and its staff were few in number. There were no standing commissions. In this, the Church of England stood in sharp contrast to the Vatican. The first Doctrine Commission of the Church

---

4   R. Rouse & S.C. Neill (eds), *A History of the Ecumenical Movement 1517-1948* (London: SPCK 1954), p. 299.

5   R.J. Lahey, 'The Origins and Approval of the Malines Conversations', *Church History*, 43 (1974), pp. 366-384.

6   Lahey, 'Origins and Approval of the Malines Conversations', p. 380.

7   G.K.A. Bell, *Randall Davidson, Archbishop of Canterbury* (3rd edn, London: Oxford University Press 1952), p. 1284.

of England was formed in 1922 under the chairmanship of William Temple and reported in 1938.[8] It then ceased to meet until the 1960s, when a permanent Doctrine Commission was formed. That temporary commission apart, the Church of England had no mechanism *as a Church* for saying anything authoritatively on Christian belief. Even the synodical system that now dominates the polity of the Church of England was very recent; it was not formed in its present shape until 1919, when a series of representative bodies were created, starting at the very bottom with parish church councils and culminating in the national Church Assembly (the forerunner of today's General Synod).[9] There were certainly precedents in the nineteenth century, though they were patchy and had no legislative power. By implication there were no norms, there was no pattern, there was no precedent or mechanism for the reception of the Malines Conversations in the 1920s. And on the wider international scene, alongside the evolution of the Church's bureaucracy went a growing participation on the part of the Church of England in formal ecumenical instruments, including Faith and Order, Life and Work, the International Missionary Council, and eventually the World Council of Churches when it was formed in 1948. As a result of all these institutional developments, the Church of England now can declare its mind in a way that was simply not possible in the 1920s: by the beginning of the twenty-first century, it had a functioning national representative system, national institutions covering different aspects of its life and mission, and paid, full-time, professional 'civil servants'; these things barely existed in the 1920s. This helps to explain why, when news of the original conversations broke, there was such controversy. From the Anglican side the Malines conversations were arguably unbalanced: it was an exclusively Anglo-Catholic group taking part. Although at the time Anglo-Catholicism was ascendant in the Church of England, the limits of its influence were already being tested.[10] Since the development of formal ecumenical dialogue in which Anglicans have been involved really got under way in the 1960s and 1970s, either the Communion as a whole, or the Church of England specifically (in the case of national dialogue) has endeavoured to reflect the breadth of Anglican opinion in the composition of its negotiating 'team', as otherwise the risk that a group would conclude an agreement with little chance of being

---

8   Archbishops' Commission on Christian Doctrine, *Doctrine in the Church of England* (London: SPCK 1922).

9   See K.A. Thompson, *Bureaucracy and Church Reform. The organizational response of the Church of England to Social Change 1800-1965* (Oxford: Clarendon 1970), pp. 129-78.

10  Anglo-Catholics had just lost a crucial battle over the franchise for the new representative system, for example: see J. Morris, *The High Church Revival in the Church of England: Arguments and Identities* (Leiden: Brill 2016), pp. 244-54.

recognized and accepted by the Church of England as a whole, and the Anglican Communion, would be unacceptably high.

But then, the participation of the Roman Catholic Church in ecumenical dialogue, and in international, national and local ecumenical initiatives since the Second Vatican Council has transformed the ecumenical challenge. John XIII's establishment of the Secretariat for Promoting Christian Unity in 1960, which later became the Pontifical Council for Promoting Christian Unity, provided an institutional mechanism for advancing the ecumenical cause at the very heart of the Catholic Church. The development of bilateral and multilateral dialogues since Vatican II involving almost every conceivable relationship between the Catholic Church and other historic Christian traditions has put relations between Anglicans and Roman Catholics in an altogether different light from the 1920s. The official dialogue between Anglicans and Catholics has been running for over half a century and has produced a formidable library of documents creatively addressing important elements of disagreement.[11] Anglicans and Roman Catholics, through these official statements, are arguably closer to a mutual theological understanding than they have ever been. From an Anglican perspective, this development has been, paradoxically, both stimulating and complicating. Within just over half a century, relations between Catholics and Anglicans across much of the Anglican world have moved from suspicion to warmth and co-operation. But at the same time – and following in the footsteps of earlier agreements such as that between the Anglican Churches and the Old Catholic Churches concluded at Bonn in 1931 – Anglicans have secured far-reaching agreement with other Christian traditions, with relationships of full communion and interchangeability of ministers between, for example, British and Irish Anglicans and Scandinavian and Baltic Lutherans via the Porvoo Agreement, and ever closer relations with the Methodist Church of Great Britain after the signing of the Anglican-Methodist Covenant in 2003, to name just two.[12] The closer the goal of unity seems to get, the more complicated and multi-dimensional it becomes: a viable ecumenical strategy is one that does not allow any one set of bilateral relations to proceed so far that it upsets all other inter-church relations in which the Church is engaged. The pursuit

---

11  There are two useful 'mid-way' surveys: C. Hill & E.J. Yarnold (eds), *Anglicans and Roman Catholics: The Search for Unity* (1994), and W. Purdy, *The Search for Unity. Relations between the Anglican and Roman Catholic Churches from the 1950s to the 1970s* (1996); and a third volume gathering the ARCIC II documents together and offering some reflections on them, in A. Denaux, N. Sagovsky & C. Sherlock (eds), *Looking Towards a Church Fully Reconciled* (London: SPCK 2016).

12  For a survey of these developments from an authoritative witness to many of them, see P. Avis, 'Anglicanism and Christian Unity in the Twentieth Century' in J. Morris (ed.), *The Oxford History of Anglicanism, Vol 4: Global Western Anglicanism, c.1910 to the present* (Oxford: Oxford University Press 2017), pp.186-213.

of Christian unity is like juggling an ever-expanding number of balls: keeping them all in the air at the same time requires ever faster work. Moreover, formal ecumenical dialogue now comes with heavy institutional expectations and organization: much preparation is needed, with careful ecclesiastical diplomacy, and the attendant risks of wide ramifications from unfortunate or ill-placed comments. There is something to be said, then, alongside the immense progress made by official ecumenical mechanisms, for the informal, the personal, the exploratory and provisional, for the small-scale evolution of special sets of theological conversations that can be risk-taking and nimble, that can run ahead if need be of the officially-stated positions on any one side and prompt the Churches to take a fresh look at things – just what the Malines conversations group has been trying to do.

From these considerations of evolving ecumenical institutions and strategy we should now turn briefly to the emergence of a distinct ecumenical method, for what is possible now in ecumenical circles is informed by almost a century of development. Here, the original Malines conversations were indeed trailblazers. In the 1920s, there was little precedent for conversations between two well-established world communions on different sides of the Reformation divide.[13] In effect, participants in the conversations had to improvise a method, producing papers from each side, hearing each other's presentations and then discussing them in a spirit of critical sympathy, and attempting to agree points on particular disputed matters. It's particularly striking, for example, that the third and fourth conversations focused almost exclusively on the papal primacy. The memorandum from the third, drawn up by Benjamin Kidd and presented from the Anglican side, stated five points of agreement: first, that the Roman Church was found and built by St Peter and St Paul; second, that the Roman See is the only historically known apostolic See of the West; third, that the bishop of Rome is, as Augustine said of Pope Innocent, 'president of the Western Church'; fourth, that he has a primacy of all the bishops of Christendom, so that without communion with him there is in fact no prospect of a reunited Christendom; and fifth, that to the Roman See the Churches of the English owe their Christianity through Gregory.[14] These were points that the Anglicans agreed amongst themselves. It's startling to think that this

---

13  There was a precedent of sorts from half a century earlier in the Bonn reunion conferences of 1874 and 1875 between members of the Church of England and of the Old Catholic Churches of what later became the Union of Utrecht: see C.B. Moss, *The Old Catholic Movement. Its Origin and History* (London: SPCK, 1948), and more recently, M. Chapman, *The Fantasy of Reunion: Anglicans, Catholics, and Ecumenism, 1833-1882* (Oxford: OUP, 2014).

14  These points are set out in Halifax *et al., Conversations at Malines*, p. 32; Kidd's own papers on the Papacy can be found in Halifax, *Original Documents*, pp. 123-34; 151-8; & 175-86.

is what they thought could be agreed between both sides, and the third and fourth points in particular indicate just why there was so much controversy when these points became more widely known back in Britain: they would never have been accepted by many Anglicans at the time.[15] If the conclusions, then, were contentious, nonetheless the *method* adopted here was full of significance for the future. One of the Anglican contributors (unnamed, but one can imagine Charles Gore saying this) wished also to insist that organization is relatively of secondary importance and that dogmas are the things of primary importance; the report from the Roman Catholics accepted this entirely and insisted further on the necessity of unity of doctrine.[16] There was an implicit ordering of doctrine and organization, in other words, which again would later be reflected in the emergence of dialogue after Vatican II.

From that, incidentally, follows the question of language. The original conversations had to begin to grapple constructively with the question of how one church tradition, with its distinct history and culture, listens to another. A crucial linguistic – but of course also conceptual – difference was in the way Anglicans thought in terms of fundamentals and non-fundamentals, but Catholics in terms of *de fide* and non-*de fide*. For a conversation between two different cultures to take place, there has to be mutual recognition, and mediation. None of this could be taken very far at Malines in the 1920s; but the problem was encountered, even if not explicitly addressed. Only much later, with the benefit of greater experience and resources, would Anglicans and Roman Catholics seriously begin to explore such issues, inspired in part by fresh movements of theological reassessment in both Churches, signalled for example by Michael Ramsey's attempt to fuse order and Gospel in *The Gospel and the Catholic Church* (1936), and by Yves Congar's resuscitation of the spirit of Johann Adam Möhler in his *Divided Christendom* (1939). The language of *koinonia*, or 'communion', which featured so strongly in the work of ARCIC II, for example, provided just such a means of mutual recognition.[17] The method of receptive ecumenism, influential in ARCIC III, may prove another instance.[18] The current Malines conversations group has drawn on these and

---

15  A measured and supportive view, nonetheless, was expressed by the *Times* on publication of the report in early 1928, though it admitted that the 'time has certainly not arrived for conferences on reunion by officially appointed delegates of the two Church of England and Rome.' *The Times*, editorial, 19 January, 1928.

16  Again, this point was recorded in Halifax et al., *Conversations at Malines*, p. 38.

17  See especially ARCIC II, *Church as Communion: an agreed Statement* (London: Church House Publishing, and Catholic Truth Society 1991).

18  See the commentaries on the ARCIC III document, *Walking Together on the Way*, produced by O. Rush (Catholic) & J. Hawkey (Anglican), and published by SPCK in 2018.

other sources.

The controversial, difficult reception of the original Malines Conversations also reflected a history of prejudice about Roman Catholics from the Anglican side and doubts about the Anglicans from the Roman Catholic side. Putting it at its bleakest, from the late sixteenth century on a deep suspicion existed on the part of Anglicans about Roman Catholics, and the Anglican experience of the English Roman Catholic Church in particular reinforced a certain kind of sectarianism. Although a small, 'recusant' English Catholic community survived throughout the long centuries of persecution, the rapid expansion of Catholicism in Britain in the nineteenth century was a product of Irish immigration.[19] English Anglican prejudices were fuelled by Ultramontanism, a movement easily (but wrongly) cast as an authoritarian throwback, underlined it seemed by the declaration of Papal infallibility at the First Vatican Council. The most prominent Anglican layman of his day, William Gladstone, provoked a storm of controversy with his pamphlet on *The Vatican decrees* (1874), sub-titled 'A political expostulation'. That the Prime Minister, no less, High Churchman as he was, could write what his modern biographer has called 'a remarkable blend of political theory, Protestant anti-Popery, and Tractarian *angst*' was a sign of the continuing vitality of the polemical tradition that associated Roman Catholicism with treason.[20] The Catholic culture of 'integralism', which engendered a kind of religious and social sub-culture seemingly alien to mainstream British society, if anything reinforced this essentially political suspicion.[21] Some of this had dissipated, it's true, by the beginning of the First World War, but Catholics in Britain remained a largely marginalised and somewhat separatist community even into the 1920s and 1930s, with anti-Catholicism still alive and well amongst some social groups and in some cities with a strong history of sectarian division, such as Liverpool, Manchester and Glasgow. Malines in *that* context looked extraordinary.

Just as we can describe the lingering tensions and suspicions, however, we also need to take account of the very shifts and turns underneath the surface that expressed a growing mutual appreciation between Anglican and Roman Catholic theologians. From the Anglican side, of course, the driver was particularly the Oxford Movement, and the way in which many of its

---

19  J. Bossy, *The English Catholic Community 1570-1850* (London: DLT 1976), E. Norman, *Roman Catholicism in England. From the Elizabethan Settlement to the Second Vatican Council* (Oxford: Oxford University Press 1985).

20  H.C.G. Matthew, *Gladstone 1809-1874* (Oxford: Clarendon 1986) p. 247.

21  For a mid-twentieth century discussion, see Y. Congar & B. Gilligan, 'Attitudes towards Reform in the Church' *Cross Currents* 1 (1951), pp. 80-102.

leaders – even those who did not convert – were interested in French Roman Catholic theology. This was particularly true of Pusey. William Franklin has traced a series of parallels and connections between the Catholic Tübingen school of theology, the French liturgist Prosper Guéranger, and Pusey, reflecting the same set of preoccupations at the root of liturgical renewal in the Catholic and Anglican Churches in the late nineteenth and twentieth centuries.[22] Another interesting connection was the reception of Anglo-Catholic theology by French and Italian Catholics in the nineteenth century. The circle that was particularly interested in Anglo-Catholicism was the liberal Catholic circle of Montalembert and Lacordaire. Here is Lacordaire, travelling in England in the 1850s, describing the religious revival in England, and he meant principally in the Anglican Church: 'one feels throughout this country that the era of religious liberty has here begun its reign and is producing its due effects: they are building, founding, creating an art for the Church'.[23] He went on to say that Protestantism had its weaknesses and did lead some people out of Christianity, but this was not its general effect, and he went on to praise the way in which the Bible was taught and how that encouraged Christian notions in the population large. There is also a very telling passage by Montalembert on the beneficial effects of the Oxford Movement: the Puseyites, he said, had engendered 'a profound respect for religious traditions, and consequently for Catholic authority'.[24] Malines did not come not out of the blue, but as a result of growing mutual interest between Anglo-Catholics and the continental Catholic tradition.

Once you put that growing theological appreciation alongside the fading of anti-Catholic prejudice in Britain in the early and mid-twentieth century, you can see how the scene was to change so dramatically from the 1960s on. One under-recognized part of this was the social transformation of the Catholic Church in Britain, away from its predominantly working-class Irish roots, towards a more socially and culturally diverse community, with nonetheless full integration into the professions.[25] A critical view of this development as a form of 'embourgeoisement' was advanced by Anthony Archer, who argued

---

22 R.W. Franklin, *Nineteenth-century churches: the history of a new Catholicism in Württemberg, England, and France* (New York & London: Garland 1997).

23 *Correspondance du R.P. Lacordaire et de Madame Swetchine, publiée par le Cte de Falloux* (Paris: Auguste Vaton 1864), p. 508, cited in J.N. Morris, 'High Churchmen and French Catholics', in ibid., *The High Church Revival in the Church of England. Argument and Identities* (Leiden: Brill 2016), p.159.

24 Charles de Montalembert, *The Political Future of England* (new edn., London: John Murray 1856) p. 201.

25 See especially M. Hornsby-Smith, *Roman Catholics in England: Studies in Social Structure since the Second World War* (Cambridge: Cambridge University Press 1987).

that Vatican II reinforced the growing middle-class nature of English Catholicism.[26] However one describes the changes in the English Catholic Church since the 1960s, they have actually produced a context, nonetheless, in which Catholics and Anglicans now locally feel much more alike, and are much more easily able to relate. That is perhaps just one example – though in this context a vital one – of how much closer relationships between Anglicans and Roman Catholics have become possible over the last half century.

# THE TRANSFORMATION OF GLOBAL CHRISTIANITY

And yet, once again, as some opportunities open up, others perhaps fade. Just as the Catholic Church in Britain has changed, so have the Anglican and Roman Churches on a global scale. The Malines conversations in the 1920s had one very specific and recent consideration in the background that, surprisingly, was barely registered in the published reports of the conversations: there must have been a sense of solidarity between Anglicans and Belgian Catholics after the First World War. Belgium was the reason Britain went to war in 1914. The war did extraordinary damage to early ecumenical relations between, for example, the British and German Churches.[27] Consequently there was a strong desire in ecumenical circles in 1919 to try to rebuild ecumenical relations. Another easily forgotten dimension is that Britain and Belgium had colonies then: it may even be that the conversations were controversial partly because of the weight attached to talks between church leaders from two imperial powers. All of this has changed dramatically since the 1920s. Up until 1939 the world was predominantly a European world, and yet now we live in a post-colonial world. The process of decolonisation massively changed the context of the ecumenical movement. In some ways it heightened the expectation of change and intensified the desire for unity, but it also complicated the means. There could no longer be a realistic hope that conversations between two groups of national theologians – or at least representatives from *national* Churches of worldwide communions – would actually lead to substantial change, because ecumenical dialogue now had to be embedded in worldwide structures of authority of representation with a great deal of internal dialogue, internal disagreement and diversity. A further, difficult dimension of the changed world is the particu-

---

26  A. Archer, *The Two Catholic Churches. A Study in Oppression* (London: SCM 1986).

27  See comments on this in Keith Clements' biography of Joseph Oldham: ibid., *Faith on the Frontier; A Life of J.H. Oldham* (Edinburgh: T & T Clark 1999), pp. 121-62.

lar problem of transitivity – that is to say what happens when one 'national' Church concludes an ecumenical agreement with another Church, but one that is not received or accepted by other ecumenical partners elsewhere in the world. This obviously does not affect the Roman Catholic Church in the same way, but it is a significant problem for Anglicans. For example, the Episcopal Church and the Evangelical Lutheran Church of America (ELCA) have a relationship of full communion, which means they have interchangeability of ministries; the Episcopal Church is a member of the Anglican communion, and in theory therefore it ought to be possible for an American Lutheran minister (from the ELCA) to come to Britain and function as a clergyman or a clergywoman in the Church of England; but they cannot do so, but rather have to be conditionally re-ordained.[28]

But even this does not capture the most startling development in world Christianity. For that, at least as it bears on our theme here, we have to turn to what has been called the changing 'statistical centre of gravity' of world Christianity, and what follows can be no more than the briefest of summaries.[29] On the one hand, Christianity has seen a steady decline in western Europe over the last century, spawning an already vast and constantly expanding literature on the causes and course of this decline, as well as significant challenges to the claim that this 'secularization' is inevitable.[30] On the other hand, and contrary to what some commentators and post-colonial theorists expected, Christianity has grown spectacularly in much of sub-Saharan Africa, and in Asia.[31] As a consequence, it's argued, the centre of gravity of world Christianity is shifting away from Europe, southwards and eastwards. From an estimated 1% of the Catholic Church's membership in 1900, African Catholics had become over 20% by the end of the century.[32] Likewise, growth in the Anglican provinces of Africa in particular after the middle of the twentieth century was spectacular, though precise figures are hard to come by.[33] This has important consequences

---

28  This was achieved in the agreement *Called to Common Mission* of 1999/2000 in the US and paralleled in Canada by the Waterloo declaration of 2001; these agreements match the Porvoo agreement (see above), but there is no automatic relationship of transitivity across the Atlantic.

29  The term was made famous by T.M. Johnson & S. Y. Chung, 'Tracking Global Christianity's Statistical Centre of Gravity, AD 33–AD 2100', *International Review of Mission*, 93 (2004), pp. 166-81.

30  For two contrasting accounts, see R. Rémond, *Religion and Society in Modern Europe* (Oxford: Blackwell 1999), and G. Davie, *Europe: the exceptional case: parameters of faith in the modern world* (London: DLT 2002).

31  See P. Jenkins, *The Next Christendom: the Coming of Global Christianity* (3rd edn, Oxford: Oxford University Press 2011).

32  See https://www.livescience.com/27244-the-world-s-catholic-population-infographic.html, accessed November 2018.

33  For a brief overview, see D. Goodhew, 'A story of growth and decline', *Church Times*, 6 January 2017; the statistics on church membership are notoriously unreliable.

for ecumenical relations. Most obviously, the context in which ecumenical relations have to be considered is immensely more complicated than a hundred years ago. There are many more local contexts to be considered, with their own characteristic features and challenges; the range of views to be taken into account has broadened considerably; new or unforeseen considerations of culture need to be taken into account; the scope and reach of ecclesial authority is greater and more complex than ever before; to name but a few. If the Malines conversations looked partial and perhaps one-sided even in the 1920s, think how incomplete and lop-sided the informal discussions of the new conversations must necessarily be! And therefore, the justification for such group cannot be a pretended representative character, for it cannot have one: it can only be a group of informed enthusiasts, working away underneath and behind – under-tunneling, as we say – the official dialogues and formal relationships.

# NEW CAUSES OF DIVISION IN ANGLICANISM

But all these changes also have to be considered against the background of the immense changes in Anglicanism in the last forty years, which appear to have thrown up new obstacles to unity between Anglicans and Roman Catholics even as the official dialogue was making headway in addressing some of the most salient points of theological disagreement. It is a matter of considerable scholarly disagreement just what exactly lies behind the divisions that have opened up in most of the western Anglican churches. Some argue that Anglicans have capitulated to secularism or humanism, liberalism, and permissiveness; others that all churches with an eye on survival must adapt to their changing context.[34] There cannot be simplistic explanations of ecclesial change, needless to say: churches are complex, multi-dimensional institutions that sit inside, and relate to, different social strata and different cultural, ethnic and political identities in a myriad of ways. What is undeniable is that broader social and cultural changes in western society in the last half-century or so have impacted considerably on church life, stimulating movements of change and of resistance.

Here there is space to mention briefly just two, and even then largely in relation to the Church of England, though arguably these are the most significant new obstacles to the reunion of the Anglican and Catholic Churches. By

---

34 Sharply contrasting positions can be seen in E. Norman, *Anglican Difficulties: A New Syllabus of Errors* (London: Continuum 2004), and M. Percy, *Anglicanism: Confidence, Commitment and Communion* (Farnham: Ashgate 2013).

far the most salient new point of disagreement between the Catholic and Anglican Churches – at least at the official level – is the question of the ordination of women. Not all Churches of the Anglican Communion have accepted the possibility of women's ordination, and most remain divided on the matter to some degree, though the extent of the division varies considerably. There is a long 'back story', which can be traced at least from the beginning of the twentieth century, of a growing movement for change in the Church of England.[35] An early advocate was Maude Royden (1876-1956) who, though an Anglican, occupied a preaching pulpit at the Free Church City Temple in London during the First World War, and even before the war had emerged as a supporter of women's ordination.[36] But although the theological arguments in favour were gaining ground in mid-century, it is unquestionably true that the forceful emergence of a movement in favour in western Anglicanism in the 1960s and 1970s was linked with the wider movement for women's rights in those decades. In the Church of England, the diaconate was opened to women in 1987; the priesthood in 1992; and finally, the episcopate in 2014. Opposition to each of these steps frequently emphasized the ecumenical objections from Rome and the Orthodox. In the case of Rome, prompted by a growing lobby for women's ordination with the Catholic Church, John Paul II emphatically denied its possibility for priestly ministry (which derivatively therefore includes the episcopate) in *Ordinatio Sacerdotalis* in 1994; this judgment has been affirmed by Pope Francis on several occasions. The implications for reconciliation of Anglican and Catholic ministries are clear: even if official acknowledgment of the absence of a *formal or theoretical* doctrinal difference over ordination and ministry could be secured from both sides, the Catholic Church's effective extension of the doctrine of ordained ministry to include male gender as an essential condition means that an *actual* mutual recognition of ministries is not currently possible. Nonetheless, there are plenty of Catholic theologians and church people who argue that this is not a closed matter.[37]

Even wider divisions within the Anglican Communion have opened up over sexual ethics, and particularly over same-sex relations. Here, again there is a considerable 'back story' of theological argument and reflection, with Norman Pittenger, the process theologian, an early advocate acceptance of same-sex

---

35 S. Gill, *Women and the Church of England. From the Eighteenth Century to the Present* (London: SPCK 1996).

36 S. Fletcher, *Maude Royden: A Life* (Oxford: Blackwell 1989).

37 See, for example, M.J. Daigler, *Incompatible with God's Design: A History of the Women's Ordination Movement in the U.S. Roman Catholic Church* (Lanham, MD: Scarecrow Press 2012).

relationships.[38] And again, developments in the western Anglican Churches were unquestionably related to wider movements of change, and particularly the 'Gay Liberation' movement. In the US Episcopal Church, same-sex relationships were affirmed as deserving of support and equality before the law by the late 1970s, but the formal acceptance of same-sex marriage is much more recent. The election of Gene Robinson, a gay divorcee, as bishop of New Hampshire in 2003 triggered a wider conflict within the Communion, not just the Episcopal Church.[39].The Church of England has taken some steps along the same road, extending expressions of pastoral support to same-sex relationships, but has stopped short of adapting its doctrine of marriage to encompass them, and formally (though in practice this has often proved unenforceable) has declined to acknowledge the possibility of sexually-active same-sex relations for those in the ordained ministry.[40] For the Catholic Church too same-sex relations have become a controversial and internally divisive question, though the nature of ecclesial authority in the Catholic Church and the universal character of the *magisterium* mean that there is no substantial disagreement at the official level across the Church as a whole over formal acknowledgment of them within the ordained ministry, and of course the Church remains committed to the practice of clerical celibacy. Here, then, how serious is the obstacle thrown up by differences between Catholics and Anglicans over same-sex relations is harder to assess, given the extent of internal Anglican divisions.

# CONCLUSION

So what, finally, are we to make of this complex, changing history? How do we take stock of where we are? Whilst in the 1920s no one could be sanguine about the difficulty of reuniting Anglican and Catholic Churches, the main obstacle was thought to be essentially theological: it lay in the profound doctrinal differences which had opened up between Catholics and Anglicans at the time of the Reformation, and which had been strengthened in the intervening centuries by mutual misunderstanding. To the Anglo-Catholics who took part in the original conversations, the key goal was to achieve agreed positions on disputed points of doctrine. Their efforts were impressive and ground-break-

---

38 See, for example, N. Pittenger, *Time for Consent: A Christian's Approach to Homosexuality* (London: SCM 1970).

39 S. Bates, *A Church at War: Anglicans and Homosexuality* (London: Hodder & Stoughton 2005).

40 The determining document for the Church of England remains *Issues in Human Sexuality: A Statement by the House of Bishops* (London: Church House Publishing, 1991).

ing. But they were not enough. Neither Church was ready to receive what the conversations had concluded. Neither Church, in any case, had the mechanisms in place to make something of the agreement that was achieved. Perhaps, too, it's fair to say that without much prior experience of ecumenical conversation, hopes of rapid progress towards reunion were somewhat naïve. The extraordinary progress that has been made in mutual understanding between Anglicans and Catholics since then, buttressed by the formidable work of ARCIC, has been nothing if not simultaneously a journey of discovery into the sheer difficulty of genuinely reconciling long-separated Christian traditions. Learning not to be naïve is real learning. It is a vital condition of further progress. Unity will not come without that lesson being taken to heart. And if, in discovering how difficult this goal of reunion really is, we also find ways of seeing beyond the fresh divisions that have opened up within and between our traditions, so much the better.

Reactions to ecumenical initiatives commonly take one of two forms – either a surprise that such initiatives are necessary at all, given that 'we have so much in common anyway', or a weariness that we're still *talking* about unity and haven't just got on with it, when 'so many other things ought to draw our attention'. As I've argued, neither reaction, however, does justice to the complexity of the ecumenical task, which requires different traditions to reach out to each other across a gulf in mutual understanding brought about by divergent histories. Achieving church unity is not like solving a jigsaw puzzle. It demands patience, willingness to learn from each other and to change, an attention to sometimes painful memories, above all a commitment to grow together in proclaiming and living the Gospel; all of this is costly and difficult. It is a tortuous and often frustrating journey, if also a joyful one.

# Paul McPartlan

We have to put things in the proper context: is Christ proclaimed? That's the crucial thing. That's exactly what Pope Francis is coming back to, as the fundamental question: is Christ proclaimed? Of course, he's always shooting down any sort of triumphalism. If we believe that we have these things that are precious, let's treat them with proper humility and actually try to live them, instead of just tub-thumping. He's inviting us to have a richer list of the elements, isn't he? Catholics tend to think of the sacraments and assert the importance of having all seven. But what about the Word? What about the works of mercy? These are elements of the Church and I think that's a very helpful kind of expansion of this language to take account of what matters, namely, is it Christ who is being proclaimed? Don't be too churchy, too institutional; realize that this is the ultimate thing: is Christ being proclaimed? So, it's the word, it's the works of mercy, as well as sacraments and whatever else. Keep an awareness of all the elements and don't just have your favorite Catholic list of the elements. There's a bigger list maybe.

Paul McPartlan
MCG VI, 100

# Bishop David Hamid

What is vitally important to recognize is that even in a time of what has been called by some, an ecumenical winter, Anglicans and Roman Catholics have an officially mandated commission to enable us to work together in real Christian witness and life. This has never happened before, and as far as I can tell has never happened with any other bilateral relationship. One of the fruits of fifty years is that we have an instrument with the express purpose of putting flesh on the bone of the theological dialogue's agreements and to work to implement the consequences of that agreement. And this is to be celebrated.

Bishop David Hamid
MCG IV, 50

# Chapter 7

# Humanity, Society and Church: Reading the Signs of the Times

## CYRILLE VAEL, O.S.B.

We are placed squarely between the times of modernity and that which is yet to come and yet unnamed. Making the right choices is crucial. (Jacques Derrida)[1]

# INTRODUCTION: THE COMPLEX CULTURAL SHIFT OF THE AMBIENT WORLD

We all clearly know the successes and the failures of disembodied rationality, modernist-inspired liberalism, and Marxist-socialism, but those of long-term postmodernist influences are not yet clear. In particular, the impact of post-modernism on religious institutions remains an open-ended question. We are still assessing the impact. Since postmodernism acknowledges that the world is undergoing a vast, global, and intense transformation, we can state that our contemporary world still hasn't grasped how to characterise itself based on what it is, but only on what it recently ceased to be.[2] The dynamics at work in our current society are marked by a multitude of deep cultural shifts that are reshaping the way we perceive, interact with, and understand the world around us. They are largely driven by the decline of Eurocentric thinking, the rise of deconstruction as a philosophical method, the ensuing legitimation crisis, and the emergence of transhumanism as a dominant paradigm in the intellectual marketplace. These developments have ushered in a new era of

---

1   From a letter to Jean-Louis Houdebine, see Jacques Derrida, *Positions*, Translated by Alan Bass (Chicago: University of Chicago Press 1981), p. 93.

2   Stephan Toulmin, *The Return to Cosmology: Postmodern Science and the Theology of Nature*, (Berkeley: University of California Press 1982) p. 213.

thought, challenging traditional worldviews, and offering novel perspectives on the human condition.

For centuries, Europe has been the hub of intellectual, political, and cultural discourse. However, since the end of the twentieth century, we have witnessed a marked decline in Europe's dominance. This shift can be attributed to factors such as globalisation, decolonisation, and the rise of non-European powers. The decline of Eurocentric thinking has paved the way for more inclusive, diverse, and interconnected worldviews.

This erosion entailed a global dynamic of 'deconstruction', as elucidated by thinkers such as Jacques Derrida,[3] who accepted the challenge of questioning the traditional comprehension of metaphysical thought established in binary oppositions. This has emerged as a powerful intellectual tool for critiquing and dismantling traditional notions of meaning, truth, and authority. This development has profoundly influenced fields ranging from literary theory to political philosophy, and all kinds of structures. Deconstruction challenges all established hierarchies and calls into question the very foundations of knowledge production, and authority.

The deconstructionist movement and the shift away from Eurocentric thinking have led to a crisis of legitimacy within academic and traditional knowledge institutions. As dominant paradigms are dissected, and historically underrepresented voices are given greater weight, concerns over the very legitimacy and authority of existing systems are seriously emerging. This crisis is marked by the increasingly difficult challenge of reconciling established traditions and ethics with new perspectives and an exploration of alternative methods of accreditation and acknowledgment.

The rapid exchange of information and digital connectivity has exponentially reinforced and deepened this fundamental change in contemporary society, resulting in an increasingly dynamic and competitive intellectual marketplace. Ideas flow freely across borders and different perspectives are readily available. Transhumanism, a movement dedicated to enhancing human capabilities through technology, has emerged as a powerful intellectual force within this marketplace. Its radical vision of a transhuman future challenges traditional notions of human nature and existence.

Transhumanism proposes that through scientific and technological breakthroughs, humanity can surpass its current limitations. This idea includes enhancements such as biotechnology, nanotechnology, and integration of

---

3  Jürgen Habermas, *Legitimation Crisis*, Translation by Thomas McCarthey, (Boston: Beacon Press 1975) p. 68-75.

artificial intelligence. As transhumanism becomes more prominent, it prompts deep ethical, social, and philosophical contemplation regarding human identity, consciousness, and morality.

The shift away from Eurocentric perspectives, the rise of deconstruction, the subsequent crisis of legitimacy, and the emergence of transhumanism in the intellectual landscape represent a profound shift in contemporary thinking. These occurrences challenge established principles and create new avenues of investigation, marking a time of intellectual pluralism in which human potential and the borders of knowledge are continually being redefined.

The integration of this huge and complex cultural shift into religious settings, including Christianity, poses a multifaceted and evolving terrain and demands urgent and serious study. As the scholarly and intellectual landscape continues to evolve, it is essential for the Church that critical engagement with these phenomena takes place, so as to develop a deeper understanding of what is emerging, and in order to shape the future direction of the global cultural and intellectual pursuits. Can our Churches – with their extensive and illustrious heritage – accept the reality of *'nulla unquam inter fidem et rationem vera dissensio esse potest'*,[4] so that they may integrate the current global cultural shifts, the sciences and their development, as real and urgent opportunities for theological reflection today and in the future?

# SOME CONSEQUENCES FOR THEOLOGICAL THOUGHT

Since the rejection of a classical metaphysical thought, the nature of reality is no longer to be found in objective truth but in phenomenological linguistic events.[5] This does not mean that translation of traditional concepts into contemporary understandings automatically obtains the status of exclusive truth. Metaphysical objectivity is replaced by sociological subjectivity. This explains somehow the shift from 'deductive theology' to 'inductive theology' (in this perspective we can understand the obvious need of an ascending theology of the Eucharist).[6] It also explains the numerous contextual theologies now much more in vogue. Ambient social subjectivity leads to a tendency towards

---

4   'There can never be any real disagreement between faith and reason'. First Vatican Council, *Constitution Dei Filius, chapter 4. Text and translation, see Norman P. Tanner, Giuseppe Alberigo et al. (eds) Decrees of the Ecumenical Councils, Volume II: Trent – Vatican II (Georgetown: Sheed and Ward 1990), p. 808.*

5   Ernest Gellner, *Postmodernism, Reason and Religion*, (Routledge, London, 1992) p. 35.

6   Cf. Daniel J. Adams, *The Paradox of Contextual Theology*, (Taejon Press, 1990) pp. 248-279.

the rejection of human autonomy. The human person is part of a larger social matrix which includes history, culture, economics, religion, politics, philosophical worldview, and so on. Actual theological forms do not fall from the sky but are constructed within complex socio-cultural matrices. This shaped an anti-foundationalist character within contemporary theology, that seeks to dissociate theology from exclusive objective foundations, such as rules, creeds, and dogmas. These become part of the ever-changing contexts of culture and history and therefore cannot serve as frozen foundations for theological life and work. Ethics rather than doctrine became central to the task of theological construction. For this reason, we see the emphasis upon praxis. Theology is not only to be thought, but also to be lived. Nowadays orthopraxis replaces orthodoxy. But this is not without a reference to the maxim *'lex orandi, lex credendi.'*

This all results in a pluralism of theologies with no single viewpoint assuming dominance within the Church. Theologically speaking, we live in an intellectual marketplace which includes not only contemporary (postmodern) theologies, but also those considered as 'modern' and 'premodern' in their basic assumptions. In itself, this deconstruction process is not bad, but the very process presupposes that we see the challenge behind it. Yet theologians are, as Johann Baptist Metz called them, 'the last universalists'.[7] The result is contemporary fragmentation, to the point where it is now often easier to dialogue with people of other faiths than with those within our own tradition (likewise interculturality nowadays can be experienced more harshly within a single cultural model, than between different cultural models). Theology has become so wedded to specific socio-political interests that it is often impossible to tell where theology ends and ideologies or politics begin. As we said, 'non-foundationalism' in theology seeks to minimize the importance of rules, creeds, confessions, and Church Tradition. But here lays the great challenge of the fact that theology always needs to be enculturated, which means that it is obvious that theology often stands in judgment over culture. So, theology, at least as we understand it in the Christian sense, does have its parameters. In this context, the 'foundation criteria' become *ipso facto* problematic.

But can't these fragmentations be poured, in some sense, into polarities of theologies: God and the World; Christ and Culture; Text and Context; the Universal and the Particular; and so on? Indeed, but if we look at the sermons and so many other texts proclaimed in the ecclesial environment, they tend

---

7   Johann Baptist Metz, *A Passion for God. The Mytical-Political Dimension of Christianity* (New York: Paulist Press 1998) p. 133.

to focus too much on horizontal exegetical comments in reductive language, on Church understandings, on moral implications or on pietistic psychology. They seldom reveal a path of initiation into deeper understandings of the dynamics of Creation, Revelation, the Incarnation and Redemption. These are the central events and doctrines of the Christian faith, involving all the polarities: 'the Word became flesh and dwelt among us', and identified himself as 'the Truth, the Way and the Life.' So 'Truth' does exist. But postmodern deconstruction makes clear that 'Truth' is not a frozen doctrine, but the 'Way', the 'Life' itself, and hence is always contextual.

So, I believe that deconstruction by postmodernism has its purpose, because it echoes the structures embedded in Creation: we refer to texts such as 'Adam & Eve', 'Cain & Abel', 'the Tower of Babel', and so on. It is the process of deconstruction that obliges us to engage on the way of deification through life, of reconciling life and the knowledge we pretend to have of this life. In part, this is the path of *kenosis*. These processes of deconstruction even give us tools for a new reading of the central core of the Christian message. This requires a direct return to the sources of Revelation and the Scriptures, and especially to the person of Jesus Christ as we see him in the gospels. This, of course, requires a purification concerning our memories of the restrictive denominated 'Christianity-centred' theologies that have blurred the universality of Jesus Christ as Logos. The question, philosophically speaking, is how can we find a way from hermeneutics, which confiscated an autonomous existence (and is hence fruitless), towards a non-static metaphysical thinking, which seems to be necessary again. Personally, I think it would be worthwhile to consider how a postmodern reading can offer us the tools to re-discover a metaphysical language.

Two small examples may illustrate our reasoning:

1 There is nothing wrong with the concepts and words handed down from Tradition. It is the ever-changing meanings, interpretations and translations that become increasingly obsolete if we give them the status of universal static authority. These are valuable in themselves, useful for a limited time and space, but not the final universal solution. It is easy for Church doctrine to criticize contemporary philosophy, particularly that of the last thirty years, because it has broken down a whole construction of values that we thought were eternal, and of which a certain one-dimensional interpretation of history thought it was the 'Tradition'. This might have been so for a certain period. But we must be conscious of the fact that losing our energy in criticizing what seems to be inevitable, we have very little energy left to discover the enormous challenge of this deconstruction. The effects of deconstruction clearly participate

in Nietzsche's 'God is dead.' Since the Pragmatism of Richard Rorty,[8] we could say that the deconstruction culture spreads over at least three realities: the 'ontological', the 'anthropological' and the 'linguistic-logics'. To the ancient and medieval ontological reality, which sees the necessity in things, our contemporary thinking opposes an anti-essentialism. This means that the desperate search for an unchanging and unique foundation on which the order of things is based, expresses an illusion of soteriological and historical nature. Obviously, anti-essentialism sounds the death toll for certain conceptions of an immutable God as Creator, but it might open a perspective to discover a more soteriological concept of the Creator God at work throughout history. To the modern anthropological reality opened up by René Descartes and explored by Immanuel Kant, which locates necessity in the structure of our mind and intellect, our contemporary thinking opposes an 'anti-foundationalism' based on a psychological nominalism.[9] This anti-foundationalism might invalidate certain concepts of a God as Saviour, who imposes justification through faith to the extent that we expect objective and irrefutable guarantees from him, concerning our identity and the sense of life. But it could liberate our faith from an idolizing theism that still makes that faith far too dependent on knowledge. And to the modern linguistic reality, which searches for the necessity in language, our contemporary thinking opposes an 'anti-representationalism', which is not without an intrinsic link to the Old Testament prohibition of certain imagery. This opens many perspectives bridging contemporary understandings to old traditional concepts of our Jewish Christian Tradition. The point is not to criticize a certain metaphysical thinking – for this had its truth and value in a certain period and place – but since Heidegger, we have witnessed the death of its monopoly. The death of God prophesized by Nietzsche does not mean the death of the God of Revelation, but implies rather the death of a religion and a God firmly founded on closed, frozen ontological thinking, always identical to himself; the death of a creation without evolution or history and which remains in itself as it was created in the beginning; the death of the 'Being' itself, in the measure that we see this 'Being' as a unity in stability.[10] This however does not mean the death of the God of the Revelation throughout history. We could analyse this further under another title, but for

---

8   Cf. Santiago Zabal, 'Richard Rorty: Life, Pragmatism and Conversational Philosophy', 2017. In LARB. (https://lareviewofbooks.org/article/richard-rorty-life-pragmatism-and-conversational-philosophy).

9   Cf. Michael James Davis, 'Rorty on Knowledge and reality', 2005. In *ANU Open Research Repository*, (https://openresearch-repository.anu.edu.au/bitstream/1885/251915/1/Michael%20Davis%20-%20 Rorty%20on%20Knowledge%20and%20Reality.pdf).

10  Cf. Scotty Hendricks, '"God is Dead": What Nietzsche really meant', *Big Think*, January 2022 (https:// bigthink.com/thinking/what-nietzsche-really-meant-by-god-is-dead).

the moment it is enough to note that this death of Nietzsche's metaphysical God opens up an enormous potential for the rediscovery of the God of Abraham, Isaac and Jacob; for revelation through history, in other words for Tradition.[11] Hence, our Tradition could find a breath of fresh air if its classic philosophical perspectives could be enlightened by contemporary thinkers like William James, Richard Rorty, Charles Peirce, John Dewey, Jacques Derrida, Michel Foucault, Jean-François Lyotard, Jean Baudrillard, and others.

2 The Church in the 20th century placed itself to some extent under the motto of 'Unity in Diversity' but the praxis has shown us how bitterly difficult this seems to be to realize. This is partially due to the underlying problem of which we are generally unaware: 'Universality in Unicity'. But already the Church Fathers knew this, as it is a key problem in understanding the whole pedagogy embedded in the structures of creation. Here the old tradition of some of the Church Fathers seems to be quite friendly to postmodern thinking. The point is not to find together a new ultimate vocabulary or form for contemporary understanding, but to see how 'universality' is present in the 'unique' and in 'differentiated forms' in time and space: from the Church Fathers to our deconstructive philosophers.

# SOME CONSEQUENCES FOR ECCLESIOLOGICAL SELF-UNDERSTANDING

Countless are the questions echoed: can the actual hierarchical structures of power and authority adapt to new models of organizational structure and governance? Will the channels of transmission at least become aware of their inefficiency, based as they are on outdated reforms from the last decades? Can conscious religious and liturgical language evolve into new forms in keeping with new understandings of human and world views? Will the Church be able to articulate a cogent vision of a humane global society based on Christian notions of peace and justice? Or will it become a bastion of unexamined tradition, or of what it holds as tradition?

However, such questions are rather secondary. Of course, the Church should have a voice in shaping the emerging new world consciousness, but the Church needs to change in several ways if it is to be a vital force in influencing

---

11  See the three key study points of Bennahmias Richard, 'Postmodernité, Pragmatisme et Théologie Chrétienne Evangélique', *Revue d'Histoire et de Philosophie Religieuses,* 73 no. 2 (1998) pp. 57-77.

the shape of the future. The Church needs to see and engage with the world based on its radical roots in God's revelation but informed by current views of the nature of the ever-changing actual reality of life. To do so, Church people need to look beyond the actual parochial institutional concerns and deliberately develop a broader view of the world and of the role of the Church as a transforming agent. To this end, multi-disciplinary approaches prove to be enormously helpful and a non-judgmental way of framing new situations, encouraging us right from the outset to think outside the box.

We must be aware that despite the long-standing cultural visibility of religious organizations, religion in our actual society has also harboured an individualist temper inimical to institutionalism. This penchant for religious disestablishment sees religious institutions as inherently alienating. It was increasingly embodied in actual values of individual autonomy, self-reliance, rugged individualism, localism, ruralism and different forms of pseudo-democracy. These have promoted religious populism and suspicion of any authority and encouraged a need for the dispersal of power in all spheres of social and cultural life. The question of the status of religious institutions in contemporary culture has therefore become problematic. The culture-shaping power and authority of these institutions has declined over time. Where religion still has an influence, it tends to be over specific types of issues, and only in the realm of culture (symbols, liturgical experience, prayer life or moral appeal) rather than in terms of structural power (dogmatism, rules, politics, or coercive networks). Personal religious beliefs consistently have greater influence in society than formal or institutional teaching.

However, it should be mentioned in the margin that while the more culturally normative religious traditions have declined on the one hand, many of the conservative, traditionalist, and fundamentalist ones have achieved new visibility and strength. In addition, various new religious movements of non-Western cultural derivation have also achieved an institutional presence and grown with varying degrees of success. Equally we witness that while mainline 'liberal' and 'progressive' churches have declined, many of those on the political right have grown. However, this development is not in itself a direct consequence of postmodern tendencies, but rather a residual reaction stemming from Christianity's troubled encounter with modernity since the Enlightenment. Fundamentalism in its various modalities is intrinsically reactive.[12] Its genesis lies in the crisis of modernity, rather than in postmodernity.

---

12   Cf. William Dinges, 'Religious Institutes and Postmodernism', (*The Way*, 36 no. 3, London (2022) p. 215, (https://www.theway.org.uk/back/36Dinges.pdf).

The radical relativism and incipient nihilism of 'hard' postmodernism has merely exacerbated this reaction, as have other political and social developments which are totally unrelated to postmodernism. There is nonetheless every reason to believe that certain types of religious institutions may thrive in the culture of postmodernity precisely because they are seen as an antidote to the radical relativism of an age that proclaims not only the death of 'God' but also of 'humanity', entailing in an even more dramatic fashion the spectre of nihilism, despair, and catastrophe.[13]

One of the most significant consequences in actual religious life over the past three decades has been the decline of the mainline denominations. The Catholic Church, for example, has experienced serious institutional instability and malaise, stemming from dramatic changes in class structure and from the contested interpretation of the meaning and implementation of the reform initiatives of the Second Vatican Council.

Among lots of other consequences of this complex cultural shift in ecclesiological self-understanding, I would like to enumerate four aspects,[14] which may be useful for further reflection.

## 1. Crumbling of the Institutional Denomination Cement

What is significant is the pervasiveness of the perception that it is no longer possible to believe in any compelling way that one denomination in particular (or Christianity in general) is necessarily truer than any other religion. For contemporary people religious truth is no longer seen in objective categories, but rather in terms of what is subjectively plausible, because it is felt as an acute spiritual need. Religious institutions simply have little relevance for their religious identity. These institutions are peripheral to concerns with a broader and purely subjective spiritual quest.

## 2. Divorce of Spirituality and Institute

An important yet under-explored aspect of religious individualisation is the disassociation of spirituality from institutional affiliation. For numerous modern-day Christians, attending to one's own spiritual well-being is no longer intertwined with a significant or convincing relationship with a disciplined community, an organised historical heritage, or a dogmatic denomination. Due to an authentic existential requirement that is always individually and

---

13   Cf. Panu Raatikainen, 'Jordan Peterson on Postmodernism, Truth and Science', in Sandra Woien (ed.), *Jordan Peterson. Critical Responses* (Chicago: Open Universe 2022).

14   Cf. Dinges, 'Religious Institutes and Postmodernism', p. 215.

privately experienced, spirituality has taken on an eclectic and self-directed nature. Indeed, individuals are no longer pursuing intellectual solutions to questions or strict institutional representations of them. Instead, they seek a profound understanding of God and humanity, as well as inner wisdom to help them live a holistic and genuine existence. Institutional loyalty can no longer be assumed as a given. Loyalty to the Church and adherence to a singular set of dogmas no longer suffice as reliable indicators of loyalty. We can no longer take institutional loyalty for granted. The days when we could rely mainly on loyalty to the Church and general agreement to a uniform body of dogmas are gone.

Spirituality has become an element in the culture of 'personal necessity', or a lifestyle choice. Whilst this is often criticised as another commodity fetish in a free-market economy of ever multiplying material and symbolic goods, we should not forget that the solitary spiritual 'argonaut' of today finds the 'life giving water' in the wake of transmitted traditions, so there is after all a certain shape of connection to a collective, a religious institute or community. We must recognize the significant differences between private and personal religion. Objective religious encounters are personal and thus relational, as private religion does not exist. The spiritual quest is now often a purely individual task divorced from institutional loyalties and commitments and devoid of any form of hierarchical control or social inheritance. Because of the huge pressure of our contemporary non-stop performing society, this personal quest for spirituality is frequently coloured by psychological needs. That is why rituals, liturgies, with their religious symbols, are often experienced as therapeutic.[15] While churches can provide individuals with a poetic and imaginative symbolic imagery that brings them effectively closer to the ultimate questions of life, the same churches as denominational institutions are devoid of any compelling social or spiritual relevance or necessity.

## 3. Deconstruction of Meaning and Symbols

Since the decline of metanarratives, no objective categories of 'right' and 'wrong' hold any authority. Truth and falsehood are often seen as nothing more than categories justifying the dominance of one group over another. Because truth is conceived as a perspective suited to individuals or social groups, there is no inherent truth to be radically disclosed anywhere. All texts (includ-

---

15 Cf. Rieff Philip, *The Triumph of the Therapeutic. Uses of Faith after Freud*, (New York: Harper and Row Editions 1966).

ing the religious) are marked by indeterminacy.[16] But religious traditions are in fact carriers of metanarratives. They make claims that posit objective or absolute premises. They postulate hierarchies of truth and tie these assertions to institutional frames. Claims of this nature however, along with their epistemological undergirding, are difficult to sustain in the actual postmodern context. They are drained of confidence, even where the hegemonic pretensions of scientific empiricism are also called into question.

The postmodern cultural ethos is also implicated in the evisceration of religious symbols. It is a guiding assumption that there can be no frozen ideas about the form and meaning of concepts and texts. This assumption extends to the world of symbols. Furthermore, according to Michel Foucault and other scholars, symbols do not represent specific entities but rather operate as discursive systems. But here too, we witness something which is not completely new because the contemporary context is not the first time in which the Christian tradition has had to struggle with the issue of control over the meaning(s) of its core symbols. It is even in the nature of a symbol to have multi-variant meanings and interpretations. However, symbols have inherent multiple meanings beyond their official signification by so-called 'power groups'. Yet, they remain connected to particular cultural, historical, and communal events, which involve a shared interpretive dynamic. Thus, it is possible to comprehend common references linked to the dynamics of revelation across history.

That is why, for example, it is sometimes quite painful to discover how much energy is invested in a non-stop search for finding new ways to represent symbols, for translating liturgical language into more contemporary images and words which should from now on be unanimously relevant for all people. This is filling up the Danaïdes' barrel: someday, these 'more contemporary images and words' will also become obsolete to the people of tomorrow (and are probably already irrelevant to people of other cultural ambiences). This approach only displaces the problem. Here, the medicine or therapy painfully reflects the superficiality of the diagnosis. Tradition, symbols and 'old vocabulary' are no longer necessarily understood as stagnant language, as something which is dead because it describes a thing which no one understands anymore. Symbols are by nature a non-reductive language, and thus ensure a necessary openness so that their meaning is never exhausted. We must never forget that the degree of understanding of liturgy is parallel to, or even determined by, the degree of

---

16 Cf. Kort Wesley, 'Religion, Texts and Literature in Postmodern Contexts', *Journal of the American Academy of Religion, 58 no. 4 (1990), p. 576.*

development of one's own kenosis. The underlying problem appears as a dashboard indicating inadequate transmission channels.

## 4.　Trans-denominationalism

One consequence of the weakened social coherence and weakened significance of institutional religion is trans-denominationalism, which can be understood as the interchangeability of religious identity.[17] Denominations may still have some historical significance, but in our postmodern society, denominational identities are essentially interchangeable. The reality is that the relevant factor for religious identity today is no longer the denomination to which one belongs, but where one stands on the spectrum of cultural 'conservatism' or 'liberalism'. Otherwise, contemporary spirituality is mainly expressed through cultural or ethical language rather than through set rules or dogmas. The defining criterion of religious identity is one's cultural or ethical orientation rather than institutional affiliation. This cultural-ethical aspect of the trans-denominational orientation regularly shows situations in which individuals attend a church of a certain denomination for one liturgy, but a church of a different denomination for other spiritual needs (better preaching, aesthetically more edifying prayer, and so on) which they don't find in their 'home' church. For those who accept to read the signs of the times, the ecumenical challenge of this trans-denominational phenomenon is both enormous and extremely interesting.[18]

History shows that religion and spirituality require institutional expression in order to endure, just as society cannot exist without its institutions. There is nothing of value that we do not continue to perpetuate through some form of institutional expression. Therefore, ecclesial institutions will endure in the culture of modernity/postmodernity not only because they are intrinsic to religion, but because they are maintained by the imperatives of social reality itself in reference to age cohort, social mobility, family patterns, ethnic ties, conformist cultural trends, and so on. However, today's inquiry is not about the destabilization of religious institutions caused by postmodernist processes but rather how these institutions will change and respond strategically to these processes. But somehow, in a Christian context, this is not a novel concept,

---

17　Stephen Dray, *From Consensus to Chaos: An Historical Analysis of Evangelical Interpretation of 1 Timothy 2:8-15 from 1945-2001*, (Boca Raton, FL: Universal Publishers 2006) p. 25.

18　Kimlyn Bender, *Confessing Christ for Church and World. Studies in Modern Theology*, (Downers Grove, IL: IVP Academic 2014) p. 71.

but rather another variation of the longstanding 'Christ and Culture' debate.[19] The peculiarity of this problem today is that certain values central to modernity/postmodernity, including openness, diffusion, pluralism, contextuality, anti-hierarchy, anti-bureaucracy, small-scale organic co-ordinations, do not result in a robust institutional commitment. The issue at hand is not the longevity of church institutions, as those that effectively channel these novel cultural, intellectual, and societal forces will persist, alongside the unlikely persistence of those that do not. Such is the continuing dialectic between 'church' and 'sect' throughout the premodern, modern, and postmodern eras. The vital energy of these groups has come into question.

The primary issue at hand is that of transmission. The Church cannot regain its vitality, strength, or integrity solely by implementing elaborate new tactics, launching flashy programmes, sublimating rigid rules, trying to be more organised, or working harder.

# CONCLUSION

The Canadian philosopher Charles Taylor, who analyses the evolution of tradition in his book *The Malaise of Modernity*,[20] refers to the powerful idea of the 'Law of Three'. Basically, it states that every change or new development in the physical world is the result of not two, but three independent forces: not just 'yes' and 'no' (or 'thesis' and 'antithesis' in Hegelian terms), but 'yes', and 'no', plus an additional energy that brings the two opposing forces into meaningful connection – although without fusion – at a new level. These three forces are called 'affirming', 'denying', and 'reconciling'. The steering of a sailboat is a fitting metaphor. Many assume that a sailboat moves through the water thanks to the wind filling its sails, and the water pushing against its keel. However, any sailor knows that a boat doesn't sail in this state, it turns into the wind and comes to a standstill. Only with the inclusion of the helmsman, who coordinates the wind and water for a selected trajectory, does forward motion occur.

The Church appears to be confronting a dilemma, as it mechanically assumes either the role of 'affirming' or 'denying' (representing the first and second force) under the misconception that this is the only way to remain faithful to eternal truths (whether located in memory or tradition). It will be difficult to continue in this way. It merely makes the boat head up into the wind and come to a standstill. Instead, we must realize that in a religion whose 'core mandala'

---

19  For further exploration of this topic, please refer to the study by Helmut Richard Niebuhr, *Christ and Culture*. New York, Harper, 1951. (*https://archive.org/details/christculture0000unse/mode/2up*).

20  Charles Taylor, *The Malaise of Modernity*, (Toronto: House of Anansi Press 1991), p. 135.

is the Trinity and whose incarnational theology proclaims both the necessity and the goodness of an ever-changing, dynamic world, we must learn how to harness the third force, 'the reconciling'. The Church must prioritize connection, learning how to bring things into relationship at a new level, to support a whole new level of God's self-revelation throughout history. This is not pandering towards conservatism neither towards progressivism, but rather 'midwifing' the future.

The way forward is through the development of meaningful spiritual practices, a renewal of corporate spirituality, a profound shift of consciousness in the way we see humanity, society, Church and so on. These deep inner changes will only be achieved when we become aware that tradition and progress, like most antinomic concepts, are not to be opposed. In fact, the two concepts merge: tradition is a living reality, which therefore includes in itself the principle of development and of progress. Tradition is like the river which always carries its source in itself, flowing and growing towards its outlet. Memory is not just remembering the Divine Touch somewhere in the past, it is seeing the Divine Touch continuing to create, sustain and redeem all of life.

The mechanical sliding into a categorical 'yes' or 'no', into 'pro' or 'contra', into exclusive dualism, into argumentation and unfruitful oppositions, simply makes us blind to the third force, hence blind to the Tradition, to the transmission, to the memory. Like the oldest son in the Parable of the Prodigal Son, we stand frozen and self-righteous in front of the Banqueting Hall: undoubtedly correct in our assertion of integrity, but undoubtedly alone and thus without any future. Because, in any case, the party will go on without us.

# Interlude

# Notes on Liturgy and Ecumenism from a Lutheran

## GORDON LATHROP

Much in the current practice of liturgy in the Christian Churches has tended toward both signaling and encouraging their unity. The recognition of a widespread shared *ordo* for the Sunday assembly has been remarkable: many Christian Churches commonly gather remembering baptism, hear the scriptures read and preached, pray for the needs of the world, greet each other in peace, give thanks at the table and receive the gifts of this eucharist, and find themselves sent to a needy world. If Christians are thus doing something like the same things in their gatherings, in the same order, surely more expressions of unity will not be far behind. More: local assemblies mostly use vernacular language in enacting this *ordo*. In many Churches throughout the world the scriptures are read according to a very similar three-year lectionary and interpreted as speaking of the mystery of salvation in the death and resurrection of Christ. Indeed, many of the goals for liturgical reform in the diverse Churches are articulated in profoundly similar ways: an accent on the baptismal dignity and full participation of all in the assembly, for example, and a similar accent on the clergy as serving this assembly in its gathering around Christ. And Christians of diverse confessions now speak of 'a liturgical ecclesiology', an understanding of Church that begins with actual assemblies gathered around Christ in word and sacrament.

Among Anglicans and Roman Catholics, one can note an exchange of gifts: the liturgical reforms of the Second Vatican Council have profoundly influenced current worldwide Anglican reform. But the long Anglican experience of liturgy in the vernacular to enable communal participation has also deeply influenced Roman Catholic work.

But there is a problem. This tendency toward unity is not always the actual experience when we attend each other's assemblies. Many local congregations have not caught this shared spirit of reform or have enacted it poorly. Decisions in particular Churches – such as the Roman Catholic abandonment of what had been shared liturgical texts in the latest vernacular translations of the liturgy for mass – have signaled disunity rather than unity. Matters of specific ecclesial cultures – popular devotions, exercises of Christian fraternities, national holidays and national flags, certain kinds of vesture, the role of the rector or the pastor – sometimes take central place, displacing the centrality of the shared *ordo*. In some places, this *ordo* has never been welcomed. And, for all of the increasing sense of baptismal unity, full eucharistic sharing is still not possible.

How shall a Christian who longs for the manifest unity of the body of Christ react to these liturgical experiences?

I hope she or he will do so without despairing of the common Christian movement for liturgical renewal nor of the search for more visible unity. I hope, rather, that such a Christian will seek to be present in what can sometimes feel like an alien assembly as a small sign of unity: taking part as much as is welcomed and as much as conscience allows; seeking to see the shared *ordo*, even when it is obscured; praying for these other Christians; being the silent sign of a broader Christianity than may be manifest here; asking for forgiveness for one's self and one's own community; rejoicing that the mercy of God is surprisingly alive even in a broken Church; and realizing that these stances are ones that she or he often needs to take in whatever is her or his regular congregation. And I hope that, when occasion allows, she or he will engage in what the Lutheran-Reformed dialogue of Germany and of North America has called 'mutual affirmation and admonition'. If the liturgy has been strongly centered around the mystery of Christ in word and sacrament, available for the participation of all the people and sending to a needy world – especially if it has done so in ways that may be new and refreshing to the ecumenical participant – let it be affirmed. But if matters of ecclesial or national culture have taken central place, if the clergy have not served and the assembly has not been honored in its baptismal dignity – if the fruits of the ecumenical liturgical renewal have not been present – let the ecumenical participant, when the occasion allows and in humility, graciously admonish her or his hosts, seeking to be open to receive both affirmation and admonishment in return.

Liturgical practice can still function to signal and encourage growing visible unity between the Churches.

Part III

# THE HORIZON: SHARED SACRAMENTALITY

# Chapter 8

# 'Unveiling Mysterion': Reanimating the Sacrament by Rooting it Back into its own Soil

## THOMAS POTT, O.S.B.

A few years ago, on a cold Saturday evening in November, I walked through Venice, absorbing the smells and sounds of the *Serenissima*, with the firm intention of carrying them with me when I would leave the city again. The *campi* and *calli* were crowded with people, surrounded by colourful storefront windows. Other people, like me, already tired and looking forward to some reinvigorating culinary pleasure for restoring the inner person, were in search of their predestined place on a heated terrace. Suddenly, the solemn sound of a church bell rang out in the sky, and slowly but surely began to make its way through the disconnected frequencies that filled the noisy Queen of the Adriatic. While noticing that no other people seemed to be disturbed in any way in their activities, I myself, like a deer, pricked up my ears to find out where this beautiful and enticing sound came from. Only one bell was ringing, but its sound, deep and full of overtones, clearly intended to descend into the inner ear of those whose ears it touched; from there, the heart could be moved, aiming to set the whole body in motion seeking to discover the place from where the sound emanated. In order to expose such a dynamic, such a persuasive force, the sound couldn't but represent a reality bigger, stronger and nobler than itself: something beautiful and worthy enough to fill the sky with sound and to call all who can hear to attention. Consigning my search for a terrace to the realm of the vain attractions of this world, I looked around, screening the sky above the houses. Could I find a *campanillo* capable of containing the kind of bell which so insistently appealed to those inner layers of my memory where the sound of church bells is stored? Soon I spotted the dark silhouette of a tower, probably on a *campo* not far from where I was. I focussed on the *cam-*

119

*panillo*, listened to the bell with great attention and started walking towards the place which mysteriously called me to it.

However, after a few steps, other considerations arose in my mind. Why did I really want to go there? What did I expect to find? For what other reason than a common Saturday evening Mass was the bell attempting to gather people to church? Once I arrived at the church door, entered the sacred – but probably badly lit and chilly – place, what kind of 'event' could I reasonably be expecting to attend? Above all, would it be at the level of solemnity represented by the mysterious appeal of the church bell which invited me to come to church in the first place? From experience, shouldn't I expect that the ringing of the bell itself might be the most solemn moment of everything it announced, of what would follow? Should I really take the risk and go there? Or should I stay where I was, meditatively absorbing the sound of the bell and serenely continuing my activities once the ringing stopped? I confess that the decision wasn't difficult...

But during that whole evening – and long since – I have reflected on that awareness which suddenly came over me. Why is it that liturgy so often seems to have lost its capacity to communicate sanctity to the human being – body, spirit, and soul – like a church bell does, with its undeniable solemnity and celebrative resonance? Why is it that liturgy generally seems to aim at captivating our intellectual faculties when the ringing of bells, the sound of organs, the smell of incense, the poignancy of figurative art, the impact of ceremony and ritual convey a kind of intense presence that the intellect cannot grasp?

The experience of this liturgical universe is contained, theologically and philosophically, through the word with which the Greek Church Fathers, and the Eastern Churches to this day, render the concept of 'sacrament': *mysterion*. Although *mysterion* is historically and culturally rooted in the pagan mystery cults and never expresses in the Bible what we understand today as sacrament, the Church Fathers came to use this concept to name the New Testament sacred acts of baptism and eucharist. This is because they perceived the same dynamic of communication and presence in the pagan, Hellenistic mysteries, on the one hand, and in the ecclesiastical rites of baptism and eucharist, on the other.

The Eastern Christian meaning of *mysterion* cannot easily be understood without implicitly referring to the Neoplatonic scheme of archetype and reflection on which Plato's theory of ideas is based, as described in the 'Myth of the Cave' (*Republic* VII, 1-3). In this scheme, which is dynamic by essence, the believer, the initiate, participates in the mystery by means of the archetype's punctual and concrete reflection. The archetype communicates itself through its reflection, it makes itself present, in order to make those to whom it is being communicated participate in its being. Like a symbol, it conveys and reveals something that remains elusive in itself, something in which our human condition does not allow for perfect and complete participation. In this scheme, the *mysterion*, the sacrament, is neither the archetype nor the reflection itself, but the believer's participation in the essence of the archetype thanks to its reflection. Applied to Christian liturgy, the *mysterion*/sacrament is not Christ, dead, buried, risen, ascended into heaven and who will return (this is the archetype), nor the bread and wine, his body and blood (this is the reflection or, in patristic language: the 'antitype'), but our participation in Christ by eating and drinking, our communion in his body and blood.[1]

There is thus an inner relationship between archetype and reflection: the archetype is truly present in its reflection, even if in a mysterious – a 'mystery-filled' – and veiled way. Initiation is therefore an essential component of *mysterion*. In this sense, with the Greek Church Fathers, the term *mysterion* does not denote inaccessibility or invisibility, but the 'mysterious' connection between archetype and reflection for the initiate. Therefore, from its etymological meaning, *mysterion* is not a static concept, as 'sacrament' can be due to its prevailing juridical connotation. *Mysterion* is a dynamic term that denotes the transcendence of sensory perceptibility. The core of *mysterion* is the awareness of a presence that communicates itself and invites participation in it. That is why *mysterion* must be attractively beautiful, truthful, and unifying. Indeed, beauty is an essential substance of *mysterion*, of sacraments. Without beauty a sacrament is stilted theology, bearing in itself no more than a remote memory of reality. Beauty, even in its most primordial shape, is oxygen to the blood of a living sacrament.

The concept of *mysterion*, as the cradle of sacrament, should help make clear that 'sacramentality' – of the liturgy, of the Church, of life – is not derived from the theological and juridical reality of sacraments in the way we use to understand them, but rather the other way round: sacraments are punctual and concrete expressions of sacred presence and communication, of which 'sacramentality' is the generic name. Today, rediscovering the concept of *mysterion* remains essential if, like the protagonists of the Liturgical Movement a century ago, we wish to revive the Church, its liturgy and, generally speaking, theological culture. Vatican II theologically rooted the sacraments in the Church, understood itself as 'primordial sacrament.' But it failed in applying

---

1   R. Hotz, *Sakramente im Wechselspiel zwischen Ost und West*, Ökumenische Theologie Bd 2 (Zürich-Köln: Benzinger 1979), pp. 40-41.

the concept of *mysterion*, as dynamics of presence and communication, to the life of the Church and to liturgical reality. Instead, it has tried to theologically 'educate' *mysterion*, integrating it into its systematic thinking of sacraments as effective signs of divine grace, validly dispensed by the Church according to categories without any real relevance for the idea of *mysterion*. This merely intellectual approach with respect to sacramental discipline is something many churches hold in common. It is the reason why in many churches the relationship between liturgy and sacraments, on the one hand, and the reality of life and the truth of faith, on the other hand, generally doesn't get beyond the level of conceptuality and ritual formality. At the same time, the failed fructification of liturgical discipline by the dynamics of *mysterion* is one of the reasons why encounter and dialogue between divided Churches focus on theologically and intellectually defined categories, rather than on the reality of life and the shared faith in a God who saves, which Christians express and celebrate in their liturgies. *Mysterion* is not opposed to truth as theology may define it; instead, *mysterion* upholds the idea that theologically defined truth will never completely express our living faith in a living God, that it will never be able to substitute the commitment of our life for God's own work of Creation and Redemption.

The application of theological categories, without an honest appraisal of the authentically Christian – 'orthodox' – character of what is being transmitted in the liturgy of another Church, is responsible for the now 'traditional' non-recognition of Anglican orders by the Roman-Catholic Church. In Leo XIII's Bull *Apostolicæ Curæ* (1896), Anglican orders were declared 'utterly null and totally void' on the basis of a sacramental theology which, compared to patristic theology, had evolved in a reductive way. Rediscovering *mysterion* would mean, not so much to intellectually discover an ancient theological, philosophical, cultural, and anthropological concept, but to join the dynamics of it, which exist, work and produce 'effectiveness', even if theologically we are not aware of it. In the light of such a rediscovery of *mysterion*, the Catholic Church cannot honestly maintain its negative position on the validity of Anglican orders without questioning its own orders.

In what follows, I will focus on the concept of sacramentality as that dimension of sacramental theology which manifests the most obvious connotations from the patristic and Eastern Christian concept of *mysterion*. I will present three complementary points of view on sacramentality: (1) sacramentality and the question of validity; (2) sacramentality and ecclesiology; and (3) sacramentality, liturgy and life.

# SACRAMENTALITY
# AND THE QUESTION OF VALIDITY

At the second meeting of the Malines Conversations Group (Canterbury, 2014), Archbishop Rowan Williams said, 'Maybe that's the sort of theme that could offer scope of what to think about further: what is actually being said and what practised.[2] A more polemical version of the same idea is expressed by Leo Tolstoy: 'If there be a sacred thing, it is surely not what they call Sacraments, but just this very duty of unmasking their religious deceptions when one detects them.'[3]

Typical expressions of traditional Catholic sacramentology may be found in the recent debate on the possibility for divorced couples to contract second marriage (Synod of Bishops of 2014-15). In an interview with *Corriere della Sera* of 14 December 2014, Cardinal Angelo Scola proposed to reconsider the problem of the relationship between marriage and eucharist in a 'radical' way. Concretely, he advocated to 'remain faithful to the doctrine', but to facilitate the procedure of annulment. Thus, in order not to disdain the sacrament, an easier way to conclude that *there isn't one* should be found... This understanding of sacramentality is far away from its own roots in the Greek concept of *mysterion*, in which the sacrament is not so much a holy state of affair as rather a lively participation in the dynamics of creation and incarnation. But also, designated in such a way, it becomes normal and legitimate to reduce liturgy and life to what it produces in juridical terms, saying that what in the eyes and memories of testimonies and offspring is – or was – a *mysterion* of God's loving presence among his people, has been void and null from the very beginning. Testimonies become pretenders, 'liars',[4] children become illegitimate...

This Scholastic way of considering the sacraments, illustrates the typical Catholic claim on theological objectivity, based on the 'one' acceptable theological model, which applies even to churches separated from the Catholic Church and to so-called 'Ecclesial Communities'. Thus, it is inevitable and normal that our non-recognition of the 'validity' of sacraments of other Churches turns their pastors into 'liars'. That is what Archbishop Rowan referred to at the second meeting of the Malines Conversations Group (Canterbury, 2014), when he spoke about 'false memories': 'This memory is false insofar as it reports the only way how to tell the story. And look, listen, here are

---

2  MCG 2014, p. 106.

3  Leo Tolstoy, *Last Steps: The Late Writings of Leo Tolstoy*, edited by Jay Parini (London: Penguin Classics 2009), p. 148.

4  Cf. infra, note 5.

other people who are telling a story about that, and it is not the same as yours. Are they liars?'[5]

But Catholic sacramental discipline is not totally estranged from the concept of 'economy'. In fact, canon CIC 1127, §1, states: 'If a Catholic party contracts marriage with a non-Catholic party of an Eastern rite, the canonical form of the celebration must be observed *for liceity only*'; furthermore, §2 adds: 'If grave difficulties hinder the observance of canonical form, the local ordinary of the Catholic party has the *right of dispensing from the form in individual cases*.' If that is true for marriage, which is so well regulated in the Code of Canon Law, why would it be impossible to *dispense from the form in individual cases* with regard to ministry and order?

The specification 'in individual cases' brings us to another theme: ecclesiology.

# SACRAMENTALITY AND ECCLESIOLOGY

It is clear that the whole dynamics of mutual recognition are directed towards the restoration of communion among churches. The 'communion' at stake here refers itself, though, to one particular theological system, to one particular system of ecclesiological self-understanding. Theological systems tend to dictate how reality must be understood, sometimes even with the best intentions. But a system never can substitute itself for reality. To quote Rowan Williams again, on memory: 'If, though, there is one story of the Church, one real memory, an authentic memory, then of course, there is one real apostolic identity, which would be what it is, whatever else was going on – leaving aside one of the points that, purely historically, people don't always register, which is the fact that at the Reformation the Catholic world changed at least as much as that world which evolved on the other side.'

However, the recognition of sacraments of another church only makes sense when one is on the way towards restoring unity. The regulations for accepting 'schismatics' in the communion of the Catholic Church, in the canons of the first Ecumenical Councils, are based on how those 'returning' had originally been initiated into the mystery of Christ. A modern, seemingly 'ecumenical' version of this can be found in Vatican II, in the principle of *subsistit in* (LG 8). As a consequence of this principle, 'many elements of sanctification and of truth are found outside of its [the Catholic Church] visible structure. These elements, as gifts belonging to the Church of Christ, are *forces impelling toward*

---

5    MCG 2014, p. 109.

*catholic unity*.'[6] Thus, the recognition of the validity of sacraments, by definition, occurs in a – more or less smoothly – unionistic perspective. There is
no use in declaring 'valid' the sacraments of another church if not in view of
individuals or groups of individuals wanting to join 'the other communion'.
This is clear when we consider the regulations of *Anglicanorum Cœtibus* in the
light of *Apostolicae Curae*: the only sacrament in Anglicanism which may be
considered 'valid' is Christian initiation. It may appear strange, though, that
confirmation/chrismation is not to be 'repeated'.[7] In fact, logically spoken, it
shouldn't be considered 'valid' since Anglican priests and bishops are not –
for the Catholic Church – what they 'pretend' to be and what indeed *they are*
for their faithful.

However, in virtue of *subsistit in*, the Catholic Church has been able, theologically speaking, to 'declare valid' all the sacraments of the Orthodox
Church (apart from the ordination of deaconesses).[8] Generally speaking, the
Orthodox do the same, although not in virtue of the Catholic concept of *subsistit in*, but in virtue of Economy (*oikonomia*). Economy, however, in principle
and ultimately, is applied only *in individual cases*. If, in the name of Economy,
an individual is recognised or treated as validly baptised or ordained, without
that person desiring to embrace the Orthodox Church, the only reason for recognition, theologically, is for the sake of courtesy…

In this context, it is interesting to compare the present reluctance of many
Orthodox to fully accept Catholics as true brothers and sisters in Christ on the
basis of considerations regarding the possible validity of the Catholic sacraments, with the time of Peter Mohyla (17th century) when scholasticism was
massively introduced into Orthodox sacramental theology. Even if it changed
the way of theologically 'thinking' about the sacraments, the scholastic theological system didn't practically effect either the sacramental rites, nor canonical categories regarding 'validity', remaining therefore merely as a sort of theological supra-structure. I was able to observe a typical example of this, some
years ago, at an Orthodox marriage in Saint Petersburg. Faithful to Scholastic
sacramental doctrine, the priest asked groom and bride if they wanted freely
to take each other as man and wife. The groom answered, as the priest told me

---

6   *Lumen Gentium*, 8, https://www.vatican.va/archive/hist_councils/ii_vatican_council/documents/vat-ii_const_19641121_lumen-gentium_en.html

7   Article 5 of the 'Complementary Norms for the Apostolic Constitution *Anglicanorum Coetibus*', issued by the Congregation for the Doctrine of Faith, concerns the Sacraments of Initiation only for the lay faithful who wish to belong to the ordinariate. Nothing of the kind is said about the clergy.

8   Cf. Canon 754 of the *Code of Canons of the Oriental Churches* (1990): 'Only a baptized man is able to receive sacred ordination validly', invalidating in such a way the never abolished ordination of deacon-esses in the Byzantine Churches.

later: 'I don't have another choice', at which the priest raised his shoulders and continued the celebration of the *mysterion*...

Finally, what is the meaning of all this in terms of the official Catholic position on Anglican orders from a sacramentological and an ecclesiological point of view? First, a lot of honest dialogue and sincere *rapprochement* has been witnessed during the twentieth century, but decisive ecclesiological mentalities have remained where they were in 1896 (with *Apostolicae curae* and its method). Secondly, Catholic ecclesiology has gone through a process of purification and reform, but the *ressourcement* has not been profound enough and the *aggiornamento* has been overpowered, at crucial points, by the spirit of 1896. Finally, the paradigm of our liturgy, according to an evocative observation of John Baldovin,[9] is like the typical medieval Italian town on a mountain – 'my church, my school, my baker's, my doctor, my cemetery' – similarly, our typical ecclesiological paradigm never really entered the twentieth century, let alone the twenty-first.

# SACRAMENTALITY, LITURGY AND LIFE

At the Great Council of the Armenian Church in Hromkla, Cilicia, 1179, S. Nerses of Lampron pronounced the following words:

> We have always blessed this bread for the glory and memory of Christ, and one is the blessing, one the name of Christ, that we, the nations, pronounce over it, each in a different language. And having entered our enmity, we accept from each other the same bread before it is blessed in the name of Christ and we eat it without scruple; but when we recall Christ's name over it and we make it his body by the same blessing, the Armenian loathes to participate in the blessed sacrifice of the Greek and the Greek in that of the Armenian. And the bread that by the same prayer, by the same blessing, we call Christ, that each of us consecrates by the grace of the same Spirit, henceforth we despise this bread from each other; before the blessing we ate it without abhorrence and, having blessed it in the name of Christ, we have it in abomination.[10]

---

9  Private conversation.

10  Cf. Georges-Henri Ruyssen, SJ, *Eucharistie et œcuménisme. Évolution de la normativité universelle et comparaison avec certaines normes particulières* (Cerf: Paris 2008), epigraph. Cf. Th. Pott, 'L'"hospitalité eucharistique": réflexions théologiques et pastorales' in A. Lossky and M. Sodi (eds), *Rites de Communion*, Conférences Saint-Serge LVe Semaine d'Etudes Liturgique, Paris, 23-26 juin 2008, (Città del Vaticano: Libreria Editrice Vaticana 2010), p. 163.

At the Plenary Session of the Orthodox-Catholic theological dialogue in Amman (2016), at such a short distance from where people are persecuted and murdered because of their identity, where people have had to flee their homes, where people exactly know what peace, ministry and communion mean because they are cut off from them, it was clear to all that Christians are not killed because they are Orthodox, Protestant or Catholic, but precisely and straightforwardly because they are Christians. Does this communion in blood make any sense for theology or even for liturgy? But to what extent can a liturgy, which confines itself to what happens within the church walls, be called 'Christian'? When people from different ecclesial denominations share the mystery of life, as married couples or simply as persons in love, as prisoners in concentration camps, as seafarers in storms on the ocean, as benefactors in affected areas, do they have a 'lesser communion' than the specific one our theological dialogues are striving for, a 'lesser communion' than the one we are allowed to share in the Eucharist?

The problem with sacramental theology, like the one expressed by *Apostolicae Curae* or by Cardinal Scola's 'radical thinking', is that sacraments have lost contact with liturgy, liturgy with life, and theology both with liturgy and life. This is the heritage of which Catholic ecumenical theology in general, and *Apostolicae Curae* in particular, are testimonies in themselves. Theology often tends to be self-sufficient and to overshadow reality as if it were reality itself. Yet, theology really is nothing more than a navigation system, intended to guide the Church through daily life, through *real* life. The problem with theology is that the word itself seems to bestow reality with some sort of 'untouchability', after which any growth or change of reality itself risks being seen as a denial of divinely revealed Truth. However, this doesn't apply to theology alone, but also to liturgy and to piety, which, according to A. Schmemann,[11] through losing their original mutual harmony, have also lost the organic contact with their sources. Liturgy, no less than theology, doesn't have its source in itself, but in creation and in redemption. Theology, liturgy, and piety, each in their own way but under the guise of divine authority, keep each other in a kind of stranglehold. The sacramentality of the world, of the word, of the eucharist, of the Church, of ministry, of life itself, instead of being lived and celebrated in liturgy, instead of being endorsed by theology, is reduced to an exercise of piety by the first, to an item of belief by the second.

---

11    Alexander Schmemann, 'Liturgical Theology, Theology of Liturgy, and Liturgical Reform', *St Vladimir's Theological Quarterly* 13 no. 4 (1969), pp. 217-224, here: 223

# CONCLUSION

In our time, more than ever before, sacraments have become the symbol *par excellence* of non-communion and exclusion. At the same time in which communication and 'virtual communion' are being projected across the globe, ecclesiology and liturgical theology jealously protect the autonomous status which the eucharistic species have acquired through the ages. But if sacraments and eucharistic communion remain above all a theological problem, communion in Christ's body in the world, by the force of the same Holy Spirit who sanctifies the gifts and the communicants and who calls people to his service, will end up progressively being identified in other ways – let us hope it does! Life goes on even without theology. The heritage will remain intact, like the typical medieval Italian town on a mountain, but life will have fled from it and only a few theologians of the old times will claim its memory.

Undoubtedly, there is not much time left. Even if sacramentality could find its way back to the universal symbol of communion and the sharing of life, contained in the sharing of a meal, the common meal itself is at risk in many of our contemporary societies where eating together is no longer a basic crucible of education and transmission. If it is already difficult to reform our theological mentalities, the widening gap between liturgical tradition and contemporary society will challenge all our concepts to an extent that no reform has ever yet had to deal with.

# Robert F. Taft, S.J. (†2018)

Anyone who knows a little history of theology is aware that at the time of the original decision denying the validity of Anglican orders there was in vogue in Catholicism a view of Christian presbyterate as 'priesthood' overdeveloped from the time when the early (probably) African apologist Munucius Felix (ca. AD 130-300) could declare: 'Aras non habemus—We [Christians] have no altars!' Here, as with all historical reality including religious phenomena, context is everything. And it is well documented that the theology of Christian ministry underwent a progressive 'sacerdotalization' in the course of its evolution, once the need to resist recurrent Judaizing tendencies had abated.

Robert F. Taft, S.J. (†2018)
MCG II, 267-8

# Cardinal Joseph Tobin

In the *Catholic Order of Discipline*, there are actually three categories of sacraments: valid sacraments, invalid sacraments, and valid but illicit sacraments. Valid sacraments are where Jesus is present, invalid sacraments are where he's not, and valid but illicit sacraments are those where he is present 'but he's not happy...'. It makes the point that the functionality that served us well in some eras perhaps doesn't serve the truth as well today.

Cardinal Joseph Tobin
MCG III, 154

We are, individually and communally, clay pots, made of base material and very easily broken. Nevertheless, we hold a treasure in ourselves and in our midst. And among the greatest of these riches is the knowledge of the possibility of forgiveness and reconciliation: that we can admit our sinfulness and yet not despair; that we can believe in the possibility of forgiveness and of a new creation; that it is possible to advance in the ways of the Spirit; that, individually, or as a Church or as a race, we are not, doomed always to be as mediocre as we are. The brokenness of her members and our appropriation of worldly values and behaviors may serve to obscure the sacramentality of the Church.

Cardinal Joseph Tobin
MCG III, 172

# Chapter 9

# Sanctification of Memory and the Disclosing of the Holy City

MICHAEL NAI CHIU POON

This chapter aims to explore the way forward in ecumenical dialogue at the start of the third millennium. The title underscores two ideas. First, sanctification of memory points to the intensely personal, inner, elusive and yet Spirit-led search for true knowledge. Memory is the sphere in which, as Augustine suggested in his *Confessions*, humans know God and are led to discover their most inner being in God; in whom haunted, inarticulate and irreconciled memories are purified and transformed by love. It is a discovery, as Augustine put it, of 'Beauty so ancient and so new' (*Confessions* X, 27, 38). Second, the disclosing of the Holy City refers to the heavenly Jerusalem in the final two chapters of *Revelation*. The Church's future and the true tasks of ecumenism are shaped by this eschatological hope. I shall suggest the social vision 'united, but not absorbed' the Malines Conversations held out a century ago is uniquely relevant in today's world. Can peoples whose memories and identities are locked in violent and interminable conflicts with one another be reconciled? I end this chapter by exploring what ecumenical conversation could look like if the history of the Church is essentially tragic. If martyrdom is the norm of the pilgrim Church, what posture should ecumenical dialogue take?

## 'GOD'S NAME, HIS MEMORY, ARE ALL MY SOUL DESIRES'

The Lauds canticle 'Hymn after victory over the enemy' (Isaiah 26), appointed for Tuesdays in Week Three in the Liturgy of the Hours offers a programmatic guide to this exploration. This canticle enjoins the faithful to cry out to God: 'Your name, your memory, are all my soul desires' (verse 8). Strikingly, the 'righteous' (verse 7) who offer this prayer are confronting hostile and violent earthly powers – the 'other lords' (verse 13) – that seek to erase their names and memories. One would have expected the righteous to make a passionate plea to God to preserve their threatened identity. Surely, their blood, like that of Abel, should have cried out to God. The canticle instead points to a more eloquent prayer (cf. Hebrews 12.24). Desiring God's name and his memory, more than Abel's plea, connect them to God's redemptive acts. They put their trust in the God who throughout history has revealed himself and commissioned his servants in times of deep crisis to take part in his saving acts. Thus, God announced to Moses in the burning bush: 'This is my name for all time, by this name I shall be invoked for all generations to come' (Exodus 3.15).

Desiring God's name and his memory enables the faithful to see the reality of the 'strong city' amid a social order in the present world that openly rebels against God. Yet, they are not merely looking for solace in the future. Neither are they seeking deliverance from the world. Remarkably, the Liturgy of the Hours puts Revelation 21.14 at the beginning of the canticle: 'The city walls stood on twelve foundation stones.' The names and memories of the righteous in the Old and New Israel that have been obliterated in this world are in fact kept safe, transformed, and re-ordered in the final messianic banquet at the Holy City of God. The faithful therefore can find strength, together with John at Patmos, to live in *this* world and in *this* city on earth, with the certain hope that heaven will come down to the world, the world will be embodied in city, and city as true communion between God and creation.

While the righteous are still in the present world, they *desire* God's name and his memory. They *desire* because God – 'I am who I am' – is beyond what they can name. Yet unless God has disclosed himself to them in some genuine measure, they would not be able to desire after him. Their names and their memories are in fact the very means by which God spurs them onward in the dynamics of salvation, where all names and memories find their true meaning and proper places in the city of God.

# UNITED, BUT NOT ABSORBED

The watchword 'united, but not absorbed' that Lambert Beaudiun proposed in the Malines Conversations a century ago aptly holds out a social vision that is of huge continuing interest. To be sure, for him and his peers, the vision referred largely to the reunification of the Church of England to the Apostolic See. Its realization depended largely on clarifying the ecclesiastical status of the See of Canterbury, more specifically, on its patriarchal jurisdiction, in relation to both the English dioceses and to Rome. The proposal was dismissed by both the Catholics and the Church of England at that time. Nonetheless.

the vision is even more relevant and challenging at the beginning of the third millennium.

What's in a name? How can peoples today turn away from interminable social conflicts to helping one another disclose what is real and life-giving? How can peoples engage together in a common quest of what is real? How can present-day multicultural society safeguard the memories of all its peoples? There is no easy answer to this. Present-day societies impose huge pressure on their citizens to conform to state ideology to ensure social harmony. Such state policies often lead to suppression of the languages, habits, and memorials of those whom they regard to be troublemakers.

Clearly, it is difficult to do justice to any description of the present-day. The post-colonial and post-missionary grids the late twentieth century sought to give a more authentic expression of their world are no longer useful in the twenty-first century. Global South/North and other binary concepts also run the risk of misrepresenting real life. More recent social movements of thought and practice, driven by globalization and biotechnological revolution make the world even more complex. Indeed, reality is elusive. It cannot be fully described by any theoretical account of it. Theoretical accounts in fact can become tyrannical tools of social control. In a globalizing world where boundaries are fused and imagined, identities are mapped and remapped, and narratives contested and constructed, peoples do not fit conform to conventional types.

The vision 'united, but not absorbed' is of enduring significance because it holds out a Christological vision of humanity. What the Word Incarnate Jesus Christ is, according to the Chalcedonion Definition of the Faith, 'in two natures unconfusedly, unchangeably, indivisibly, inseparably, the distinction of natures being by no means take away by the union'; so the people of God from all languages and all nations should be, 'united, but not absorbed'.

The prospect of full communion with one another, as a united people but not absorbed, is of importance to humankind. The people of God that is called out from all nations with names and memories that are embodied in their languages, customs, laws, and institutions, should be a witness to this commonwealth. As such, ecumenical dialogues, and the Malines Conversations Group discussions particularly, are entrusted with the prophetic task to hold out a vision of authentic communion before the world. For this reason, the Church, both at local and universal level, need to give a fuller theological account of the foundation of its faith and practice. That is, it should not only be able to state what it stands for. More important, it needs to explain more fully the sources, habits and principles that shapes its decisions and agreements. Particularly, it needs to explain how the encounter with the particular and the real situations, leads it to probe more deeply the theological nature of its own habits, laws, and institutions, and therefore to allow these fresh insights to reshape them accordingly. To think theologically in this way is incumbent on the Church, for the sake of the common good of humanity.

Thinking theologically is not an obvious task in the present-day. This is especially challenging for Churches that are associated with the historical trajectories of the Reformation. Pope Benedict XVI, when he was prefect of the Congregation for the Doctrine of the Faith, asked Anglicans to clarify 'the concrete structure of authority in the Anglican community', in the wake of the release of official statements by the Anglican Roman Catholic International Commission.[1] This question is arguably for all Churches of the Reformation. Ecclesiastical authority does not only refer to the managerial power. It concerns the viability of Christian life. The people of God, as individuals and corporate body, do simply live in the past. Orthodox theologian Georges Florovsky underscores that the historical memory of the Church is not only a remembrance of bygone events. For him, tradition is the constant abiding of the Spirit. It is a charismatic, not a historical, principle.[2] How does the Church, then, determine, in response to new movements of the Spirit, what do and what do not arise from the organic growth of the understanding of the sacred deposit of faith? How does the Church determine what is legitimate development in matters of doctrine and discipline? Who speaks for the Church, and what are the structures of discerning, deciding, and receiving truth?

Both Orthodox and Catholics are more ready to approach these questions. Churches of the Reformation however do not see the unity and catholicity of the Church needs to take visible form. The principle of primacy is absent in their respective doctrine of the Church. They would therefore find it difficult to explain how the Church universal and local come together in deciding and agreeing on matters of faith and order. Some Churches may not even see this as a liability. The Christian world communions of these Churches are not expected to decide on faith and order matters. These are left to the local Churches, each with their own autonomous governance structure. This makes official ecumenical dialogues frustrating. For members from such Churches strictly-speaking are unable to present a consistent theological stance except that of their own individual opinion. Members that belong to the same Church may

---

1 Joseph Ratzinger, 'Anglican Catholic Dialogue: Its problems and hopes' in *Church, Ecumenism and Politics*, (Slough, St. Paul's Publications 1987) p. 66

2 Georges Florovsky, 'The Catholicity of the Church' in *Bible, Church, Tradition: An Eastern Orthodox View* (Belmont: Nordland Pub. Co. 1972), pp. 37-56.

hold conflicting views. It is unclear therefore, how ecumenical agreement can structurally relate to the authentic life in the Churches, global and local. There is simply no structure for reception. Such impotence can also become endemic within each Christian world communion. For instance, in the Anglican Communion, the autonomous Provinces and the united Churches that make up the Communion do not have a uniform understanding of metropolitan authority. The unique status of the Church of England as both the Established Church and the historic centre of the Anglican world makes the structure of authority in the Anglican Communion even more complex. For on the one hand, the Church of England needs to respond to political expectation at home; and at the same time, is expected to be standard bearer in matters of faith and order for Anglican Churches worldwide. The dramatic turn of events that led to the decision to allow women in the episcopate in 2014 is a case in point. Churches may therefore find themselves locked in toxic and interminable internal dispute on doctrinal and disciplinary matters because the member Churches cannot take hold together 'the supernatural sense of faith' (*sensus fidei*). This can lead to escalating chaos and eventually breakup within a Church.

Faced with such daunting prospect, a Church may be tempted to give up hard theological wrestling. Instead, it takes a practical approach to preserve its own organizational stability. After all, without institutional stability, a Church can hardly engage the wider world. A Christian world communion would, along such reasoning, use a strategy of distinctive co-existence to manage diverse practices among its constituencies. Pastoral provisions would readily be made available to meet the needs of those who hold different convictions, so long as they remain within a single organization.

Such comprehensiveness however would undermine authentic doctrinal development in the Church. Lobby pressure would take the place of theological thinking. The Church would become less alert to the enduring theological questions that have been handed on down the generations. This also make it less able to be perceptive to the real theological issues that present-day societies pose, e.g., on present-day questions of human/gender identity.

# SANCTIFICATION OF MEMORY: THE LITURGICAL LOCUS

The Roman Canon in the Roman Missal aptly depicts the essential connection between memory and communion. The opening section, the *Te igitur*, of the Eucharistic Prayer points the faithful to the reality of communion in the holy, catholic Church – 'our Pope, and our Bishop, and all who, holding to the truth, hand on the catholic and apostolic faith.' Clearly, this memorial of the blessed passion (*Unde et memores*) lies in the heart of this communion. Moreover, the memory of the body that was given up and the blood that was shed (*hoc facite in meam commemorationem*) breathes life to the meaning of history:

- Remember (*momento*) 'all gathered here', the local Church;
- In communion with Mary, the apostles, and the early Christian martyrs and saints 'those whose memory we venerate' (*communicantes, et memoriam venerantes*);
- Remember also (*memento etiam*) those who rest in the sleep of peace;
- The fellowship (*societas*) and company (*consortium*) of the apostles, martyrs and saints.

The apostles, martyrs and saints therefore become living voice for the present. Their specific testimonies and forms of obedience are devoutly handed on through the liturgy. Through faith they still speak and summon the Church in all ages to imitate their examples. The Eucharistic Prayer arguably sets the tasks of guarding, uniting, and governing of the holy catholic Church (in the *Te igitur*) in this martyrdom and saintliness context.

To be sure, the General Instruction on the Roman Missal lists 'the public authorities and the salvation of the whole world' among the intentions to be included in the Prayer of the Faithful. Nonetheless, the Roman Canon is re-markably silent on the place of earthly authorities. It stands in sharp contrast to the picture that is presented in the Prayer for Christ's Church militant here on earth in the Holy Communion service in the Church of England Book of Common Prayer. The universal Church finds itself in an ordered Christian world, where Christian kings, princes, the monarch, the government, bish-ops, and curates find their places in pursuing the common aspiration for truth, unity and concord.

The Roman Canon therefore speaks with especial relevance to today's world. It underscores the authentic real situation in the present-day. The Church does not find itself in a settled Christian society that can depend on earthly author-ities to 'indifferently minister justice.' Rather, it holds to the truth and hands on the faith amid organized opposition to Christ's lordship. The public cele-bration of the memorial of blessed Passion is subversive; an open defiance to earthly claim of lordship and kingship. It is an act of solidarity with the names and memories of the faithful that have been exterminated in killing fields of tyrannical earthly powers.

The Letters to the Churches of Asia in Revelation 2 to 3 underscore this reality. The seven Churches are united not only in their suffering, but also in the divine call to faithfulness amid intense pressure to compromise. The public reading and sharing of letters among the Churches are an intense form of ecumenical conversation and learning where specific points of weakness, strength, and challenge of each Church are exposed to the other. To be united, but not absorbed, is an eschatological reality. Their unity on earth, however vulnerable it is, is kept safe by the Lamb who is worthy to disclose the true meaning of history (Revelation 5). Each is required to 'prove victorious' with particular forms of obedience. The act of remembering in the Eucharist, draws the worshippers into this communion of martyrs and saints.

# SANCTIFICATION OF MEMORY: THE MISSIOLOGICAL LOCUS

Augustine teaches us in his Sermon 21 that love is 'what we love with'; what we should love is 'a good beyond words, a good that does good, a good that is the creator of all goods (*ineffabile bonum, bonum beneficum, bonum bonorum omnium creatorem*)' (*Sermo* 21.2). So, it is also for unity. Unity is found in uniting; the good we seek in unity reaches beyond all human imagination that finds its true fulfillment in final consummation in God.

To be united, and not absorbed, therefore finds its true bearing in reaching out to the poor, hungry, marginalized, homeless and stateless in Western societies as much as in the rest of the world. The uniting takes place at points of social chaos, where Christian and human identities are threatened by insatiable passion for earthly gains. Not absorbing is a spirituality of encountering the other as Thou, with attention, reverence and devotion. To seek to preserve the names and memories of others, till they can find their home in God, is the ecumenical task of the present-day.

\* \* \*

Ecumenical dialogue is an inner journey that involves loss and gain. It is a Spirit-led adventure in which names and memories are purified and find their true meaning in the name and memory of God the Trinity. Pope Benedict XVI underscores in the essay to which I refer earlier the importance of truth in this journey:

Greater unity is really to be found in the fact that the separated communities are passionately seeking the truth together with the firm intention of imposing nothing on the other party that does not come from the Lord and of losing nothing entrusted to us by him. (87)

The remembering in the divine liturgy, and the uniting at the fringe of settled and institutional life, disclose the gift and task of communicating communion in the present-day. That they may be one is the gift of the Crucified and Ascended Lord to those who prove to be victorious in the City of God.

# Bishop Geoffrey Rowell (†2017)

At a meeting I had with the then Cardinal Ratzinger, after some interesting conversation about Newman's theology, I referred back to our earlier conversation, reminding him of his strong affirmation that the reality of the Eucharist in an ecclesial community whose orders he did not recognize as valid was 'never, ever nothing'. If that was the case, given that he was receiving me as an Anglican bishop, and even more received Archbishops of Canterbury as such, where was the 'never, ever nothing' in relation to the judgement of *Apostolicae Curae*. 'We cannot', he said, 'do anything about Leo XIII's words, but there are, however, other ways of looking at things.' Sadly, he did not go on to specify what those might be, but merely referred me to theologians in the CDF who would be glad to help.

Bishop Geoffrey Rowell (†2017)
MCG IV, 199

# Sarah Coakley

The fundamental 'difference' to be negotiated is *not* male and female, let alone the Romantic 'masculine' and 'feminine', but rather the ultimate difference between God and humanity; and this, we might say, only Christ has 'negotiated'. *This* crossing of difference is indeed a 'cosmological disturbance' of unrepeatable status. What happens in the Eucharist, then, happens on the *limen* between the divine and the human, where the miracle of divine enfleshment challenges and undercuts even the most ingenious secular theorizing about the order of this world.

Sarah Coakley
MCG V, 103

We need to provide a new response to the issue of what it is for the priest or minister to act *in persona Christi*. True to my focus on the category of desire, I shall argue that Rome and the Orthodox are entirely right to seek the Christic clue to eroticism and gender in the Eucharist; but that Rome's particular attempt to debar women from the altar and to 'freeze' the gender binary back into mandated (and 'complementary') roles finally fails in its very articulation.

Sarah Coakley
MCG V, 83

# Chapter 10

# Ordination in the Church of England: Theology and Practice in the Common Worship Ordinal

## DAVID STANCLIFFE[1]

When priests make the Declaration of Assent publicly before being licensed to any cure of souls they rehearse their loyalty not only to the 'faith uniquely revealed in the Holy Scriptures and set forth in the catholic Creeds', but to the Church of England's 'witness to Christian truth in its historic formularies, the Thirty-nine Articles of Religion, The Book of Common Prayer and the Ordering of Bishops, Priests and Deacons.'[2] Priests respond to the bishop's Preface in these words: 'I declare my belief in the faith which is revealed in the Holy Scriptures and set forth in the catholic creeds and to which the historic formularies of the Church of England bear witness'; and significantly they conclude 'and in public prayer and administration of the sacraments, I will use only the forms of service which are authorized or allowed by Canon.' This is why the texts used in worship are subjected to rigorous scrutiny not only in the House of Bishops, but though the laborious revision processes of the General Synod.

As there is no confessional statement or body of teaching in the Church of England remotely parallel to the corpus of papal pronouncements or the Augsburg Confession, we depend substantially on liturgical formularies to hold our doctrine of the Church, its ministry and mission. Surprisingly, therefore, few bishops seem to take much interest in the liturgy. Worship tends to arouse strong feelings rather than theological engagement, and decisions about the forms of service to be used in worship are made in the General Synod of the

---

1  Some material in this essay is drawn from a chapter in *Grasping the Heel of Heaven: Liturgy, leadership and ministry in today's church*, ed. Aidan Platten, (Norwich, Canterbury Press 2018) – a collection of essays to honour the ministry of Michael Perham. David Stancliffe was the chair of the Church of England's Liturgical Commission during the formation of the liturgical texts in question.

2  *Common Worship; Services and Prayers for the Church of England* (London: Church House Publishing 2001), p. xi.

Church of England. Drafts produced by the Liturgical Commission (following a formal request from House of Bishops) are introduced into the Synod by the House. They are debated, revised in a multi-stage process, and finally authorised by Synod before they can be published and used.

One of the reasons why the Ordinal is important is that this is where you can find the Church of England's theology of the distinctive orders of ministry clarified.[3] *Saepius Officio*, the formal response of the Archbishops of Canterbury and York to the Papal Bull of 1896 *Apostolicae Curae* declaring Anglican orders to be 'absolutely null and utterly void', was drafted by my predecessor as Bishop of Salisbury, John Wordsworth, and his robust defence of what the Church of England thinks it has always been doing as well as saying in the rites of Ordination – specifically referred to in the Declaration of Assent – is important for any reconciliation of ministries in the future.

At my episcopal ordination I had invited Bishop Sigisbert Kraft, bishop of the Old Catholic Church in Germany, to take a full part lest the validity of my orders should ever be in question. Since Pope Paul VI's gift of his ring to Archbishop Michael Ramsey in 1966, what the Roman Catholic Church does and what it says have been at variance, so during the revision of the ordinal in the late 1990s and early 2000s, I was concerned to ensure that the Church of England should have an ordination rite that could never again be called deficient.

As well as considering what an ordination does, it is important to consider what it says about the Church and its theology of ministry. Is an ordination only like a graduation ceremony or a rite of installation – a public recognition of something that has happened, or does something take place to alter the relationship between the ordinand and the Church?

When the House of Bishops was beginning to look at the revision of the Ordinal, I felt that the House might be helped by a preliminary paper to help think through some of the issues around not just what an ordination did, but what it expressed before we got down to drafting texts. Central to this was to make explicit the theology of each of the three orders since the distinctive nature of diaconal ministry was only just recovering from being seen as little more than a probationary period before ordination to the priesthood.

Ordinations are occasions where the ordering of the Church's common life is made visible. The ordination rite gives shape and order to the life of the whole Church of God. That community of faith is called to continue the work of Christ: it is into his body that we are baptised and thus empowered by the

---

3   *Common Worship: Ordination Services (Study Edition)*, Church House Publishing, 2007 contains the rites discussed here, and includes 'A brief history of Ordination Rites' by Paul Bradshaw.

Spirit to become God's agents and instruments in bringing about his new creation. It is Christ's ministry that we share, and as Christ is the head of that body,[4] so the ordained ministry represents the ministry of Christ as Head of the Body. There is a distinctive responsibility within the *laos* for the *kleros*.[5]

Although it can look as if the bishop is setting one or more of the people of God apart from the community of faith and transmitting to them a distinct power, the way in which the rite is celebrated makes it clear that ordination is the act of the whole community, presided over by the bishop, that not only publicly authorises a particular member of the community of the baptised to bear a representative responsibility, but also constitutes the Church as the ordered expression of the divine life. So, care has to be taken in text and symbol, as well as in presentation, not only to uphold the common baptismal foundation of all Christian ministry, but to clarify the distinctiveness of those called to be and authorised as ministers in the three historic orders.

The call of all the baptised is made clear at the start of the rite. We are to follow Christ, to be made corporately into a royal priesthood so that we may 'declare the wonderful deeds of him who has called us.' The whole Church is to witness to God's love and to work for the coming of his kingdom. It is to serve this royal priesthood that those standing before the assembly are to be ordained into a distinctive order. While all the baptised are called to exercise their gifts in their discipleship, not all are called to be public, representative ministers.[6]

So, what is distinctive about ordained ministry? There is only one ministry, and that is Christ's. Ordination as a minister makes visible in a particular person a distinctive call to Christ's ministry in his Church. Ordination places a person within that catholic order and is not primarily concerned with the way in which that ministry will be exercised in the local context. It is the needs of that particular local context – whether parish or chaplaincy – that will form the way in which that universal diaconate or priesthood is exercised in a particular cultural context.

It is the task of an ordination rite therefore to make clear in one liturgical act the particular focus of the ministry to which the candidate is called. As in other rites, like the funeral or marriage services, this liturgical rehearsal of a series of stages in a candidate's development in response to the Church's call is articulated by the rite: by the candidates' presentation, by their public

---

4   Eph 4:15,16.

5   1 Pet 5:3

6   John N. Collins, *Are all Christians ministers?* (Newtown: E. J. Dwyer 1992)

examination and the assembly's assent to their ordination, by their visibly exercising the formal responsibilities of the ministry into which they have been ordained, by being equipped with the distinctive symbols of office, and by returning the candidates, authorised, and acknowledged, to the particular communities in which they will exercise that universal ministry. This is how the Church makes clear that the candidate has a particular authority to minister in Christ's name within the body as a whole. But in the ordination rite, the emphasis is on what God in Christ has done and continues to do rather than on the particular people being ordained and their diverse gifts.

# TOWARDS A DISTINCTIVE THEOLOGY OF EACH ORDER

Ordination therefore is more than articulating publicly what the Church is doing. In an ordination it is God who empowers his people and orders his Church. The ministry in which we share is Christ's, and the sign of the candidates' incorporation into Christ's whole ministry that is common to all ordinations is prayer with the laying on of hands.

A clear theology of the distinctive nature of each order is important. So often the theology of orders in the Church of England seems to be founded on little more than a description of the functions of various ministers. As a result, many people in the Church of England think that the three orders are bishops, vicars and curates (or sometimes bishops, clergy and readers!) with function and hierarchy as the basis of the distinction. This assumption is understandable given the way in which various references in the Epistles approach ministry in terms of discerning gifts and linking that to function.

By contrast with this more pragmatic approach, I believe that the right place to start is with the work of Christ himself.

Here is a simple matrix. God in Christ does two things for his people: first he shares our life, then he changes it. This is the heart of the faith, and it is the Church's task to engage God's people in the process of engagement and transformation and to ensure that this pattern is absorbed, practiced, and handed on.

While this paradigm of the relationship between Incarnation and Redemption, and the way this is handed on provides a model for how to structure a pastoral visit (listen first, and then decide what to offer that change may happen) or how to construct a liturgy (challenged by the ministry of the word to expect transformation in the celebration of the sacrament), in this context the paradigm is most significant as a means of teasing out the distinctive ministries of deacon, priest and bishop.

The diaconate focuses God's direct and personal engagement with us, his sharing our nature in Christ's incarnation, his being rooted in the particularity of time and place. This opens the door to a ministry of attention, service, and the brokering that goes with the concept of Christ as the agent or herald of God. If Christ is the 'deacon of God',[7] then the deacon is one who is commissioned to undertake a specific task or deliver a specific message. At the heart of this incarnational ministry therefore are the twin categories of embassy and engagement.

The priesthood focuses what St Paul describes as 'the upward call of God in Christ',[8] the reconciling, redemptive action of Christ's perfect self-offering on the cross. This sacrificial movement of response to a God who 'calls us out of darkness into his marvellous light' sets redemptive change at the heart of the sacramental ministry of the priesthood. Movement and change are central to the paradigm of a missionary priesthood, but never at the expense of that unity with one another and with Christ in the one sacrifice offered at the one altar.[9]

Episcopal ministry embraces both diaconal and priestly ministry, but its distinctive focus of this apostolic and prophetic ministry is pastoral oversight. The mission of the twelve, and of the seventy, inaugurates the distinctive Pentecostal mission of the Church. This apostolic ministry enrolls God's people in this process of engagement and transformation and makes sure that this pattern is handed on. That is why distinctive episcopal ministry is focused liturgically in those occasions like baptism, ordination and the ratifying of initiation in confirmation. Those are celebrations where baptized Christians tumble to it that that is what they are, and begin to take adult responsibility for sharing in the Church's apostolic mission and ministry and its prophetic witness. It is here that the bishop's ministry as the focus of unity and the agent of communion with other parts of the Church is given expression in the ministry of pastoral oversight.

None of this means that bishops are the only ministers engaged in the Pentecostal task: it is clearly shared with other ministers and with the priestly people of God. But it is the bishops' responsibility to see that the Church is Pentecostal and apostolic, engaged in holding together the diversity of gifts in a way that builds up the body in its witness to the world. Nor is this is all that

---

7  See Ignatius, *Epistle to the Trallians*. 3.1 and Mark 10:45

8  Phil 3:14

9  See Ignatius, *Epistle to the Magnesians*, 7

the bishop does. It is the bishops' responsibility to see that the whole Church is engaged in that process too, and to lead the Church out from the safety of the sheepfold to engage in its mission to an indifferent world.

This sense of overlap is true of the other orders too. The diaconate is not an inferior order, where deacons never find themselves engaged in distinctively priestly or apostolic tasks: it is simply that the diaconate has a prime responsibility to remind the whole Church to engage with reality first, before attempting to transform – or more properly, to let God have the opportunity to transform - our lives. Diaconal ministry undergirds everything else, and all ministers need to have this held constantly before us.

# THE CONSEQUENCES OF APPLYING THIS CHRISTOLOGICAL PARADIGM

First, it ought not to be possible to exercise priestly ministry without first being a deacon. So often priests forget that they are always deacons too and plunge in with an agenda for change without first spending time and energy in that incarnational, diaconal engagement. When this happens, their ministry often fails to be rooted in the reality of a local context and fails to engage with what is actually happening. This is the root of much frustration and disappointment. Our Lord spent some thirty years in preparation, saying not a public word, and only three years of active ministry. Diaconal ministry is a constant and indispensable foundation for all priestly and episcopal ministry.

A second corollary – the mirror image of the first - is that ordination directly to the priesthood is not theologically appropriate, any more than we would entertain direct ordination to the episcopate. As Gregory Nazianzus said 'That which God did not assume, he did not redeem.'[10] Just as there can be no redemption without incarnation, so priests and bishops who have no diaconal foundation to their ministry are at risk of offering a ministry that has no point of engagement, but moves directly into the imposition of redemptive change.

A third corollary is that the diaconate cannot be merely a probationary period for the priesthood. It is a ministry in its own right and has an integrity of its own that needs to be respected, even for those whose ultimate vocation to the priesthood has been recognised. The total ministry of Christ's Church in a particular community is best served by the visibility of both diaconal and priestly ministry. When these two orders are exercised together in the service

---

10  Gregory Nazianzus, *Epistola* 101.7; cf Athanasius, *De Incarnatione,* 54.

of the community – and specially when this is visible in the liturgy, this complementarity models for the whole community what God has done for us in Christ – sharing our life, and then changing it. The episcopal thread in priestly ministry – made visible when at a licensing the bishop says 'Receive this cure of souls which is both yours and mine' – will always be hovering around how the community is energised – or not – in its mission as a result of this process of engagement and transformation.

A fourth corollary is that what an ordination is doing is easier to grasp when ordination to a single order is being celebrated. When priests are ordained at the same time as deacons – and this was allowed for in the ASB as in the BCP and is still practiced in some dioceses today – then the distinctive focus on a particular aspect of Christ's saving work is less clear. This is not just a matter of needing to choose distinctive readings for each order. It is also important that the 'charge' to the candidates and the way in which those ordained express their particular order in that liturgical celebration should give a clear message about the distinctive witness of that order. And if we wanted the complete picture, then an episcopal ordination is not always easy to arrange at the same time!

# EXPRESSING THE DISTINCTIVE NATURE OF THE ORDER IN EACH ORDINATION RITE

The basic rite of ordination is the laying on of hands with prayer within a celebration of the eucharist, but there are a number of points at which the distinctive focus of each order can be expressed. The first is in the Presentation. Traditionally in the Church of England it has been the archdeacon who has presented candidates, but would there not be more sense in someone who has had a hand in their formation presenting candidates for ordination to the diaconate? And who should present candidates for the priesthood? The most obvious person is probably their training incumbent. For the episcopate, the Crown's formal presentation might well be best exercised for suffragans by the diocesan bishop involved in their nomination and for diocesans a member of the Crown Appointments Commission.

A second element is clearly the readings. Readings for the distinctive ministry of the priest, like those which focus on the ministry of reconciliation, for example, are clearly out of place for the ordination of a deacon.

The charge is a significant element in the Anglican tradition. It is one of the places, together with the ordination prayer itself and the collect and post-communion prayer, where the theology of each order is articulated distinctly. The charge to priests in the Book of Common Prayer has been very significant in shaping our theology of priestly ministry over the centuries, and many priests know it by heart and return to it regularly for self-examination on the anniversary of their ordination. But there was never a charge of comparable weight for the ordination of deacons. So while the flavour of the BCP text was kept well in the ASB rite for the ordination of priests, the charge to deacons said little more than that they were to minister in the Church and assist the priest under whom they serve. This was grudging in what the deacon may do, gave no sense of a distinctive diaconal role visible in the ministry of Christ, and served merely to reinforce the functional image of a trainee in an inferior order. With renewed interest in the diaconate as an equal and independent order, a longer charge with more theological weight has been crafted.[11] Revision of the priestly and episcopal charges acknowledged the growing significance of collaborative styles of working which required modification of the historically dominant sheep/shepherd model.

At the heart of each rite, the whole assembly is called to prayer for the coming of the Holy Spirit and engages in a litany. The presidential prayer that follows includes a preface-type thanksgiving to God for the gifts he has given and for calling the candidates and has at its heart an epicletic formula, repeated in the Anglican tradition with the laying on of hands over each candidate (if there are more than one). The prayer concludes with intercession and a doxology, sealed with a great Amen. Priests join the presiding bishop in the laying on of hands when the ordination is to the priesthood (as bishops join the archbishop for the episcopate). Care needs to be taken that the laying on of hands does not interrupt the sense of the complete prayer overmuch: in some places the assembly's continuing prayer is sustained by a murmured chant invoking the Holy Spirit.

A fifth element relates to the handing over of distinctive symbols to the newly ordained to symbolise their order. In the 1550 *Form and manner of making and consecrating Archebisshoppes, Bisshoppes, Priestes and Deacons* and in subsequent Ordinals, giving a copy of the New Testament took the place of the handing over of the Book of the Gospels to deacons and a copy of the Bible in place of the chalice and paten to priests. In the ASB, the possibility of

---

11 Draft versions of a distinctively diaconal charge were found particularly helpful at ordinations where the candidates were for the 'permanent' diaconate, though now all deacons benefit from a more robust theology of the diaconate than that offered in the BCP or ASB. Church of England House of Bishops Paper HB(01)22, paras 156-158 comments on the ASB charge.

giving the chalice and paten to priests and the pastoral staff to bishops in addition to the Bible at this point was restored.

As well as these essentially theological considerations, the basis of which has broadly been accepted in the *Common Worship Ordinal*, new features were mooted included dispersing elements of the ordination rite throughout the Eucharist. Presenting candidates at the start, moving the charge to after the sermon so that the assembly's ratification of their worthiness may follow the candidates' response to the bishop's questioning, and transferring the presentation of 'tools for the trade', like a bishop's pastoral staff or individual copies of the Bible, to the *missio* or Sending Out were among the suggestions, and it was only the last that provoked any opposition.

In the BCP, following an older tradition, deacons were ordained after the epistle and then immediately given the New Testament so that they could at once do what they were ordained to do, and read the Gospel among the assembly. That clearly illustrated their commitment to live out the incarnational ministry that had been entrusted to them: taking the Gospel book and reading the passage among the people modelled the Word of God being made flesh and pitching his tent in our midst. With all ordinations now coming after the Gospel and sermon, distributing personal copies of the New Testament at this point to newly ordained deacons did not make much sense. What are they to do with them? And the same was true of the handing over of the pastoral staff to newly consecrated bishops at this point. In the Church of England, where the ordination of a diocesan bishop cannot take place in their cathedral and include the enthronement,[12] they cannot use their staff at this point in the liturgy and it has to be taken from them almost at once. And what are newly ordained priests and bishops supposed to do with a Bible at this point in the service, when the Liturgy of the Word has just ended? If the Bible is to be given at this point, I argued, ought it not to be The Bible, the large lectern Bible which is handed to each candidate in turn, rather than the distribution of a mound of individual copies? This would parallel the newly ordained deacons being given the book of the Gospels – the richly bound text that was processed into the cathedral at the start of the liturgy by the deacon of the rite as the icon of Christ coming among his people.

Considerations like these led to the suggestion that copies of the New Testament should be distributed to newly ordained deacons at the end of the rite, so

---

12 A diocesan bishop in the Church of England has to pay homage to the sovereign after consecration and before enthronement. Unless the sovereign were willing to come to episcopal ordinations in the cathedral, as is the case in Denmark for example, it seems unlikely that the unity of consecration, homage and enthronement could be achieved in one celebration, as things stand.

that they can be sent out with 'the tools for the trade'. And would this not be a better place to give new priests their copy of the Bible and bishops their pastoral staff? Bishops could at least walk out with them even if not invited by the consecrating archbishop to join in giving the blessing. Detaching these symbols from the central rite of ordination might also help make clear that the *porrectio instrumentorum* and any verbal formulae that might accompany them are not instrumental in effecting ordination. All the Churches are agreed on this now, even though the assumption that they were played a part in the papal declaration *Apostolicae Curae* of 1896 that Anglican orders were 'absolutely null and utterly void'.

If anything beyond the ordination prayer and the laying on of hands is required at the central point in the rite, I suggested some visual underlining that might explicate the distinctive focus of each order, which of course would be optional.

For deacons, the custom of the bishop divesting himself of his vestments, tying a towel round his waist and washing the newly ordained deacons' feet has commended itself as a visible sign of the way in which a new deacon's ministry should be exercised and the relationship between the deacon and their bishop made visible. Such a practice – originally part of the baptismal rite before becoming an independent rite separate from the Eucharist of the Last Supper on Maundy Thursday where it is now most commonly celebrated – roots the deacon's ministry in the gospel and helps to make sense of diaconal ministry to many in the congregation, especially to those who are not regular churchgoers. No words are said, but a chant such as *Ubi Caritas* is sung, and if John 13:1-11 has been read as the gospel, the deacon may finish the passage (John 13:12-20) after the Bishop has finished and vested again. After the exchange of the Peace, the newly ordained deacons can begin to give liturgical expression to the ministry to which they have been ordained by laying the Holy Table and preparing the gifts, and then taking part in the distribution of Communion.

For candidates for the Priesthood, a telling symbol of their self-surrender before the majesty of God is to prostrate themselves flat on the floor during the *Veni Creator* and the Litany. Ordinands who have experienced this speak of its power – and it conveys their sacrificial dependence on God vividly to the assembly.

The distinctive gospel for priests (John 20:19-23) speaks of the risen Christ breathing over his apostles. (This visible handing over of the Spirit was given literal illustration in the Coptic Church where the Patriarch – if unable to be present – would breathe into a bladder that would be taken to the ordination and burst over the head of the candidate!) The western tradition offers a symbol which is more readily recognisable as embodying the outpouring of the Holy Spirit, and links ordination to its roots in baptism: the anointing of the newly ordained, and specially this time the hands that are to bless and absolve. Though such symbolic acts are secondary, they may speak powerfully to people in the assembly of the outpouring of God's grace on those who have been chosen and appointed to hold the priestly ministry of Christ before his Church and given authority to preside at the celebration of the sacraments.

And the newly ordained – perhaps priests and bishops even more than deacons, with their traditional relationship with the bishop – need some kind of welcome into their respective orders. This says something important about entering a catholic order, whether diaconal, priestly or episcopal, and makes it clear that the newly ordained minister has a responsibility to and in the whole Church, not just to the local community. It certainly looks very odd to see the newly ordained returning to the seat they occupied as a candidate, as if the ordination had made no difference to how the Church was ordered. The time for returning people to their local church, whether this is bishops to the people of their dioceses or priests to the people of their parishes, is at the end of the service, as part of an extended dismissal rite where a representative – a churchwarden for priests or a lay chairperson or Lord Lieutenant for bishops – might accompany them out.

Ordination can be a powerful sign to the very parochial parish that the Church's priestly ministry is not primarily about serving their needs – that is an essentially diaconal task – but about linking that cell of the Church's life with the universal priesthood of the Church and drawing them into that one perfect self-offering of the Son to that Father. But that universal ministry needs constantly to be re-earthed in the local, the particular – in fact the parochial. So the way in which priests (or bishops) are given back to their people is important. It may not require any words, like many of these signs, but the significance of the bishop handing back priests who have just been ordained to their training incumbent and members of their parish should not be underestimated. If the ordaining bishop moves around the cathedral – or even outside after the liturgy has formally ended – reuniting the newly ordained with their parishes, it would say a lot about the unity of that ministry 'which is both yours and mine' – both catholic in concept and local in expression.

But it is important that people are not led to think that the only place in which the newly ordained priests or bishops can exercise their ministry is in their own local parish or diocese. When ordaining bishops invites the newly ordained priest(s) to stand alongside them at the altar during the Eucharistic

Prayer, vested as the bishop is, this sends out a powerful signal about the way in which collegiality is modelled. Of course ordaining bishops can ignore the newly ordained, send them back to sit in the seats where they sat as candidates and continue with the eucharistic celebration as if they had no need of them. Strictly speaking, the bishop does not need them. But is that the signal it is intended to convey, or would a more inclusive gesture say something better about the nature of the Church and the collegial nature of priestly and episcopal ministry that the newly ordained now share with the bishop?

# CONCLUSION

What conclusions do I draw from this reflection on the nature and practice of ordination? First, that there is an implicit ecclesiology – an often subliminally imparted teaching about the nature of the Church and its mission – in the rite. Second, in order to chart the development of doctrine, we need to be more aware of the implicit teaching in our liturgical formularies. Third, while the rubrics in a rite are as subject to the Synod's authorisation as the texts, the Synod has never sought to try control *how* the rites are celebrated. Yet is in *how* the rites are celebrated that the underlying theology can be made explicit.

And indeed, how you model the life of Christ in your liturgical ministry is what develops habits that spill over from their worship into how the deacon, priest or bishop behaves and so exhibits who they are becoming in the communities in which they are set. The inability of some priests to engage with people is a betrayal of their diaconate. Conspicuous failure to live a life that is in any way sacrificial is a denial of the sacrificial ministry of a priest. An evident lack of interest in the life and witness of the Church beyond your own parish or diocese either historically or geographically cuts the roots of any claim to catholicity. It is easy for the Church's ministers to collude with current fashions of management, self-concern, and congregationalism and to forget that they represent the prophetic, incarnational and sacrificial ministry of the one into whose ministry they are ordained.

# Chapter 11

# The Celebration of the Sacrament of Ordination in the Roman Catholic Church

## JORIS GELDHOF

Before going into various aspects of the liturgy and theology of ordination, a persistent terminological confusion must first be cleared up.[1] The Roman Catholic Church considers not only priestly ordination to be a sacrament, but also ordination as bishop and deacon. Deacons, priests and bishops are the three ordained ministries it recognizes. In addition to those three offices, there are many tasks and services for which people can be appointed (such as acolytes and lectors) as well as things (such as altars and churches), which can be consecrated. In addition, people can be consecrated or dedicated for various roles in the ecclesiastical, pastoral, and religious life of the Church (such as virgins and abbesses, for example), but in all these cases one does not speak of sacraments. So, the most convenient way to be terminologically – and immediately theologically – correct is to speak consistently about the sacrament and liturgy of ordination, and not to narrow it to priesthood on the one hand and not to broaden it to acts of consecration in general on the other.

The present chapter proceeds in three steps. First, some essential background information from Bible and tradition is provided so as to understand the composition of the rites of ordination as they are currently celebrated in the Roman Catholic Church – whereby we limit the scope to the Roman Rite. Second, we focus on the liturgies of ordination of deacons, priests, and bishops.[2] It will be made clear that there is a great amount of structural similarity

---

1   The present text is to a large extent a translation of the chapter on ordinations in Joris Geldhof, *Liturgie en sacramenten: een inleiding* (Leuven: Acco 2022), pp. 125–135.

2   The best available study about this in English is Susan K. Wood, *Sacramental Orders*, Lex Orandi (Collegeville: Liturgical Press 2000).

between these celebrations, and that the differences are interesting details. Third, some theological comments are offered.

# THE ORDINATION OF DEACONS, PRIESTS, AND BISHOPS: SOME ESSENTIAL BACKGROUND INFORMATION

It seems that already by the end of the first century and the beginning of the second, a threefold model of leadership had developed in the earliest Christian Church communities. The New Testament and some other early Christian sources bear witness to this development, although it is no longer possible to ascertain with certainty what the precise phases were, and where they did or did not first become (successfully) established. Therefore, one assumes that this evolution was not linear, and certainly not that it was directed from a single centre. However, there is quite early evidence of a model with bishops, priests, and deacons at the head of the community who were appointed or ordained for this purpose in a special way and under special conditions.

The etymology of the words 'bishop', 'priest', and 'deacon' is relevant to their theological meaning.

1 The word bishop is derived from the Greek *episkopos*, which echoes the verb *episkopein*. That verb means to watch, supervise, oversee, keep the overview, check, etc. Literally, then, a bishop is a kind of overseer or supervisor, someone who keeps an eye on things.
2 'Priest' is derived from a Greek word meaning 'elder', *presbuteros*. Usually, this noun is used in the plural to mean a college of elders (*presbuteroi*; presbyterate), to which administrative and judicial responsibilities were entrusted in many ancient societies. Another Greek word often rendered with 'priest' is *hieros*, which in Latin largely corresponds to *sacerdos*. However, the two terms are not synonyms. It could be said that *hieros/sacerdos* is limited to the cultic function of a priest (the one who offers the sacrifice), while *presbuteros* refers rather to the community-forming, leadership, and governing roles of the priest.
3 Finally, 'deacon' is obviously related to *diakonia*, which means service or ministry. Indeed, a deacon has traditionally had primarily a role in the Church's charitable works.

It is sometimes assumed that there has been an evolution from a collegial presbyteral to a monarchical episcopal model in the ancient Church. At first the responsibilities would have rested with a group of elders who held various positions, but this later would have evolved into situations where one figure, specifically that of the bishop, came to be at the head of the community and held ultimate responsibility. In Paul's letters, among others, several of these tendencies would play in the background and be reflected. In any case, Paul's letters are an extremely important biblical source both for liturgical-sacramental development and for the theology of ministries in the Church. In that context, consider also the infamous passages in which he talks about all kinds of charisms in the Church.

A crucial passage in the New Testament that speaks of the appointment of certain persons for the purpose of performing a specific task is the account from the Acts of the Apostles of the early growth of the community of Christian believers in Jerusalem.

> Now during those days, when the disciples were increasing in number, the Hellenists complained against the Hebrews because their widows were being neglected in the daily distribution of food. And the twelve called together the whole community of the disciples and said, 'It is not right that we should neglect the word of God in order to wait at tables. Therefore, friends, select from among yourselves seven men of good standing, full of the Spirit and of wisdom, whom we may appoint to this task, while we, for our part, will devote ourselves to prayer and to serving the word.' What they said pleased the whole community, and they chose Stephen, a man full of faith and the Holy Spirit, together with Philip, Prochorus, Nicanor, Timon, Parmenas, and Nicolaus, a proselyte of Antioch. They had these men stand before the apostles, who prayed and laid their hands on them. (Acts 6:1–6)

In this notorious passage, the combination of prayer and laying on of hands after careful selection is particularly noteworthy.

Elsewhere in the New Testament the profile of leaders in the community is considered in more detail, as, for example, in Paul's first letter to Timothy.

> The saying is sure: whoever aspires to the office of bishop desires a noble task. Now a bishop must be above reproach, married only once, temperate, sensible, respectable, hospitable, an apt teacher, not a drunkard, not violent but gentle, not quarrelsome, and not a lover of money. He must

manage his own household well, keeping his children submissive and respectful in every way – for if someone does not know how to manage his own household, how can he take care of God's church? He must not be a recent convert, or he may be puffed up with conceit and fall into the condemnation of the devil. Moreover, he must be well thought of by outsiders, so that he may not fall into disgrace and the snare of the devil. Deacons likewise must be serious, not double-tongued, not indulging in much wine, not greedy for money; they must hold fast to the mystery of the faith with a clear conscience. And let them first be tested; then, if they prove themselves blameless, let them serve as deacons. (1 Tim 3:1–10)

Interestingly, in this passage nothing is said about priests. However, these are discussed later in the same book (1 Tim 5:17-22).

From all these verses it is clear that the personality, reliability, and versatility of ministers is a primary concern. For not just anyone can be entrusted with an office. This is unambiguously confirmed in the letter to Titus:

For a bishop, as God's steward, must be blameless; he must not be arrogant or quick-tempered or addicted to wine or violent or greedy for gain; but he must be hospitable, a lover of goodness, prudent, upright, devout, and self-controlled. He must have a firm grasp of the word that is trustworthy in accordance with the teaching, so that he may be able both to preach with sound doctrine and to refute those who contradict it. (Titus 1:7–9)

On a more structural level, it appears that by the beginning of the second century Christian communities had already organized themselves around the threefold model of a bishop at the head of a presbyterium, i.e., several priests. Deacons were not part of the presbyterium but performed special duties under the supervision of the bishop. For this state of affairs, the letter corpus of Ignatius of Antioch is decisive. In his view of the Church, the bishop is a crucial figure for building the Church and passing on the treasure of faith.

Another highly important source for understanding the early development of the ordination ministry is the *Traditio apostolica*. In fact, this collection of text fragments begins with instructions on the ritual appointment of a bishop. One interesting aspect is that at a bishop's ordination, other bishops must be present. So there is such a thing as a college of bishops, for which the twelve apostles were a symbolic model. A weighty task assigned to bishops was participation in synods and councils.

The bishop shall be ordained according to the word that we said before, having been chosen from the whole multitude and being without sin. When he has been named and he pleases them, all the people shall gather themselves together with the presbyters and the deacons on the Lord's day, all the bishops who have laid their hands on him giving consent. The presbyters also standing and waiting with all of them shall keep silent together and shall pray in their heart that the Holy Spirit come down on him; and as they request one of the bishops, everyone standing, he shall put his hand on the one who will be made bishop and pray over him.[3]

As time progressed, a predominantly hierarchical church model took hold, affecting both the liturgy and theology of ordination. Much attention went to the badges of honor presented to ministers during solemn rites, while the invocation of the Holy Spirit over the candidates and the role of the gathered people were pushed to the margins. In a sense, Vatican II reconnected with the earliest tradition. Symbolic of this is the replacement of the bishop's ordination prayer, with the new prayer directly inspired by the above passage from the *Traditio apostolica*, which was assumed to be grafted onto the liturgical practice of third-century Rome.

# THE LITURGICAL CELEBRATION OF THE SACRAMENT OF ORDINATION: AN OVERVIEW

The first *editio typica* of the liturgical book arranging ordinations after Vatican II dates back as far as 1968, showing that this was truly a priority for the liturgical reformers. The title of the book was *De ordinatione diaconi, presbyteri et episcopi*. In 1990, the *editio typica altera* appeared, entitled *De ordinatione episcopi, presbyterorum et diaconorum*. Two things stand out: the order has changed and priests and deacons are in the plural. The change in title moreover reflects an advancing theological understanding, namely that the fullness of ministry is the bishop, in which the priests share and in which the deacons participate.

Yet another theme is relevant in this context. Indeed, on the feast of the Assumption of Mary in 1972, the then Pope Paul VI issued two motu proprios, *Ad pascendum* regarding the diaconate and *Ministeria quaedam* regarding

---

3  Paul F. Bradshaw, Maxwell E. Johnson, and L. Edward Philips, *The Apostolic Tradition: A Commentary*, Hermeneia (Minneapolis: Fortress Press 2002), p. 24. The quote is taken from the Sahidic version of the text, which for this section of the *Traditio apostolica* is the most extensive.

the so-called lower ordinations. These documents had a very concrete impact on the liturgy. The pope was forced to implement provisions of Vatican II in a more concrete way, such as the reintroduction of the permanent diaconate and (thus) the existence of married deacons. On the other hand, he abolished the subdiaconate and tonsure. Entry into the clerical state henceforth coincided with the diaconate itself, but a rite for the acceptance of candidates as deacons and priests was established. At the same time, the pope retained three 'ministries' (expressly not ordinations), which could be entrusted to the laity (specifically, men), 'according to a venerable tradition of the Church': lector, acolyte and extraordinary minister of communion.[4]

The 1972 liturgical book for the Institution of Ministers and the Blessing of Persons incorporates the provisions of both motu proprios of Paul VI. It consists of three parts: (1) the admission of candidates to the diaconate and priesthood, (2) ordination to deacon, priest and bishop, and (3) appointment to various ecclesiastical ministries. The ordination celebrations in each case distinguish between the ordination of one or more candidates. For the situation of married deacons, the new Latin Ordo provides separate elements.

As the table below shows, the celebrations of ordinations to the ministry of bishop, priest, and deacon have a similar structure. Very importantly, these celebrations must be held on a Sunday or feast day during a Eucharist, and it is explicitly stated that a large group of people gather for it. There are surely echoes here of the ecclesiology of the 'people of God' of Vatican II as well as of the Liturgical Movement's call for 'active participation'.

| Bishop | Priest | Deacon |
|---|---|---|
| Introductory rites and Liturgy of the Word | Introductory rites and Liturgy of the Word | Introductory rites and Liturgy of the Word |
| Presentation of the candidate<br>• Question of a mandate from the Holy See<br>• Reading the apostolic letter<br>• Consent (people) | Presentation of the candidates<br>• Question of worthiness<br>• Election (bishop) and consent (people) | Presentation of the candidates<br>• Question of worthiness<br>• Election (bishop) and consent (people) |

4   Recently, under Pope Francis slight but significant changes have been made with respect to expanding some of these ministries to women. For a discussion of this whole dossier, see Alphonse Borras, 'Festina lente. De l'empressement du pape François pour les ministres institués', *La Maison Dieu* 313 (2023), pp. 119-154.

| Address/homily | Address/homily | Address/homily |
|---|---|---|
| Examination | Examination | Examination |
|  | Promise of Obedience | Promise of Obedience |
| Litany of the saints | Litany of the saints | Litany of the saints |
| Laying on of hands and prayer of consecration | Laying on of hands and prayer of consecration | Laying on of hands and prayer of consecration |
| Anointing of the head | Anointing of the hands |  |
|  | Investiture<br>• Stole<br>• Chasuble | Investiture<br>• Stole<br>• Dalmatic |
| Explanatory rites<br>• Book of the Gospels | Explanatory rites<br>• Paten and chalice | Explanatory rites<br>• Book of the Gospels |
| Investiture<br>• Ring<br>• Mitre<br>• Pastoral staff |  |  |
| Kiss of peace | Kiss of peace | Kiss of peace |
| Eucharist | Eucharist | Eucharist |
| Solemn blessing |  |  |

It is worthwhile to interpret and comment on some notable liturgical elements of the liturgy of ordinations.

1 In the presentation of ordinands, the bishop sits on his cathedra or episcopal chair and wears his mitre. With priests and deacons, it is a deacon who is responsible for calling each ordainand forward. The latter makes a small head bow (but does not kneel at this point). The question of the 'dignity' of candidate priests and deacons is addressed to a priest, usually the one who was responsible for or at least involved in their training. In the case of a bishop, the presentation of a candidate involves a letter from the Holy See, showing that effectively the candidate in question is chosen for the episcopate. This tradition came about because throughout history abuses had frequently occurred.

2 The address follows immediately after the presentation of the candidates, which in turn follows immediately after the reading of the Gospel. The address thus in a sense replaces the homily, whereas the intercessions are omitted (but can be seen as replaced by the litany). For these speeches,

the liturgical book itself provides written-out examples. The content of these speeches focuses on the role of ministry in the Church and is inspired by Scripture and tradition. In fact, one can think of this speech as a kind of profound catechesis on diaconate, presbyterate and episcopacy.

3  It is possible to see in the interrogation and pledge a parallel to the rite of marriage, although the formulas for ordinations are more elaborate. In the questioning of priests and deacons, fidelity to the bishop is a major focus. The answers to the questions of the bishop at the questioning are simple: 'Yes, I am', and at the promise: 'Yes, I do.' For the 'promise' part, there is no parallel in episcopal ordination.

4  An impressive part of the ordination ceremony is the litany of the saints. All kneel and the about-to-be-ordained prostrate themselves. The symbolism is that there have been great examples of holy and sanctifying lives of service in the history of the Church, and these are invoked to emulate.

5  For the gesture of laying on of hands in the case of deacons and priests, the ordinands kneel before the bishop. He places his hands on each of them individually. Then, standing upright, with the mitre on and hands extended, he pronounces the prayer of ordination over them all. Attending priests form a semicircle around the bishop and carry the alb and stole. Immediately after the prayer of ordination, the now-ordained receive the stole and dalmatic (in the case of a deacon), or chasuble (in the case of a priest).

6  In the case of the laying on of hands at a bishop's ordination, it is not only the presiding bishop but all the bishops present who lay hands on the ordained, ritually underscoring the idea of a college of bishops. It is, however, the presiding bishop who says the prayer of consecration while the candidate kneels and while two deacons hold open a gospel book above his head. Even a bishop can never consider himself above the Word of God.

7  In the case of an ordination of priests or bishops, the ordination prayer is followed by an anointing with chrism of the hands and head, respectively. The accompanying prayers by the presiding bishop express what the sacramental priesthood (*sacerdotium*, in which priest and bishop share) stands for: to be imbued with the Spirit of God through acts of service such that his salvation becomes tangible to his people and all of humankind.

8 As for the explanatory rites including the 'investiture' (the classical *traditio instrumentorum*), the deacon's emphasis is on the proclamation of the word. For during the Eucharist, his task is to read the Gospel. With the priest, the emphasis is on the gifts of bread and wine, which are offered on behalf of the people on the paten and in the chalice and become the body and blood of Christ in the Eucharist. With the bishop, the emphasis is on the insignia that symbolize his administrative functions, but they are a reminder that his primary task is the proclamation (and therefore the observance) of the Gospel. Like a marriage, the ring is a sign of fidelity; the Church is 'God's bride', to be preserved 'from every blemish'. The staff symbolizes shepherdship, and the mitre is placed 'silently' on the head of the newly ordained.

9 The kiss of peace is a rite by which union in ministry is sealed. In practice, sufficient time is often allotted for this.

10 The celebration of a bishop's ordination has a special feature at the end. The new bishop goes around his episcopal church, the cathedral, and for the first time gives his episcopal blessing to all the faithful present. In doing so, he may also address them in a more personal way.

# A COUPLE OF
# THEOLOGICAL THOUGHTS

Ordination to offices in the Church is linked to many aspects of the life of faith. It is important ecclesially, spiritually, practically, legally, ecumenically, and theologically. Consequently, the Church has never taken it lightly and has always seen it as much more than an organizational necessity or a mere convention.

In fact, all ordinations are based on and possible only through the general priesthood of every baptized person. The common priesthood means a participation in the life of Jesus Christ himself and his triple office (*triplex munus* or *tria munera*) of priest, prophet, and king. Christ exercises in his Church the function of high priest, teacher, and guide. He is the supreme *leitourgos*, the ultimate teacher both in content and pedagogy, and the archetype of good government through service (*ministerium*). In Christ, the Word and Son of God, principles and contents, matter and form, inwardness and outwardness coincide. The theology of ordained ministry has always focused on that triad and on the inseparable bond between the three different aspects. Vatican II highlighted this in a special way. This vision, besides having great advantages – including an inspiring potential, a 'traditional innovation' and a strong consistency of content – has perhaps a few drawbacks. For in practice, an organic merging and holding together of the three *munera* is anything but evident.

A particular concern relates to the relationship between the ordained ministries and the Eucharist. Classical theology teaches that all sacraments are in fact directed to the Eucharist, and derive their deepest meaning from that intrinsic bond. This is especially true of the ordained ministries, and of course of the priesthood in particular. In this context, it is interesting to reflect on Vatican II's conviction that the completion of the priesthood is to be sought in the episcopate. Thus, a bishop is not simply a priest with additional (administrative) responsibility, and the Eucharist is not simply a pastoral assignment of the (parish) pastor.

Furthermore, a theological reflection on the meaning of the ordained ministry in and for the Church can give rise to reflection on its unity, holiness, apostolicity, and catholicity.[5] In fact, deacons, priests, and bishops – whatever function they perform – are at the service of the unity of the Church, which Christ called for in his farewell prayer in John 17. This Christological emphasis also deepens the idea of the ministry's service (which is in fact a tautology) to the worldwide mission of all the baptized, to the fidelity of the apostles who were so close to the Lord, and to the universal call to holiness and sanctification of all. Thus, it is not only ecclesiology that offers opportunities to understand ministry, but also vice versa: the ordained ministry helps to understand the essence of the Church.

---

5   Adam A.J. Deville, 'The Sacrament of Orders Dogmatically Understood' in Hans Boersma and Matthew Levering (eds), *The Oxford Handbook of Sacramental Theology* (Oxford: Oxford University Press 2015), pp. 531–544.

## Interlude

# Not-nothingness:
# The Reality of Life and Holy Order
# in the light of *Apostolicae Curae*
# and *Saepius Officio*

### SIMON JONES

There's a sense in which our starting point was the same as that of our fore-bears Cardinal Mercier and Lord Halifax: the statement by Leo XIII in 1896 which has been ringing in our ears since our conversations began: 'We pronounce and declare that ordinations carried out according to the Anglican rite have been, and are, absolutely null and utterly void.'[1]

But there's a more important sense in which that wasn't our starting point, because we know it not to be true. But not only that this unrepresentative group of Roman Catholics and Anglicans knows it not to be true. Through our conversations and encounters with a range of people, we have discovered that there are certain contexts and situations in which the Church behaves as if it's not true as well. There's a disconnect between the official position, as outlined by *Apostolicae Curae*, and the reality of life and holy order as it's lived out and experienced today. The disconnect is not the whole picture, but it's part of it.

And so for this group, rather than picking up the argument where *Apostolicae Curae* and *Saepius Officio* left it, or trying to unpick the gordian knot with which they tied up our two ecclesial bodies at the end of the nineteenth century, perhaps one of the most important aspects of our work has been, and will be in the future, to hold up a mirror to see what the reality of life and holy order for Roman Catholics and Anglicans actually is, not so much in the light of *Apostolicae Curae* and *Saepius Officio*, but as it is being lived out around the world today.

---

1 Leo XIII, Apostolicae Curae, 36

When we met in Rome in 2016, Cardinal Coccopalmerio told us that: 'When someone is ordained a priest in the Anglican Church and becomes a parish priest in a community, we cannot say that nothing has happened, that everything there is "invalid."'

It is not nothing. Similarly, in relation to the Eucharist, Geoffrey Rowell recalled what Emeritus Pope Benedict had said to him: 'we cannot do anything about Leo XIII's words, but there are, however, other ways of looking at things.' 'When an ecclesial community, with its ordained ministry, in obedience to the Lord's command, celebrates the eucharist, the faithful are caught up into the heavenly places, and there feed on Christ.'

Finding 'other ways' of looking at things is perhaps another contribution which this group can make to the wider Church. Moving away from the language of validity, which so often leads us into an ecclesial cul-de-sac, to use another sort of language which reflects the reality of life and holy order, and which builds on the work which ARCIC and others have done on our understanding of *koinonia*.

If ecclesial life between denominations which do not share a relationship of full communion is 'not nothing', then what is it…?

Part IV

# THE FIRST STEP:
# HEALING MEMORIES

# Chapter 12

# History and *Apostolicae curae*: The Limitations of its Historical Starting Point

## THOMAS O'LOUGHLIN

One of the most damaging deficiencies in the training of clergy in the nineteenth century was a lack of historical understanding and openness in the historical sense. (Yves Congar)[1]

There is a basic element in human thinking that treats that which we experience everyday around us, that with which we are most familiar, as not only 'normal' but normative. The familiar, the outcome of the past, takes on for us who have known no different the character of that which should be, indeed must be. The factual is, unconsciously, identified with the ideal. The situation we are in now is the necessary outcome of the past – it is inevitable that things should be as they are. It is, perhaps the most common flaw in our thinking to confuse the way we have always seen things done, with that being the only way things can be done. Even in our society with its unprecedented rapidity of change whatever is familiar now is seen as normative; and if I want to examine any present state of affairs historically, I can move backwards and find each link in 'the' chain of events that brings me to where I am. In every situation where we are asked to consider a radical alternative, implicitly acknowledging our past error and that we should not be wholly content with our present state, the blinding tyranny of the familiar comes into play.

There is another, equally important, aspect of this psychological trait: once a change has occurred – when there is a 'new normal' – we very soon endow this new state of affairs with the same normative value with which we endowed the previous one. The new normal soon convinces us of its inevitability and

---

1  Yves Congar, 'Moving towards a Pilgrim Church' in A. Stacpoole (ed.), *Vatican II: by those who were there* (Chapman: London 1986), pp. 129-52 at 143.

that the whole scene was always this way – and this way *ab origine*.[2] Over the centuries, generations of theologians have invoked 'the Vincentian Canon' as a sure guide, yet few have stopped to ponder that that which is most familiar is that which is recognised as genuine everywhere (*quod ubique*), it has the character in our minds of being there from ages past and normative for the future (*quod semper*) and appears the only course for those who are as familiar with the facts as we are ourselves (*quod ab omnibus*).[3]

This chapter shall argue that reflecting on this trait allows us to appreciate one of the fundamental flaws with *Apostolicae curae* (13 September 1896) [*AC*]: convinced that the factual situation around them in Rome in the 1890s was that which was normative, their investigations were flawed in that it prioritised that chain of events which inevitably led their situation, their norm. Since it is the business of the historian to explore the variety of human experience in the past, that work undermines this human tendency to imagine our normal as normative. In effect, every experienced normal is relativised – and with this is established a freedom to note that the present situation could be other than it is, and, more importantly for theologians, that the future does not have to be an elongation of the past. Historical theology could, therefore, be seen as the discipline of setting out the many real options that exist for the future on the basis that such positions have been at one time or another 'normal' in the past. But before this can happen, we must examine how limited was the historical understanding that underpinned *AC*, and how that has affected subsequent Catholic attitudes and decisions because ever since *AC*'s appearance in 1896 it has been appealed to not only as a 'fact' and as normative, but indeed as a *norma normans*. Its decision has been, and is, used as the basis of an edifice of Roman Catholic teaching affecting numerous Christians in their lives and ministries, yet the normative quality of *AC* is rarely examined.

# HISTORY, OUR PRESENT, AND OUR MEMORY OF *APOSTOLICAE CURAE*

Few documents – particularly those which are legal decisions handed down by the papacy as the supreme legislative authority within the Roman Catholic Church as distinct from teaching documents such as *Rerum novarum* – from the pontificate of Leo XIII continue to be a source of actual discussion among

---

2   The first mention of this tendency in human rationality, that I can locate, is in Georg Jellinek in his *System der subjektiven öffentlichen Rechte* (Freiburg-im-Breisgau: Mohr 1892), pp. 8-28.

3   See the re-examination of the *dictum* in Thomas G. Guarino, *Vincent of Lérins and the Development of Christian Doctrine* (Grand Rapids, MI: Baker 2013).

theologians today, but *AC* is one such document. The document's direct object was an issue outside the boundaries of the Roman Catholic Church, and in that respect – in a very different world today from 1896 with regard to relations with other Churches – it continues to be a source of rancour, on the one hand, and an encouragement, on the other hand, to those who find distasteful the ecumenical endeavours that began officially in the Catholic Church in the 1960s.[4]

I well recall at the time of the visit of Pope Benedict XVI to Britain two reactions to his participation in the liturgy in Westminster Abbey on 17 September 2010. The first occurred a day or two before the visit was to begin when an Anglican theologian expressed disgust at the prospect because it would be 'a fraud unworthy of Christians.' To this theologian the challenge that Archbishop Williams should put to the pope was: 'Am I a brother bishop in a sister church or a confused layman who administers a religious organisation based on Christian principles?' For otherwise, no one was calling a spade a spade. Worse, while the papal actions in the Abbey might give the impression of fraternity and mutual respect between Churches (rather than between 'a Church' and what the Vatican refers to as 'an ecclesial community'), the legacy of *AC*, re-affirmed with complete certainty every time a man in priest's orders in the Anglican communion was ordained 'absolutely' in the Roman Church, was sending the very opposite message. Such 'doublethink' bespoke of the world of lies and was a case of Christian false witness. A couple of days later, and just after the liturgy in the Abbey, I found a message on my phone from a Roman Catholic priest – known to me as one who actively rejected the initiatives of Vatican II across the board – which ran something like this: 'the BBC commentator has just announced that the Pope is wearing Leo XIII's stole. That's a signal: he's telling them they are frauds, they're only firing blanks!'[5]

---

4   On this movement, and the key role played by the *Centro pro unione*, see Thomas F. Stransky, 'The foundation of the Secretariat for Promoting Christian Unity' in Stacpoole, *Vatican II: by those who were there*, pp. 62-87.

5   This commonly heard terminology among Catholics in Britain can be traced to a story (whose authenticity I have been unable to establish) regarding a meeting between the Anglican chaplain aboard a Royal Navy warship and Thomas Gilby OP (the Roman Catholic chaplain, and later famous as the chief editor of the 61-volume bi-lingual edition of Aquinas) during the Second World War. The Anglican wished to reserve the sacrament but did not have tabernacle; Gilby did; and so the Anglican asked if he too could avail of it. Gilby replied that this was not up to him but governed by naval regulations. The perplexed Anglican asked if the navy had any interest in such matters. Gilby cited the regulation that 'live [i.e. ammunition with warheads] and blank ammunition [which is used for practice, makes noise, but does not actually effect what a gun is there for] must not be stored in the same magazine.'
I have heard it so often that I consider it to be the conventional wisdom among many Roman Catholic clergy on *AC*. The theology of the eucharist implicit in this story may deserve study as a means of identifying some of the factors that impede ecumenical progress. To the objection that one cannot examine a possibly apocryphal story theologically, I would point, by analogy, to the value of the study of early Christian apocrypha (e.g., the *Protevangelium Iacobi*) as a means of understanding the developments in early Christianity.

I do not know what the pope wore, whether it has been worn previously, or even if the BBC had so announced it: I recall the anecdote to illustrate the level of latent passion, hurt, and bitterness that are linked to that legal judgement. Given this interest, paying attention to *AC* is an important part of theological discourse today lest the work of the Gospel, that we credibly present to humanity the vision of love and unity that is the Christ's will for the whole community of the baptised, be compromised. Here lies the importance of the work that has led up to the production of *Sorores in spe*, and the explorations that it is, in turn, generating within the Churches.

From that perspective, it is useful for Roman Catholics – and I write as a Catholic – to reflect on what *AC* might tell us about where we are today in relation to 1896 and ask ourselves if we have anything to learn from the shifts in human and ecclesial culture that have taken place in the century and a quarter since its appearance. I am not concerned, directly, with the letter's question – the validity or otherwise of Anglican presbyteral orders, nor with the ecumenical situation today, but rather what *AC* might tell us about ourselves as Catholics and how we might need to own or disown what it tells us. If we can learn from it, this, in turn, may help in ecumenical discussion.

# WHAT IS HISTORY?

All Christian theological statements have an historical dimension in that they invoke a connection to Jesus of Nazareth, the Judaism to which he belonged along with its history, and the documents produced by his early followers. Some Churches, which consciously see themselves as part of a tradition, invoke historical material as accumulated wisdom, evidence of continuity, genuine growth and evolution, and as a guarantee of their authenticity. And a few Churches, who see themselves as living corporate personalities almost transcending history to the extent that they contain within themselves their history, are so embedded in that history that the lines between historical 'fact' and theological 'assertion' become almost indistinguishable. The Roman Catholic Church falls clearly within this third category. The pope is the 'successor of Peter', and Peter and Paul are there in Rome such that its bishops come to that city '*ad limina apostolorum*'; the claim of the papacy is that Peter is the first pope; and the authority of Pope Francis is that he is Peter today in a direct line of succession. It is this 'historical dimension' of Christianity – irrespective of what contemporary historical scholarship might say about these historical claims – that makes the question of how the author of any specific Christian document understood / understands history a basic question for theological understanding.

So how did the late nineteenth century, and in particular Roman Catholic theologians, conceive history? The starting point is to note the positivism that characterised most history writing in the period. The past was a closed set of facts, and to the extent that these could be known, they could be described. One could, potentially, have an encyclopaedia of all known facts. Thus there would be a 'definitive history' of this kingdom, that Church, or that period of warfare. It might not be complete – evidence might be lost, too obscure to understand, or simply not there – but one could make the best of what one had, seek out more, and then write the 'real history'. The endeavour needed would be prodigious, 'drudgery divine' as one writer described their labour,[6] but such 'great historical enterprises' resulted in monuments of scholarship before which we still stand in awe.[7] We have but to name the *Monumenta Germaniae Historica*, the *Patrologia Latina* and *Graeca*, or the great encyclopaedias and collections such as Pauly-Wissova, Hastings, the *Dictionnaire de théologie catholique*, or the *Corpus Inscriptionum Latinarum* to see this desire to collect, document, and arrange all the remains of the past – a belief at its apogee in the 1890s – to see a vision of history as approaching a complete knowledge of the past. This spirit was captured in the Preface to the first volume of *The Cambridge Modern History*, published in 1902, in this expression of confidence:

> Ultimate history cannot be obtained in this generation; but, so far as documentary evidence is at command, conventional history can be discarded, and the point can be shown that has been reached on the road from one to the other.[8]

Such a certainly about the past surprises us – the past is a foreign country[9] – and it might alert us to how foreign is the intellectual world of *AC* with its certainty that it had 'ultimate' control of the facts relating to events in the sixteenth century.

---

6  See Jonathan Z. Smith, *Drudgery Divine: On the Comparison of Early Christianities and the Religions of Late Antiquity* (Chicago, IL: Chicago University Press 1990).

7  See David Knowles, *Great Historical Enterprises; and Problems in Monastic History* (London: Nelson 1963).

8  A.W. Ward, G.W. Prothero, and S. Leathes, *The Cambridge Modern History: I: the Renaissance* (Cambridge: Cambridge University Press 1902), p. vi.

9  The image is taken from opening of L.P. Hartley's novel *The go-between* (London: Hamish Hamilton 1953); and has become more widely known among historians since D. Lowenthal's *The past is a foreign country* (Cambridge: Cambridge University Press 1985).

However, while the authors of *AC* could not be immune from a sense of history, they saw themselves as theologians rather than historians, and so we might ask how their theological perception may have influenced their historical work in *AC*? Until well into the twentieth century Catholic 'dogmatic theology' – the clue is in the name – was a deductive endeavour. Everything that was needed for a knowledge of salvation was known: we had the revelation of God in its fulness, even if we did not fully understand it. This notion of complete possession of all we needed to know was not confined to Catholicism. Among Protestants it tended to take the form of the notion of the sufficiency of Scripture: if it was religiously significant, it is already there in the Bible, and ever better scholarship would unearth it. Among Catholics it was the confidence that in the *Depositum fidei* was a completeness of revelation, a process which ended 'with the death of the last apostle' (itself a positive historical fact), from which could be deduced by those authorised (in the light of the [first] Vatican Council this was, *de facto*, the pope) all that was needed. Indeed, in Vatican I's definition of infallibility – a logical quality of arguments – there was an assertion, *de facto*, that theology was a wholly deductive endeavour: it was the processes of deduction that were spared the dangers of false inference (i.e., fallacy), and so error, by this unique Petrine gift. When this deductive vision of theology encountered the notion of complete history, the result was an illusion of a one-to-one correspondence between statements of faith and specific events in time; and whenever this correspondence, in either direction, broke down the result was falsehood, heresy, corruption, and sin.

Likewise, there could be no real change in theology due to shifting historical circumstances, but merely variations in the levels of understanding. So to ask if the event at Emmaus (Luke 24:13-35) was 'the first Mass' (i.e., the first after the inception of the Mass at the Last Supper) or the 'the second Mass' (i.e., counting the instituting Mass – the Last Supper – as a Mass) was neither an anachronism nor some rhetorical device to promote piety, but an historical question underpinned by a theological certainty. More importantly, it meant that in all such enquiries there was little role for open-ended empirical historical research producing what was understood as the historical picture of a time, a movement, or a situation. Moreover, were someone to have pointed out that 'history' did not provide simple consistent continuities in either practices or the beliefs about practices, it would have been dismissed as simply the 'relativist' tendency inherent in such movements as 'the Higher Criticism'.

Should any new historical discovery be made it was presumed that it either fitted with what was already known or could be dismissed as irrelevant and the product of heretics. We can actually see this process at work in the lifetime of

Leo XIII. *AC* appeared just as the earliest of the great discoveries were shaking the whole edifice of 'early church history'. The first, and for Catholicism the most significant, shock was the publication of the *Didache* in 1886 with information that could up-turn their view of the origins of the sacraments;[10] and then the discovery in that same year by Urbain Bouriant of the *Gospel of Peter*[11] which he published in 1892.[12] If the first document might challenge the basis of sacerdotalism within Catholicism, the latter presented a very different memory of Peter to that of 'the first bishop of Rome'.[13]

The reception of these two documents then, and for several decades afterwards, is an index to the relationship of history and theology that forms the world of *AC*.[14] If those newly unearthed documents were genuine and orthodox, so the argument went, they would be in complete agreement with what was already known - and be superfluous as they would not add anything to our knowledge. If they did present something unknown, then that would be at odds with the *Depositum fidei* and, consequently, must be a work of human invention - and so they must be the products of heretics. Not surprisingly, both documents were found to be the works of heretical or deviant sects (though there was no agreement as to which sect of heretics or when that sect existed) which had perished.[15] While heresy had a history that could be investigated and discovered; true theology, in the strict sense, had no history.

In such a world, that the settled position of bishops over a period of three hundred years - when they had treated Anglican orders as void and manifested this by ordaining men such as John Henry Newman as if he had been ontologically a non-priest until 30 May 1847 - could be upturned was inconceivable.

---

10  See Thomas O'Loughlin, *The Didache: A Window on the earliest Christians* (London: SPCK 2010), pp. 1-5; within months editions / translations had appeared in German, French, and English.

11  See Bart D. Ehrman and Zlatko Plese, *The Apocryphal Gospels: Texts and Translations* (Oxford: Oxford University Press 2011), pp. 371-7.

12  Urbain Bouriant, 'Fragments du texte grec du livre d'Énoch et de quelques écrits attribués à saint Pierre,' *Mémoires de la mission archéologique française au Caire* 9, no. 1 (1892), pp. 91-147 at 137-42; and then a fuller study with facsimiles in M. Adolphe Lods, 'Reproductions en héliogravure de manuscrit d'Énoch et de écrits attribués à saint Pierre,' *Mémoires de la mission archéologique française au Caire* 9 no. 3 (1893) pp. 1-61 and plates I to XXXIV. As with the *Didache*, this was soon followed by translations and studies in German and English.

13  See Frederick Lapham, *Peter: The Myth, the Man and the Writings - A Study of Early Petrine Text and Tradition* (Sheffield: Sheffield Academic Press 2003).

14  See Thomas O'Loughlin, 'Reactions to the *Didache* in Early Twentieth-century Britain: A Dispute over the Relationship of History and Doctrine?' in S.J. Brown, F. Knight, and J. Morgan-Guy (eds), *Religion, Identity and Conflict in Britain: From the Restoration to the Twentieth Century. Essays in Honour of Keith Robbins* (Farnham: Ashgate 2013), pp. 177-94.

15  This notion continued to affect the study of the Didache until well into the twentieth century through the influence of F.E. Vokes, *The Riddle of the Didache: Fact or Fiction, Heresy or Catholicism* (London: SPCK 1938). Details of the various late datings of the *Didache* can be found in O'Loughlin, *The Didache*.

History confirmed inherited positions rather than brought them into question. This position, under the heading of *AC*'s understanding of tradition, was explored some years ago by George Tavard who came to the conclusion that 'Leo XIII was trapped in the theology of tradition with which he was working.'[16] One could say exactly the same with regard to his relationship to history: Leo and virtually all of his collaborators were trapped within the view of history through which they sought to make sense of the past, and one which was inadequate to cope with the complexity of historical evidence.

Their most obvious deficiency was that within their deductive notion of truth, there was virtually no place for empirical enquiry: the principal role for such enquiry within their understanding of historical research concerned what we would call a 'documents search' as conducted by searchers working for lawyers – and this sort of enquiry is noted in *AC*.[17] But historical research as understood within modern western culture is a radically empirical endeavour through which we seek answers to our questions on the assumption that any answer is an approximation from necessarily inadequate sources read across a cultural chasm. In terms of their view of rationality, history is an *inductive* rather than a deductive endeavour. That Catholic theology had to struggle in this move from the certainty of deduction to the different kind of certainty that related to inductive knowledge is a well-known trail that occupied much of the first half of the twentieth century: we have only to look to the work of Bernard Lonergan to see how he had to ground empirical endeavours within his overall epistemology[18] to observe just how different our world is in relation to that of Leo XIII. But we need to remind ourselves that in other areas of theology we have now left that deductive world firmly behind and embraced modern historical methods.

The first explicit case of empirical historical research offering an alternative, albeit *sotto voce*, to the inheritance was the reformed rites of Holy Week in 1955.[19] Here a central ritual was refashioned as a deliberate result of taking seriously how historians within the Liturgical Movement, building on a century of research, evaluated the inherited liturgy and then changed it. While the fact of the extent of the change, both in the 1950s and again in the aftermath of the Second Vatican Council, might have been played down and elements of

---

16  George H. Tavard, '*Apostolicae Curae* and the Snares of Tradition,' *Anglican Theological Review* 78 no. 1 (1996), pp. 30-47 at 47 (and see, especially, pp. 37-8).

17  *AC*, 5.

18  Bernard Lonergan, *Insight: A Study of Human Understanding* (London: Longmans 1957), pp. 33-102.

19  See R. Kevin Seasoltz, *The New Liturgy: A Documentation, 1903 to 1965* (New York, NY: Herder 1966), pp. 209-18.

continuity emphasised – or at least asserted – the reality of empirical investigation was undeniable. The clearest evidence of this is the now very obvious role that history plays in most academic studies of the liturgy. There has been a similar, if more dramatic, acceptance of history within biblical studies. Having spent most of its first five decades rejecting the central role the 'historical-critical method' played within modern biblical studies, the Pontifical Biblical Commission did a complete *volte face* in 1964 in its 'Instruction on the Historical Truth of the Gospels.'[20] In the same year, Pope Paul VI's great encyclical, *Ecclesiam suam*, appeared.[21] What few notice is that it expects that theological progress will take place with the assistance of empirical historical investigation led by open-ended questions.[22]

While it would be facile to imagine that the older deductive approach has disappeared or that a genuine contemporary view of history is to be found in every document produced by the Holy See or popes writing in their private capacity as theologians, it can safely be said that there is now a complete historical rupture, and in this case this entails an even more significant theological rupture, between statements of the *magisterium* today and that of the time of Leo XIII. When Karl Popper introduced his criterion of falsification – thus rendering our statements inherently open to improvement or rejection through the acquisition of new evidence,[23] he was giving epistemological form to the core notion that inspires historians: tomorrow we might have to revise this statement because we have new evidence, evidence better understood, a better understanding of what we are doing, or because we have different questions we need to pose of the past.

The famous sonorous conclusion of *AC* would seem to be as clear a statement regarding a matter of history as one can get – and has been so read by many Catholics:

> We degree that the present Letter and all of its contents cannot at any time be attacked or impugned ... it shall be now and for ever in the future valid and in force ... and we declare null and void any attempt to the

---

20 Its formal title, following Vatican convention, is '*Sancta mater ecclesia*'; however, it is invariably known as 'The 1964 Instruction' and is most conveniently found at: https://www.vatican.va/roman_curia/congregations/cfaith/pcb_documents/rc_con_cfaith_doc_19640421_verita-vangeli_lt.html (accessed 25 April 2022).

21 Found at: https://www.vatican.va/content/paul-vi/en/encyclicals/documents/hf_p-vi_enc_06081964_ecclesiam.html (accessed 25 April 2022).

22 See Thomas O'Loughlin, 'Fifty Years after *Ecclesiam suam* and *Sancta mater ecclesia*: the practice of the historical disciplines within the practice of theology' *New Blackfriars* 99 (2018) pp. 312-31.

23 See Karl R. Popper, *The Logic of Scientific Discovery* (London: Hutchinson 1959), pp. 78-92.

contrary which may be made wittingly or unwittingly ... by any person, by any authority, or under any pretext whatsoever[24]

Here is 'history' – unchanging facts! Moreover, this has that clear quality as rhetoric that makes it appealing: 'no ifs, ands or buts'; 'a piece of plain speaking' that can be said 'to call a spade a spade.' However, rhetoric apart, it assumes that in a finite matter regarding contingent historical events, one can conclude with a level of certainly as to some past event akin to the non-temporally affected certainty found in some branches of mathematics. In 1896 the basis of *AC*'s decision was that it had made a careful historical investigation of the facts. However, as we understand history today – a view of history now formally accepted within Catholicism – we cannot consider those investigations as the work of historians.[25]

So perhaps the first lesson we Catholics might draw from a study of *AC* is that we need to be aware of how our understanding of what we are doing when we investigate the past has changed, fundamentally, since the mid-twentieth century. This implies that we cannot engage with documents such as *AC* as if it were a document produced within our intellectual culture; to do so would be a form of fundamentalism, namely imagining texts from previous cultures can be understood to share our intellectual framework.

# SACRAMENTALITY AND LAW

It is so obvious that *AC* is not a teaching document but a legal decision, that it often goes unsaid – and, consequently, un-noticed. But if we do not see this as yet one more document produced by lawyers within a framework of legal practice, we are apt to endow it with a theological significance it is unable to bear and, in truth, should not bear. Bishops and their legal apparatus were, indeed are, continually involved in deciding issues relating to the sacraments in the blunt 'yes / no' manner needed to operate practically any complex organisation: it is, in a sense, their stock in trade. The government of the Church must continue and this requires decisions which are then simply acted on rather than subjected to yet further rounds of debate and questioning. Is that marriage valid or can it be annulled? Can that nun have permission for X? Has

---

24  *AC*, 40.

25  Incidentally, it is this shift in the methodology of history that makes Francis Clark's monumental study *Eucharistic Sacrifice and the Reformation* (second ed., Oxford: Blackwell 1967) far less valuable than the claims made of it by many who cite it in support of the decision of *AC* as being historical 'definitive'.

that priest faculties for Y? How many Masses are due in relation to a legacy of money to a priest for the celebration of Masses?[26] Many of these decisions are then brought forward to a higher court by way of appeal, and the highest court – indeed supreme legal authority – is the Holy See. We can see *AC*, therefore, as the pope acting as the highest judge in the final court of appeal. The decisions originally taken by Cardinal Pole, confirmed by later judges in that they did not overturn them, now come for a final decision – and this was given on 13 September 1896 and was to be duly promulgated.[27]

We must do justice to this necessity presented to Leo XIII – a man with a long familiarity with dispensing judgements as a civil magistrate in the Papal States prior to becoming pope – and give him credit when he acted in this manner rather than as a theological authority *in persona Petri*. This necessity can be seen in this anecdote. In the late-1970s an elderly Catholic gentlemen died and left a legacy of £1500 to 'the Parish Priest for the time being' of his parish, at 'the normal rate for stipends at the time of my death.' The solicitor looking after the estate contacted the Parish Priest and asked him to 'agree to carry out this request and send him a receipt for the money and specify the number of Masses.' The Parish Priest had qualms about the whole notion of more Masses meaning greater access to greater mercy.[28] He proceeded to write long catechetical letters explaining the theological difficulties in what was proposed. This made the lawyer furious: he was not the least bit interested in theology, but had a job to do: to discharge the will. If the Parish Priest was being uncooperative, he would seek a higher judgement and contacted the bishop. The bishop's reply was short and *decisive*: there would be 300 Masses (£5 per Mass), with himself, his two secretaries, and the twelve canons of the cathedral each saying 20 Masses. The lawyer replied that his wife was able to have a Mass said for £3 and his duty to the estate was to get the best value for the estate: to whom should he appeal? By return of post, the bishop replied that on further consultation with his chancellor, the rate would now be £3 and (avoiding complex remainders) each priest would celebrate 34 Masses. The processing of the will was concluded, the monies dispenses, the Masses said. The day-to-day

---

26 For a valuable example of how the shifts in historical method shape theological appreciation, see John Baldovin, 'Mass Intentions: The Historical Development of a Practice [Mass Intentions – Part One],' *Theological Studies* 81 no. 4 (2020), pp. 879-91; and 'Mass Intentions: Twentieth Century Theology and Pastoral Reform,' *Theological Studies* 82 no. 1 (2021), pp. 8-28.

27 *AC*, 41.

28 On such clashes between approved lawful practice and theological probity in the context of ecumenical discussion, see Thomas O'Loughlin, 'Sacramental Languages and Intercommunion: identifying a source of tension between the Catholic and the Reformed churches,' *Studia Liturgica* 47 (2017) pp. 138-50.

work of the sacramental government of the Church proceeds. We have to approach *AC* from this practical standpoint.

There is a sense of finality in every decision by supreme courts – whether that is in the Vatican, Washington, or, more recently, in London. The debate and disputes are over: life moves on! A contingent matter – and all such matters are historical – has been judged and the judge's word is final. This sense that 'cases' (*causae*) need practical resolution is captured in the dictum: *Roma locuta, causa* – a legal dispute – *finita*. However, we need to appreciate that the finality inherent in a legal system is not the same as the completeness aimed at in an investigation of the past and especially one involving matters of faith and worship where, of its nature, there is an incompleteness of understanding and language. If a court is asked to pronounce on the validity of a marriage, it not only can gather a wide variety of evidence and question that evidence in the time and culture of the judgement – the constant judicial attempt to get a thorough examination to the facts, but its judgement needs finality so that life can move on. If there is deemed to have been no marriage, an annulment can be promulgated (which is done in the name of God), and one or both parties is free to marry within the Catholic Church. Despite the rather grandiose terms invoking the certainty of the divine name – so distasteful to many in view of our memory of the rejection of such invocations of the holy name judicially in the Sermon on the Mount (Matt 5:34-37) – the certainty is a wilful, assertive certainty: 'we deem it to be so', rather than the certainty we might derive from complete knowledge. This willed certainty is necessary in any living courtroom: someone wants to remarry, and a judgement of nullity allows this. Similarly, a bishop wants to know what to do with a man ordained as a priest within the Anglican Church who now wants to serve as a presbyter in the Roman Catholic Church: *AC* gives the bishops a clear decision that he is to be ordained unconditionally.

However, while such precision in legal matters is essential in any society where the rule of law is part of the society – and Leo XIII considered the Catholic Church such a society per excellence[29] – this does not mean the conclusion is correct (in absolute truth) but only that there is an implicit certainty in every judicial action in giving the sentence. In a jury trial, the judge might personally be convinced of an accused's innocence, but must act on the assumption that the jury's verdict of guilty is correct. Even when the witnesses can all be questioned and cross-questioned, and every form of evidence

---

29  This has been explored by Yves Congar in 'Moving towards a Pilgrim Church', pp. 141-2 and fn. 22 (pp. 149-50).

collected, judicial processes err – and we are all too familiar with cases of miscarriages of justice that were only rectified after decades. But law needs its own functional certainty. However, when the evidence is several hundred years old, and we do not have certainty as to whether those who collected the evidence were seeking it for this process or simply seeking a 'quick fix' for a problem, and, moreover, there is a suggestion within the system that the existing judgements should stand, then we cannot see the judgement as having anything other than this wilful value.

But how was such a legal notion of judicial certainty in sentencing allowed to have such prominence in so complex a matter as the validity of someone's ordination? Firstly, we Catholics are so habituated to this understanding the mysteries of faith, the seven sacraments, through the patterns of rubrics and canon law that we forget that the law is secondary to the realities being celebrated, and while these actions have definite legal effects (e.g., the children of a marriage are legitimate) and are regulated by law, they are not creatures of the law. Law follows on sacraments in reality, even if in performance of individual rituals the celebrant is bound to follow the law regarding his/her performance. This limitation of law has been alluded to down the centuries with such dicta as '*sacramenta propter homines*' or '*salus animarum lex suprema.*' Secondly, we Catholics tend to imagine and locate our liturgical events within an overall legal vision. Baptism is a 'pre-requisite' for the other sacraments and makes the baptised person a subject of canon law. There is an obligation to attend Mass on specific days. That man and that woman are free to marry, and so the wedding takes place. Under which conditions can the Sacrament of the Sick be celebrated and by whom and for whom? Has someone faculties to hear confessions? In each case, we hardly distinguish the action from the legal context, and we imagine event/celebration/sacrament as 'there/not there' in the manner of a legal action. This approach, inherent in *AC*, has been problematic for the Catholic Church for centuries, but has come to the fore since the reform of the liturgy and the awareness that there is a vast gulf between a valid minimal performance by someone who, in the older language, intends 'to administer the sacraments' and someone who celebrates the liturgy as part of the pilgrim people's journey. This famous statement from the United States' bishops: 'Good celebrations foster and nourish faith. Poor celebrations weaken and destroy it.'[30] To someone working within the legal vision, this is mean-

---

30 Bishops' Committee on the Liturgy, *Music in Catholic Worship* (Washington, DC 1972), p. 6. This statement had a complex evolution in three other documents: *The Place of Music in Eucharistic Celebration* (1968); *Music in Catholic Worship* (revised ed., 1983), and *Sing to the Lord* (2007). See the commentary in Edward Foley, *A Lyrical Vision: The Music Documents of the US Bishops* (Collegeville, MN: Liturgical Press 2009), pp. 22, 32-3, 43 and 61.

ingless – indeed some see it as proximate to heresy as skirting close to a position of *ex opere operantis* with regards to one or more of the seven sacraments. However, to anyone involved in the actual liturgy in a worshipping assembly of the People of God it is no more than stating the obvious. These two perspectives constantly clash – and they can bedevil ecumenical discussions – and we Catholics need to attend to this problem within our liturgical perception.[31] Observing this difference between the necessary certainty of a legal system can help us understand some of the more blunt assertions regarding *AC*. Here is an example: in 2015 Cardinal Robert Sarah, former Prefect of the Sacred Congregation for Worship and the Discipline of the Sacraments wrote:

> In the Anglican church is it not actually the Eucharist because there is no priesthood. ... a Catholic cannot receive communion in the Anglican church, because there is no Communion; there is only bread. The bread is not consecrated, because the priest is not a priest.[32]

Here a statement, that was formulated within a legal notion of certain, is read in an absolute manner such that the actual reality of an act of worship, *coram Deo*, by which a community of the baptised seeks to offer thanks to the Father in the manner of the Christ is declared a non-event. But this reduced an actual celebration of the mystery of our participation in the divine life to the parameters of the administration of a ritual with a legal structure: it is a simple confusion to make, but it does not do justice to the complexity of our theology; and, more importantly, it traduces our recognition of the vitality of worship, a gift of the Spirit, when 'two or three are gathered in [Jesus's] name' (Matt 18:20).

Whenever we Catholics are tempted to imagine that the mysteries can be described in such an 'open / closed case' manner, or even more unworthily described in terms of 'reality / sham' or by analogy with live / blank ammunition in a warship's magazine, we might recall that the actual reality of worship, from whatever source, can only be known eschatologically in the very depths of the divine by 'the Father who sees [what is done] in secret' (Matt 6:5-8). This distinction between legal and the 'fuller' reality of our thanksgiving sacrifice is eloquently recognised in the 1993 letter from Cardinal Joseph Ratzinger:

> I count among the most important results of the ecumenical dialogues the

---

31 See O'Loughlin, 'Sacramental Languages and Intercommunion', especially pp. 148-50.

32 This can be found at: https://www.praytellblog.com/index.php/2015/12/01/more-on-ecumenism-valid-sacraments-and-cardinal-sarah/ (accessed 24 April 2022). I am grateful to Prof. John Baldovin SJ for drawing my attention to this statement.

insight that the issue of the Eucharist cannot be narrowed to the problem of 'validity.' Even a theology oriented to the concept of succession, such as that which holds in the Catholic and in the Orthodox church, need not in any way deny the salvation-granting presence of the Lord.

If the actions of Lutheran pastors can be described by Catholics as 'sacred actions' that 'can truly engender a life of grace,' if communities served by such ministers give 'access to that communion in which is salvation,' and if at a eucharist at which a Lutheran pastor presides is to be found 'the salvation-granting presence of the Lord,' then Lutheran churches cannot be said simply to lack the ministry given to the church by Christ and the Spirit. In acknowledging the imperfect *koinonia* between our communities and the access to grace through the ministries of these communities, we also acknowledge a real although imperfect *koinonia* between our ministries.[33]

Reality – we might say with thankfulness – is richer than the world of law.

A second lesson we Catholics might draw from our attention to *AC* is that Catholic theological discourse, broadly defined, occurs in a very complex space of discussion and dialogue. It does not use a single 'language' but many at the same time. Legal language has a special place with its own grammar – it is always '*hodie*' to the lawyer – and has a very specific set of problems to answer. Historical language is limited just to this day, but it seeks as best it can to speak of a day that is now long past. While the language of the liturgy must be open in a radical way and we must always reckon with the reality of mystery – even the terminology is inherently contradictory – and has an ontological lack of closure because 'The wind blows where it chooses, and you hear the sound of it, but you do not know where it comes from or where it goes. So it is with everyone who is born of the Spirit' (John 3:8).

# CREEPING INFALLIBILITY

It is often said that one of the accidents of the First Vatican Council was that there was a creeping infallibility such that every statement of the papacy is given a worth as if the Petrine office were akin to an oracle giving access in its

---

33 'Briefwechsel von Landesbischof Johannes Hanselmann und Joseph Kardinal Ratzinger über das *Communio*-Schreiben der Römischen Glaubenskongregation,' *Una Sancta* 48 (1993), pp. 347-51 at 348. Once again I am indebted to Prof. Baldovin for drawing my attention to this passage and for the translation given here.

every word to the truth. This also happens when we take statements – and all language-acts are finite, incomplete and at best we can hope for their having some *adequatio rei intellectus* – of a moment and imagine that these utterances have an absolute value. This matter is further complicated in the case of *AC* by this statement from Cardinal Ratzinger:

> With regard to those truths connected to revelation by historical necessity and which are to be held definitively, but are not able to be declared as divinely revealed, the following examples can be given: the legitimacy of the election of the Supreme Pontiff or of the celebration of an ecumenical council, the canonizations of saints (*dogmatic facts*), the declaration of Pope Leo XIII in the Apostolic Letter *Apostolicae Curae* on the invalidity of Anglican ordinations.

The context of this statement – so frequently quoted by those who are critical of ecumenical endeavours that *AC* is to be treated as an infallible statement – is rather complex. It is stated in a commentary by the Prefect upon a paragraph in a formal profession of faith which reads:

> With firm faith, I also believe everything contained in the word of God, whether written or handed down in Tradition, which the Church, either by a solemn judgment or by the ordinary and universal Magisterium, sets forth to be believed as divinely revealed.[34]

So we have a commentary, with a certain authority, upon a statement, with a certain authority, which forms part of a larger statement which is to be treated as authoritative, but is itself part of the discipline imposed upon certain members of the Church in accordance with law. Since un-picking the exact status of this comment would require a very specialist knowledge of canon law, it seems simpler to treat the whole edifice as if it were an infallible statement – which is then assumed to be equivalent to accepting or not-accepting the Church, and to being inside/outside the Church, and indeed to have the clarity of truth/falsehood. Certainly, there are many who find Catholicism repulsive who would find such a reading – here are their worst suspicions confirmed; while there are many within the Catholic Church who likewise welcome such

---

34 The commentary was issued on 29 June 1998 and the Profession of Faith was promulgated *motu proprio* by Pope John Paul II on 11 May 1998. Both documents are to be found together on the Vatican's website at https://www.vatican.va/roman_curia/congregations/cfaith/documents/rc_con_cfaith_doc_1998_professio-fidei_en.html .

arguments as putting 'clear water' between Catholics and 'others'. Religious belonging, indeed faith itself, can easily be construed in such binary terms and become the weaponized stuff of culture wars. Such 'doctrinal clarity' attracts a certain sector of the Church today just it did many in the Church in the 1890s who called for similarly clear water between the re-emerging Roman Catholic Church in Britain and the Church of England. However, it also attracts readers, and advertising, to magazines and websites, and this distorts our dialogue within the Church. While the megaphone and the tweet are the tools of a certain type of adversarial politics, they cannot be the methods of community who are bound in love as sisters and brothers (cf. Col 3:14). If we abandon that perspective, then we are no longer Christian searchers after truth, but simply religious protagonists whose behaviour contradicts the faith we claim to hold and defend.

There is also another strain of creeping infallibility less pugnacious in form, but equally liable to lead us towards a confusion and false certainty. The argument runs that 'to be on the safe side' ('*ad cautelam*') we give the benefit of any doubt to the notion that here is true teaching which is to be held to be irreformable. Now this form of rationality is not inherently false: such 'fail safe' procedures are common in our everyday life. Electricians assume all wires are live, and so protect themselves, until the opposite has been positively established; likewise, those who work in biohazard areas in hospitals adopt the worst case scenario as their starting point – and this is the correct procedure in both cases. However, when it comes to matters of faith we cannot proceed in a similar manner for to do so would involve assuming that, since we can never be wholly certain what is not the case, that every statement ever made has an absolute quality. This procedure we find risible when it is applied to every proposition in the Bible; and it is equally risible when applied to every sentence in Denzinger. There is an incompleteness in language, in historical research, and in all matters of faith – because it is faith. The incompleteness of language and history is a function of the effluxion of time and the partiality of human knowing. But as Christians we need to acknowledge a corresponding theological principle: the whole will only be and be known at the Eschaton when 'God will be all in all' (1 Cor 15:28).

So the continued debate over *AC* may have a third lesson for us as Catholics engaged in theology. We have inherited many structures within our theological cultures – our ecology of religious discourse – that gives us a propensity to collapse our probings into the mystery of faith into a string of propositions whose characteristic quality is their conformity with existing strings of propositions. Rarely is this more limiting that when we examine our liturgical mysteries where these overlap with the intentions of individual worshippers. Then instead of reverent silence presuming the good will of a fellow Christian, we tend to fall back on a mechanical view of language and religious truth: that which our system produces, that is to be taken as the truth. This spancels us in our own pursuit of theological awareness, as much as it limits us in dialogue with other Christians. Indeed, it can lull us into a fundamentalism that is destructive of the endeavour of faith seeking understanding. Likewise, it is a healthy discipline to take that basic lesson learned in biblical studies that every document is to be understood in terms of its genre, context, and (to the extent it can be known) its *Sitz-im-Leben* rather than seen under some all-embracing category such as 'canonical', 'inerrant', or 'inspired', and apply it the documents from the Vatican lest we imagine the magisterium as wholly-encompassing in its relationship with truth.

# HISTORY AND ESCHATOLOGY

For most of the last two millennia we have sought out 'history' as that which grounds our theological enterprise showing it to be well founded, with secure warrants, and in continuity with its origins. Eschatology by contrast was simply the future outcome of this present state of affairs. However, the past century has seen a revolution in the place of history in our understanding of Christianity. One of the most significant developments in historical theology in recent decades has been the turn to plurality. For centuries it had been an axiom of scholarship that we could, and should, keep searching until we had identified a single, consistent original. This original state – be it a text, a practice, or a belief – would have normative status and from it we could trace changes, additions, subtractions, and deviations. Whether these mutations were viewed positively ('developments') or negatively ('corruptions'), they might all be traced back, by a process similar to working backwards along a genetic tree, to a moment in the life of Jesus, to an 'apostolic practice', to the author's pen of a canonical text, or to a moment when doctrine was not yet subject to disputes arising from mistaken interpretations.[35] But Walter Bauer's work presented consistent and explicit doctrines as subsequent to a range of teaching,[36] David Parker – and others – presented New Testament texts as

---

35  See Thomas O'Loughlin, 'Divisions in Christianity: The Contribution of "Appeals to Antiquity"' in S. Oliver, et al., (eds), *Faithful Reading: New Essays in Theology and Philosophy in Honour of Fergus Kerr OP* (London: T&T Clark 2012), pp. 221-41.

36  Walter Bauer, Rechtgläubigkeit und Ketzerei im ältesten Christentum (Tübingen: Mohr 1934) [English version of second edition: Orthodoxy and Heresy in Earliest Christianity (Philadelphia, PA: Fortress 1971)].

living responses to situations such that seeking 'the original Greek text' came to be seen as a scholarly idol,[37] and Paul Bradshaw presented early liturgies as initially diverse with a standard 'shape' only gradually emerging rather than the reverse.[38] History now shows just how inherently problematic is any theological statement that is framed, as is that in *AC*, on past experience. History generates for us questions, not answers.[39]

However, it is eschatology that gives theology as a guide to Christian life its focus. Eschatology now plays the role once assigned to history as our theological compass and guarantee: the eschaton is wholly future (not simply some ideal state that might occur in the course of time[40]), but it also wholly determines the present. It is at the eschatological moment that the pilgrim journey of the Church Catholic will be complete. Only then will its *koinonia* be complete: the *koinonia* of all the baptised. It is at the banquet in the kingdom that eucharistic action will finally achieve its perfection when, through grace and not as an outcome of our processes be they valid or invalid,[41] 'people who come from east and west and north and south and recline at the table in the kingdom of God'.[42] It is only in that moment when the sacramental dispensation will cease that it will have reached a perfection unaffected by human limits and sin. In such a scenario, *AC* ceases to be a piece of our present reality; it become a period piece that we can use as a foil to remind us of those weaknesses in our own past that need to be overcome. Perhaps reading *AC* should tell us to replace the role 'history' once played in the arguments we have with one another with a vision representing our hope and eschatology; we can then let the messiness of our past, revealed through historical research remind us of how far all of us, all Churches, have to travel as the pilgrim People of God.

---

37  David C. Parker, *The Living Text of the Gospels* (Cambridge: Cambridge University Press 1997).

38  Paul F. Bradshaw, *The Search for the Origins of Christian Worship: Sources and Methods for the Study of the Early Liturgy* (second ed., London: SPCK 2002).

39  I have explored this in more detail in 'Time-Sensitivity as a Possible Way through Ecclesial Deadlock with Regard to the Eucharist,' *Review of Ecumenical Studies* 14 no. 1 (2022), pp. 1-11.

40  It is this false view of the eschaton as some ideal future moment in the life of the Churches as we experience them that confuses many ecumenical discussions in that they imagine there will be a time of perfect ecclesial harmony (akin to what they falsely image was once the case); see Thomas O'Loughlin, *Eating Together, Becoming One: Taking Up Pope Francis's Call to Theologians* (Collegeville, MN: Liturgical Press 2019), pp. 125-40.

41  Rudolf Bultmann made the crucial point with regard to Luke 13:28-9 that a place at the eschatological table is not the outcome of ecclesial practice, but 'rather a miraculous eschatological event'; see *Jesus and the Word* (London: Collins 1958), pp. 40-2.

42  Luke 13:29, adapted from NRSV.

# Chapter 13
# Exploring *Sorores in Spe*:
# A Hermeneutic of Hope

## JAMES HAWKEY & JORIS GELDHOF

## SITUATING *SORORES IN SPE*

Much has been written on Leo XIII's Bull *Apostolicae Curae*, and the responses to it. The responses began with a lengthy letter from the Archbishops of Canterbury and York entitled *Saepius Officio*, in which the Archbishops painstakingly responded in detail to the negative judgement on the question of Anglican Orders, whilst also introducing their own critique of the document's theological method. 'In overthrowing our Orders' the Archbishops wrote, 'he [the Pope] overthrows all his own, and pronounces sentence on his own Church.'[1]

Since then, most scholarly engagement with this text and its judgement has focussed on addressing historical inaccuracies and inadequacies, questions relating to form and intention, and since *Unitatis Redintegratio* and the emerging ARCIC process,[2] that thoroughly changed context in which Catholics and Anglicans have rediscovered an intimate family likeness, and developed a rapprochement of theology and practice.

The document,[3] *Sorores in Spe* does not directly address questions of historicity or historical context, which have been explored in much detail elsewhere, for example, in the Anglican Benedictine Dom Gregory Dix's *The Question of Anglican Orders* and more recently in Bill Franklin's centenary volume of

---

1   *Saepius Officio*, XX. *Saepius Officio The reply of the Archbishops of Canterbury and York to the Letter Apostolicae Curae of Pope Leo XIII*, (London: Church Literature Association 1977), p. 39

2   See https://www.anglicancommunion.org/resources/document-library.aspx?subject=Ecumenism&tag=ARCIC for the full library of ARCIC texts

3   See Chapter 14 of this volume. References to the text will be made through the numbers of individual paragraphs.

essays published in 1996.[4] However, the Malines Conversations Group's work on this subject certainly has engaged with these issues, not least during its 2015 meeting in Boston, with papers on the sacramentality of the Church, the role of memory and tradition, the Catholic faith and apostolic succession, and indeed the reception and heritage of *Apostolicae Curae*. One of the papers on that occasion argued that the Anglican ordinal, judged as defective by Pope Leo in terms of 'form', should be seen as but one voice amongst many within a broader humanist conversation about rites and orders prior to and during the Reformation and Counter Reformation periods. No less an authority than St John Fisher believed that the imposition of hands alone, and not the porrection of the instruments, was the essential form of the sacrament of order.[5] A deeper study of the history may well still help us wrestle with this topic.

However, *Sorores in Spe* springs from the entirely 'new context' in which Catholics and Anglicans now find themselves, to quote the *Final Report* of ARCIC I, formally endorsed by Cardinal Willebrands in 1985.[6] The Malines Conversations Group has been working since 2013 on the relationship between the reality of life and the truth of faith. Why is it that what we have come to say about one another theologically is so frequently not represented in practice? *Sorores in Spe* represents a kind of harvesting of the extraordinary levels of agreement represented by the ARCIC process, and the profound insights of the liturgical and ecumenical movements in the twentieth century which our Churches share.

# TITLE AND CONTENT OF *SORORES IN SPE*

The title of the document comes from an inscription on the joint tomb of two English queens in Westminster Abbey. The half-sisters, Mary and Elizabeth Tudor, both daughters of King Henry VIII, lived and reigned during some of the most turbulent years of the sixteenth century. Mary is well known as a deeply pious Catholic monarch, whilst Elizabeth is often described as England's first Anglican queen. Despite the personal, political, and religious animosity which characterised their relationship, they were eventually buried in the same tomb on the instruction of King James VI and I, Elizabeth's suc-

---

4   Bill Franklin, *Anglican Orders: Essays on the Centenary of Apostolicae Curae 1896-1996* (Pennsylvania: Morehouse 1996)

5   See Richard Rex, *The Theology of John Fisher*, (Cambridge: Cambridge University Press 1991), pp. 134-135.

6   See The Final Report of ARCIC I *Ministry and Ordination*, 17, http://www.prounione.urbe.it/dia-int/arcic/doc/e_arcic_ministry.html

cessor as monarch. James had more than a passing interest in the reunion of Christendom,[7] and as if to explain the implicit symbolism in their joint burial, he commissioned an inscription in Latin on the base of the monument which reads,

Partners in throne and grave, here we sleep.
Elizabeth and Mary, sisters in hope of the Resurrection.

The drafters of the document and the members of the Malines Conversations Group decided that an allusion to this could be very helpful. St Paul VI, in his sermon at the canonisation of the Forty English Martyrs in 1970, spoke hopefully of the day when the Catholic Church would be able 'to embrace her ever-beloved sister in the one authentic communion of the family of Christ.'[8] Our two Churches – with their common roots, and a substantially shared life of faith and service – still live in hope of the Resurrection, a genuinely united ministry through, with, and in Christ *caput et corpus*, alongside one another.

*Sorores in spe* explores how this relates to the question of Anglican Orders in four sections. Whilst it is a deeply theological document, it is not written to be appreciated by professional theologians alone. The first section offers a short history of Anglican-Catholic relations from 1896 onwards. Beginning with the process which culminated in *Apostolicae Curae* and *Saepius Officio*, a section on the Malines Conversations (including Dom Lambert Beauduin's famous essay *L'Eglise Anglicane: Unie non Absorbée*), it moves to discuss the achievements of ARCIC and IARCCUM, and finally celebrates an ecclesiology of symbols. Since Pope St Paul VI famously gave his episcopal ring to Archbishop Michael Ramsey in 1966,[9] prior to the first meetings of ARCIC, pectoral crosses, stoles, rings, and most recently a crozier head, have been presented as gifts by Popes to Anglican clergy. Frequently underplayed in formal reflection, this narrative offers a mutually illuminating counterpoint to the formal theological dialogue, which in the words of our document, 'reveals a different, deeper reality about mutual recognition which extends beyond the brusque, negative judgement of ordination rites in 1896.'[10] The section closes with a question which is formational for the rest of the document, 'Can statements

---

7  For a thorough survey of this terrain see W. B. Patterson *James VI and I and the reunion of Christendom*, (Cambridge: Cambridge University Press 2000)

8  https://www.vatican.va/content/paul-vi/it/homilies/1970/documents/hf_p-vi_hom_19701025.html

9  For a fuller description of this now-famous encounter, see Keith F. Pecklers, 'Taking Stock of the Present Situation of our Churches' in this volume, pp. 69-82.

10  *Sorores in spe*, 5.

which were made about one another's life and identity prior to our rediscovery of such a deep and shared sense of identity and mission, still be deployed as if such growth in mutual recognition, both explicit and implicit, had not taken place?'[11]

The second section is a journey into the hermeneutics of tradition and salvation. More about the methodology of this section will be said below, but in many ways this is the 'engine room' of the whole document. Harvesting the insights of the ecumenical and liturgical movements, with a substantial series of reflections on the Second Vatican Council, *Sorores in Spe* argues that these developments, faithful to the tradition, provide a hermeneutical key for understanding the depth of the new and shared context in which Anglicans and Catholics now know one another. La *nouvelle théologie* and wider *ressourcement* currents in the early-mid twentieth century themselves provided a new kind of language which finds a ready home in the ARCIC process, and which offered a richer and broader lens through which to consider questions including apostolic succession, the foundational reality of baptism, and the topic of priesthood. Our document argues that the topic of ordination should best be analysed through a soteriological lens, rather than relying on one or other more reductive epistemologies. This, we suggest, is a faithful reading of the challenges and opportunities laid down in the documents of Vatican II.

The third section of *Sorores in Spe* addresses the essentials of Church, Eucharist, and Ministries. Note the order here: there is an implicit suggestion that Church precedes ministry, and that ministry can only be understood within a wider ecclesiological landscape. This section explores the *lex orandi* of both our communions. Catholics and Anglicans have experienced substantial liturgical reform since 1896, and the Anglican rites of ordination (whilst each member Church of the Communion has its own rite) have undergone their own renaissance in the spirit of both the liturgical and ecumenical movements. Indeed, prior to the publication of the *Common Worship Ordinal* in the Church of England, the Chairman of the Liturgical Commission sought the views and advice of Catholic liturgical scholars teaching in Rome. There is now a close correlation between Anglican and Catholic rites, the inner logic of which can be sensed in the consensus expressed in the joint statements of ARCIC on ministry, ordination and eucharist. But perhaps even more importantly, when seen within the context of the preceding section, *Sorores in Spe* pointedly concludes that when there is such a shared pattern of liturgy, eucharist and devotion in ordination rites, 'one must conclude there is such a density of

---

11 *Sorores in spe*, 6.

sacramental grace that a narrow focus on the question as to whether the form and formula of the ordination rite are precisely correct can actually obscure the mystical reality of what is taking place.'[12] This refers, in the words of St Thomas Aquinas, to that which is the enunciated reality *itself*, rather than that which is simply enunciated about it (*actus autem credentis non terminator ad enuntiabile sed ad rem*).[13] Throughout the Malines Conversations Group's discussion of these questions, and throughout this document, there has been an insistence that the lived experience of Christian sacramental life must be one criterion by which we judge contested questions.

Importantly, this section does not ignore the reality of the ordination of women as deacons, priests, and bishops in many parts of the Anglican Communion. Anglicans are painfully aware of the language of 'new obstacle', as articulated by Pope St John Paul in 1994.[14] Anglicans also hope that Catholics appreciate their language of reception, and the theological seriousness with which many Anglican provinces have approached this question. But *Sorores in Spe* articulates how the specific historic and contemporary injustice on orders in general terms needs to be addressed before our Churches engage on the important topic of ministry and gender. To quote the document, 'The fact that women can, in most Anglican provinces, now be ordained, does not in itself mean that the Pope's condemnation of 1896 must be applied to the present situation.'[15] In short, it is clear that we need a robust, honest and theological dialogue about gender in general, and how gender and ordained ministry relate in particular. But the introduction of a subsequent further question does not render the primary question invalid. *Apostolicae Curae* operates on its own ground. And it is that ground that *Sorores in Spe* seeks to question. Our two communions have grown together in a way which makes the judgement of 1896 untenable on theological and historical grounds, but also in the lived reality of ecclesial and sacramental life. From an Anglican perspective, whilst the negative judgement of 1896 was deeply problematic on primary grounds of theology and history, it also failed to appreciate the basic reality of what was (by then) nearly 350 years of sacramental ministry in Anglican England.

The fourth and final section of *Sorores in Spe* introduces two examples of ecumenical progress and the healing of history which would have seemed impossible within the theological worldview of the late nineteenth century. The

---

12 *Sorores in spe*, 19.

13 *ST* II-II q. 1, art, 2, ad. 2; cf. *Sorores in spe*, 21.

14 https://www.vatican.va/content/john-paul-ii/en/apost_letters/1994/documents/hf_jp-ii_apl_19940522_ordinatio-sacerdotalis.html

15 *Sorores in spe*, 20.

*Joint Declaration on the Doctrine of Justification* (JDDJ) between the Catholic Church and the Lutheran World Federation is the first of these, illustrating how new insights and a shared language can overcome earlier doctrinal condemnations. The second is the ecclesial recognition by the Catholic Church of the Assyrian Church of the East, and the subsequent judgement that the anaphora of Addai and Mari (which contains no *ad litteram* institution narrative) should indeed be considered a 'valid' and genuine Eucharistic Prayer. Here, the ability to get beyond particular forms of words and therefore to reconcile what had appeared to be a fundamental liturgical anomaly, reveals an extremely flexible application of Catholic theological categories for the sake of the Church's unity. Put differently, effective sacramental life can be a sign of authentic ecclesiality, rather than the other way round. It is this effective sacramental life – already part-attested to in that language of grace amongst Churches and communities not in full communion with the Holy See celebrated in *Unitatis redintegratio* – which is another basis for the reconsideration of the negative judgement of 1896. The contemporary life of a particular Church is fundamental for assessing that Church's apostolicity. And it may well be that a re-examination of the tautologous language of 'ecclesial communities' would be a very helpful step on the road.

As well as the basic conclusion of this document relating to the condemnation of Anglican ordinations, and what this text believes to be the unsustainable theological position of 1896, *Sorores in Spe* also suggests that 'the implied judgement that the apostolic succession of the Church of England was lost at the Reformation should be re-examined in the light of contemporary ecclesiologial and liturgical understandings of the variety of means by which apostolic succession takes place within authentic traditions of Christian life and worship.'[16] The image of 'walking together', so confidently espoused by Pope Francis and Archbishop Justin Welby, compels us to an honest re-evaluation and celebration of one another's ecclesiality. As long ago as 1980, Pope St John Paul II praised the methodology of ARCIC as one which would scrutinise together 'the great common treasure, to clothe it in a language at once traditional and expressive of the insights of an age which no longer glories in strife, but seeks to come together in listening to the quiet voice of the Spirit.'[17] We are no longer nourished by enmity and controversy but by a common life in Christ. We suggest that the implications for a fresh consideration of Anglican

---

16  *Sorores in spe*, 23.

17  Address of John Paul II to ARCIC I, Castelgandolfo, 4 September 1980, available at:
https://w2.vatican.va/content/john-paul-ii/en/speeches/1980/september/documents/hf_jpii_
spe_19800904_cattolici-anglicani.html

ministry are profound and transformative.

# THE HERMENEUTICAL PRESUMPTIONS OF *SORORES IN SPE*

Thoughts about the hermeneutical principles which led us when we were drafting *Sorores in spe* essentially centre around two main clusters. These clusters have to be seen as complementary and cumulative; they mutually reinforce, undergird, and also nuance each other. It is even possible so see some overlap between both. The first of these clusters is the inspiration and wisdom drawn from the Liturgical Movement, in particular its conviction that it is not only possible, but also very enriching to construe a theology based on the *lex orandi*, or liturgy, of the Church. The second cluster is the enormous and profound legacy of the Second Vatican Council, which is not primarily something *of* the past but something *for* the future. We will subsequently discuss each of these two clusters. They both consist of four dimensions.

Two times four is eight. Eight is a number which in Christian symbolism refers to the idea of renewal through the redemption of creation. The seven days of God's creative activity and sabbath rest are complemented by the eighth day of renewing everything. Eight means the recapitulation of the entire universe – including all future, present and past generations of its inhabitants – to make it pass through the gates opened by the resurrection, and thereby bring it to completion. The ultimate task of ecumenism is to move the pilgrim Church Militant towards those gates to present to God an unblemished offering.

However, before entering too deeply into the realms of eschatological speculation, let us refocus our attention on earthly hermeneutics and human finitude. Notwithstanding this jolt towards normality, it is not without meaning that – in a time which has become addicted to the practical, the available, and the immediate, and which cannot but see opportunism and strategy everywhere – we wrote *Sorores in spe* not only for specific and concrete purposes, but also in view of a bigger picture. The contours of that picture may not yet be fully clear, but neither are they limiting. From within 'the within' we kept an eye on 'the beyond'. We were aware that what we were doing may be both timely and, strangely enough but healthily, *unzeitgemäss*.

## Ample Wisdom from the Liturgical Movement

From the beginning of the Malines Conversations Group's work, liturgy, thickly understood – i.e., not as a mere series of ceremonies guided by rubrics but as a genuine celebration of God's saving acts – has been fundamental to our study.[18] It was not always included as a topic of dialogue, but it shaped our thinking (and praying) together. In other words, liturgy was not the material with which we built our house but rather the very soil on which we built it. Moreover, as is only proper today, we took care to ensure that this would be an environmentally-friendly construction, with generous, hospitable architecture in harmony with the landscape and the climate. We hope that our work will be appreciated not as alienating, let alone polluting, its source. In any case, the twentieth century Liturgical Movement has been for us a major source of inspiration, both theologically and methodologically. Our inspiration came not only from what it achieved, but perhaps even more from the ways in which it operated.

First, the Liturgical Movement developed a distinctive way of theologizing. It substantially contributed to an awareness that theology is so much more than a scholarly commentary on the authoritative formulations of the Church's faith. Theology is not to be reduced to *Dogmatik* and *Dogmengeschichte*, no matter how insightful these concepts are and continue to be. Theology is not the art of proving that Christians are right about God's existence and that the doctrines held by the Church make sense as a consequence of the fact that it has consistently followed in the footsteps of the apostles. By *doing* it itself, i.e., not only by reflecting about it from a distance, the Liturgical Movement showed that the *lex orandi* of the Church, the inexhaustible treasure of its liturgical prayer, is directive of what it thinks and how it thinks. Liturgy is not extrinsic to the faith. It is not the case that there is first the content of faith existing independently, and then a ritual or prayerful expression of it. Liturgy shapes the faith, it is not a mere product, outcome or result of it. Worship is not simply doctrine performed ritually. The Liturgical Movement has (so far) not been able to undo the consequences of the many abounding extrinsicist and expressivist views of the liturgy, treating it always as a graspable and controllable thing, but it has shown a way through many deadlocks. *Sorores in Spe* is situated in the wake of the Liturgical Movement's strong ontological-*and*-theological claims about liturgy.

Secondly, the Liturgical Movement developed a model of *ressourcement* before this notion became associated with an innovative way of doing theology around the middle of the twentieth century.[19] There are reasons to assume that what the leading examples of the *ressourcement* movement in French

---

18 Support for a 'thick' theological understanding of liturgy could be found in the work of, among others, Aidan Kavanagh, David W. Fagerberg, and Gordon Lathrop.

19 Jürgen Mettepenningen, *Nouvelle théologie - New Theology: Inheritor of Modernism, Precursor of Vatican II* (London: T&T Clark 2010).

theological circles accomplished, was somehow anticipated by the Liturgical Movement. Its representatives, too, went back to the sources, full of expectations, openly, inquisitively, and self-confidently. They somehow leaped from contemporary concerns right into the depths and riches of early Christianity and found there an abundance of intriguing insights which were hardly if at all seen through the prism of post-Tridentine Thomisms and Scholasticisms. Scholars and pastors alike associated with the Liturgical Movement barely hid their amazement when they ventured to liberate themselves from conceptual rigidity. They had been trained to swim fixed distances back and forth in a swimming pool, but all of a sudden they discovered a lake. They had been told that swimming pools were the only places where they could swim safely, but instead they discovered that they could perform well in the open air as well.

Thoroughly versed in philology, classical languages, historical criticism, capable of rigorous conceptual analyses, *nouvelle* theologians and key figures of the Liturgical Movement rediscovered solid building stones of the Christian tradition, the richness of which had been dulled. They developed models of thinking and research which subsequent generations did not have to imitate but could use freely and creatively. In this sense, over the last decade, the Malines Conversations Group has learned to consider itself as standing on the shoulders of what *ressourcement* theologians and scholars from the Liturgical Movement accomplished.

Third, as a concrete example of what this implies, one could refer to the Liturgical Movement's unpacking of the profound layers of meaning contained in the concept of 'sacrament'. The Latin word *sacramentum* does not simply evoke seven rituals that throughout the vicissitudes of contingent history have come to play a privileged role in the Catholic faith. *Sacramentum* also renders the Greek concept of *mustèrion*, which is itself connected to idea of God's unfathomable counsels and their communication to humankind. Moreover, *mustèrion* is connected to the idea that such communication is somehow set forth in history.[20] Revelation and incarnation undeniably have a unique and a singular dimension, but not to the extent that they are confined to one identifiable moment alone. They are perpetuated in history, passed on, transmitted, especially in the Eucharist, where gratitude for God's *magnalia* or *mirabilia* is expressed and experienced.

Alongside a deep understanding of sacrament as mystery, and mysteries, and mystery/ies interwoven with history/ies, came a resistance to locating the

---

20 As exemplary illustrations of this scholarly development one could refer to the historical and theological work of Odo Casel as well as to the fine philological investigations of Christine Mohrmann.

core or the essence of a sacrament in one single moment or thing, although this had become customary in sacramental theology, canon law and ecclesial teaching. *Sorores in spe* wholeheartedly embraces a mystery-filled theology of sacraments and sacramentality. In doing that, we intentionally move away from patterns of thinking which try to establish the certainty of faith on the foundations of an absolute control over material or formulaic details. Instead of focusing on one *causa* causing one effect and one *signum* signifying one *res*, we have confidence in a multiple, multivarious, and symbolic approach to the sacraments, what they mean, and bring about.

Fourth, the Liturgical Movement was also famous for insisting upon active participation.[21] Much more important for us than straightforward liturgical activism, is the reality that liturgy is an encompassing action into which people are invited to participate with their bodies and minds, with their will, imagination, passions, intellect, and desires, with their entire existence, as whole persons. Active participation is unthinkable without an integrative and holistic anthropology; the latter should promote the former, and vice versa. Active participation is equally unthinkable without a participatory action. Following from what we have already said, the quality of that action should not be surprising: it is the work of salvation concentrated in the Paschal Mystery, with its universal significance and its unique connection to Jesus Christ. *Sorores in spe* is yet another voice singing the song of active participation. Its sound is profoundly theological, and it tries to avoid the temptations of ideology.

## The Lasting Legacy of the Second Vatican Council

Vatican II was an unparalleled historical event. It was so much more than a gathering of church people discussing contemporary concerns. It was not a business meeting with an agenda geared to preparing future policy. In addition, it cannot be properly assessed and appreciated today according to the stereotypical opposing tendencies of continuity and discontinuity with tradition. Vatican II itself *is* tradition. Catholics believe – and many other Christians appreciate – that it is part of the long chain of ecclesial gatherings through which something of God's will is passed on to humanity. Correspondingly, we have worked with Vatican II as a point of reference not primarily because of its beautiful texts, but because of its being a theological and ecclesiologi-

---

21 Jozef Lamberts (ed.), *The Active Participation Revisited – La participation active 100 ans après Pi X et 40 ans après Vatican II* (Leuven: Peeters 2004).

cal event.[22] Even if this is difficult to appreciate from a purely chronological perspective, Vatican II was for us *a*, maybe *the*, source to which to turn in a true *ressourcement* mode. Itself calling for an aggiornamento through *ressourcement*, it delivered fresh and living water, so eagerly desired by the deer of Psalm 42.

Vatican II emphasized a dynamic, symbolic and dialogical understanding of revelation. Revelation is more about the act of revealing, *revelatio*, than about the promulgation of revealed things, *revelata*.[23] It is God's self-communication in such a way that human beings can grasp it, not fully, but sufficiently, and always provisionally. It is not that one can see everything once the bride's veil is lifted, but it is enough to seal a mystery of love and fidelity. Revelation, moreover, is all about the subtlety of transparency, which helps one remove obstacles caused by obscurity or, worse, obscurantism. Christ's light doesn't allow for hiddenness. Revelation offers light in dark places; it assists, supports, and accompanies when a way out must be found. God's revelation is there not for its own sake but for the liberation of people from different kinds of enslavement. Revelation saves, redeems, emancipates, enlightens, manifests, clarifies, indicates, educates, and shows. This outstandingly verbal instead of substantive understanding of revelation, along with its underlying communicative, dialogical, and dynamic theology, replacing a substantialist or essentialist metaphysics, was a great source of inspiration for us.

Similarly, Vatican II's ecclesiology helped us immensely in articulating a theological language adapted to different layers or spheres of ecclesiality. There was a time in Roman Catholicism when it was almost natural to understand the reality of the Church as constituted solely by a specific class of people who ministered within it. This ordered hierarchy was usually paired with administration and an administrative mentality that permeated the deepest fibres of the Church's fabric. The structure of the Church resembled a factory managed by professionals interested above all in the growth of the company and the maximization of profit at the expense of its competitors. As a condition of this, a strict control over the production process as well as over the employees on the payroll, their education and their profile was considered necessary. There wasn't much room for continuous formation, let alone time for creating a safer work environment and a more pleasant atmosphere on the floor. Diversity, if allowed at all, was mistrusted rather than embraced; pluralism was a threat

---

22 John O'Malley, *What Happened at Vatican II* (Cambridge, MS: Belknap Press of Harvard University Press, 2008); Gerald O'Collins, *The Second Vatican Council: Message and Meaning* (Collegeville: Liturgical Press, 2014).

23 Avery Dulles, *Models of Revelation* (Maryknoll, NY: Orbis Books 1992).

instead of an opportunity. In sum, it seemed as if the economy of salvation had been taken over by single-issue officials. The Church offered services but did not really serve. Or, in the language of the liturgy, it offered services but did not really *celebrate*. There was mass production, but not a genuine Eucharistic enthusiasm. Fortunately, Vatican II helped clear the way so that a veritable enthusiasm for the Eucharist could once again emerge. This created the opportunity for reconsidering important themes including consecration, communion, community, unity, harmony, real presence, and sacramental grace. The primacy Vatican II has for a Eucharistic ecclesiology was an important contribution in shaping our drafting of *Sorores in spe*.

This was the case specifically when thinking about Christ's *munus triplex*. Christ's active being as Prophet, Priest, and King greatly shapes the theological imagination when trying to structure different kinds of ideas. Sharing in Christ's threefold office turned out to be a particularly powerful theme when we tried to think about the relationship between the common priesthood and the ministerial priesthood. The differences between these two do not run in strict parallel with the distinction between laity and clergy. Baptismal priesthood is always already sacramental, royal, and prophetic. Moreover, priesthood is both presbyteral and sacerdotal, and it is not only by being ordained a priest that one shares in the Church's priesthood. Sharing in priesthood and priesthood-as-something-to-share became important focuses for our ideas. Accordingly, we deepened thinking about the diaconate and episcopate as well, about the pastoral nature of all kinds of priesthood, and about the many and divergent ways this reality is lived, explained, and experienced, not only by ordained priests but also by other members of Christ's Body.

Finally, the Second Vatican Council gave rise to one of the most comprehensive liturgical reforms in the history of the Church, many of which have arguably not yet been brought to completion.[24] The Council comprised not only a revision of the books, rubrics, prayers, and texts, but a reconsideration of the whole sacramental infrastructure of the Church. This was neither window-dressing nor the construction of a new building. Both the foundations and the façade were tackled; it was in fact a major remodeling of the entire palace, including the gardens! With respect to the reforms of the rites of ordination, the reordering of this specific room was done twice; the first time in 1968, and again in 1991. The revision of the liturgical books acutely affected the Church's self-understanding. It profiled the role and the meaning of the

---

24 Kevin W. Irwin, *What We Have Done, What We Have Failed to Do: Assessing the Liturgical Reforms of Vatican II* (New York – Mahwah, NJ: Paulist Press 2013).

bishop alongside that of the gathering of the assembly; it was no longer focused on handing over symbols of power but on entrusting chosen people with a special mission.[25] There was introduced an accent on sharing, giving and testifying. All of this and so much more greatly inspired us in the process of writing *Sorores in spe*.

# CONCLUDING THOUGHTS

In this chapter, we have tried to present something of both the content and style of the document *Sorores in Spe*. The document's methodology has been shaped strongly by the theological renewal currents of the twentieth century and seeks to break down any perceived boundaries between theology and practice, liturgy and life. Its reliance on the work of the liturgical and ecumenical movements, and on the ecclesiological and sacramental insights of the Second Vatican Council make it a document for our own time. It is our belief that a reassessment of the negative judgement of 1896 is essential on several grounds, including basic questions of justice and theological integrity, before further work is done on broader questions relating to the ordained ministry, including that relating to gender. It is also our sense that an unlocking of this issue could helpfully lead Anglicans and Catholics towards a richer, more honest, and more robust ministry together in the world, as we learn to harvest the essential implications of the rich theological language we so rightly and frequently have learned to use of one another.

---

25 For a comprehensive commentary, see Susan K. Wood, *Sacramental Orders* (Collegeville: Liturgical Press 2000).

# Chapter 14

# 'Sisters in Hope of the Resurrection': A Fresh Response to the Condemnation of Anglican Orders (1896)

## Abstract

*Sorores in spe resurrectionis* (sisters in hope of the Resurrection) argues that there is an overwhelming body of evidence in favour of revising the negative judgment on Anglican ordinations expressed in Pope Leo XIII's Apostolic Letter *Apostolicae Curae* (1896). The ecclesial and sociocultural contexts *then* and *now* are significantly different. Through the intervening years, there has been a vast development of ecumenical exchange, cooperation and dialogue – including the groundbreaking Malines Conversations (1921-6). Anglicans and Catholics are now committed to 'walking together' on a way of reconciliation, harmony and common witness to the gospel. Important resources for the proposal to revise the judgment on Anglican orders include the insights of the 20th century Liturgical and Ecumenical Movements, the teachings of the Second Vatican Council and telling symbolic gestures from Church leaders. To these should be added reflection on the revised rites of ordination, both Anglican and Catholic. Much theological wisdom can be found in contemporary ordination rites to support a renewed understanding of the ministry of all the baptized, deacons, priests and bishops. A broadened understanding of ecclesiality, mystery, participation and *anamnesis* has encouraged us to look again with fresh eyes at the reality of the Church as the People of God and the Body of Christ beyond the confines of separated ecclesial bodies. Taking into account all of this evidence, both historical and theological, the Malines Conversations Group believes it is time for the negative judgment of *Apostolicae Curae* on Anglican ordinations to be revised so that our two communions can more fully embrace one another as 'sisters in hope of the Resurrection'.

# Plan

1 General introduction: rationale for this document

### I    Historical Section on Anglican-Roman-Catholic Relations

2 Apostolicae Curae and Saepius Officio
3 The Malines Conversations
4 ARCIC and IARCCUM
5 The language of symbols
6 Conclusion of the historical section

### II    The Hermeneutics of Tradition and Salvation

7 The Ecumenical and the Liturgical Movements
8 Mystery and apostolic succession
9 Vatican II: Revelation and history
10 Vatican II: The Church as Body of Christ
11 Vatican II: All the baptized participate in Christ's triplex munus
12 Conclusion of the second section on theological and hermeneutical development

### III    Church, Eucharist and Ministries: Orders and Ordination

13 Catholic rites of ordination
14 Anglican rites of ordination, with particular reference to the Church of England
15 The ministry of the baptized
16 The Diaconate
17 Priesthood
18 Episcopate
19 The celebration of ordinations
20 The Ordination of Women in the Anglican Communion
21 Recognition beyond mere language

### IV    The Hope of Healing

22 A call for reconsideration
23 A call for recontextualization

### V    Conclusion

24 A further step on the path of synodality?

# 'SISTERS IN HOPE OF THE RESURRECTION': A FRESH RESPONSE TO THE CONDEMNATION OF ANGLICAN ORDERS (1896)

## General introduction: rationale for this document

1 *Sorores in spe resurrectionis* (sisters in hope of the Resurrection) is what is written on the shared tomb of Queen Mary Tudor and Queen Elizabeth I in Westminster Abbey, London. Mary and Elizabeth were by birth half-sisters, daughters of Henry VIII of England by different mothers, at enmity for most of their lives. Mary was the monarch of England's short-lived counter-reformation; Elizabeth is often regarded as England's first Anglican Queen. At the canonisation of forty reformation martyrs in 1970, Pope St Paul VI spoke hopefully of the day when the Roman Catholic Church will be able to embrace "her ever beloved sister in the one authentic communion of the family of Christ." Since then, our two communions have grown substantially in unity of faith and service. Much has been achieved. But, there is still much to address.

One major issue yet to be resolved is the negative judgement on Anglican ordinations in Leo XIII's apostolic letter Apostolicae Curae. The Malines Conversations (1921–26) met in the shadow of this document. Instead of pursuing a debate via statements in adversarial posture, the participants preferred a method of dialogue and exchange. It is in this spirit that the Malines Conversations Group offers the following text.[1] This group believes that the painful matters of 1896 need to be addressed before handling further questions of gender and ordination. The theological worldview of the late nineteenth century was thoroughly different from our own. After over a century of liturgical revision and theological dialogue, we now walk together, encouraged to live, pray and work as if we were already one. In the words of Pope Francis and Archbishop Justin Welby's Common Declaration, 'We are impatient for progress that we might be fully united in proclaiming, in word and deed, the saving and

---

1 The Malines Conversations Group is an informal ecumenical study group of Roman Catholics and Anglicans who have been meeting since 2013 to carry forward the discussions begun at Malines in 1921. Just as the participants in the Malines Conversations did, we have sought to keep our respective authorities informed about our discussions and we have met in a spirit of friendship, seeking better to understand what are the impediments to unity today and how we can contribute to deeper reconciliation.

healing gospel of Christ to all people.' Bitter enmity is a thing of the past. Our communions are sisters in hope of the Resurrection.

# I. HISTORICAL SECTION ON ANGLICAN ROMAN-CATHOLIC RELATIONS

## Apostolicae Curae and Saepius Officio

2 In 1896, Pope Leo XIII published the Apostolic Letter, *Apostolicae Curae*, which gave his considered judgment about the necessity for those ordained priest (and therefore those ordained bishop) by Anglican rites to be re-ordained if they were to become Catholic priests. A preparatory Commission, which studied the question, was divided and failed to come to a conclusion. Their views were summarised before being referred to the Holy Office whose members voted unanimously against the recognition of Anglican Orders. The Pope followed this guidance, using teaching affirmed by the Council of Trent to argue that in the Church of England Ordinals of 1550, 1552 and 1662 there was a *defect of form* and a *defect of intention*: (i) a *defect of form* because it was not made clear that the priest received 'the power "of consecrating and of offering the true Body and Blood of the Lord" in that sacrifice which is no "mere commemoration of the sacrifice offered on the Cross";' (ii) a *defect of intention* because 'if the rite be changed, with the manifest intention of introducing another rite not approved by the Church and of rejecting what the Church does, and what, by the institution of Christ, belongs to the nature of the Sacrament, then it is clear that not only is the necessary intention wanting to the Sacrament, but that the intention is adverse to and destructive of the Sacrament.' The Pope concluded, 'We pronounce and declare that ordinations performed according to the Anglican rite have been, and are, absolutely null and utterly void.' Though the precise words were not used, the apostolic succession of Anglican bishops was considered to have been broken at the Reformation.

A year later, *Saepius Officio*, a response signed by the Archbishops of Canterbury and York, was published. Though it speaks of the Catholic Church as 'a sister Church of Christ' (II), it rejects *Apostolicae Curae* as 'a letter [...] aimed at overthrowing our whole position as a Church' and goes on to challenge both its presuppositions and its reasoning. *Saepius Officio* argues that, according to a close reading of the Anglican ordinals and the tradition recognised as apostolic by both the Church of England and the Church of Rome, the judgment of *Apostolicae Curae* was profoundly wrong. It was damaging not only to confidence in Anglican ordinations but, by the same token, to confidence in Catholic and Orthodox ordinations because a number of widely-used early ordination rites could be said to have similar defects of form and intention. It maintains that, 'In overthrowing our orders [Pope Leo] overthrows all his own, and pronounces sentence on his own Church.'

## The Malines Conversations

3   The investigation that preceded *Apostolicae Curae* was prompted by an initiative taken by two friends – Lord Halifax (d. 1934), a prominent, ecumenically-minded high church Anglican layman and Abbé Fernand Portal (d. 1926), a Vincentian Catholic priest committed to the reunion of 'separated Christians'. They believed that Pope Leo XIII, with his apparent broadmindedness, might be open to the recognition of Anglican orders. Despite their profound disappointment after the judgment of 1896, twenty-five years later Halifax and Portal saw in the Lambeth Appeal of 1920 – an initiative by the Anglican bishops directed primarily towards reconciliation with the ministry of nonconformist traditions as well as a concern to bring about closer relations with the Christian East – an opportunity for Anglican-Catholic reconciliation.

The Malines Conversations, hosted by Cardinal Désiré-Joseph Mercier, Archbishop of Malines (d. 1926), consisted of five sessions between 1921 and 1926 in which first six, and then ten, Roman Catholic and Anglican 'friends' addressed what they saw as the most divisive issues between their communions: the exercise of authority by the Bishop of Rome (the relation between the jurisdiction of the Bishop of Rome and the jurisdiction of all the bishops, both individually and collegially); the identification of new dogmas (specifically, the definition of the Immaculate Conception of Mary (1854), and Papal Infallibility (1870)) as 'de fide' (to be held by all the faithful); and the condemnation of Anglican ordinations as 'absolutely null and utterly void.'

At the fourth meeting, Cardinal Mercier surprised the participants by reading out a paper he had commissioned from 'a canonist' entitled *L'Eglise Anglicane Unie non Absorbée*. The paper, later known to be by the Belgian Benedictine Lambert Beauduin (d. 1960), sketched, in effect, a possible 'uniate' status for Anglicans in a reunited Church, which would accord patriarchal dignity to the Archbishop of Canterbury by the symbolic gift of the *pallium* from the Pope and would allow to Anglicans their own corpus of Canon Law, together with their own rites and structures. At a brief, final meeting, shortly after the deaths of Cardinal Mercier and Abbé Portal, complementary reports of the Conversations were drawn up by the remaining Anglican and Catholic participants.

## ARCIC and IARCCUM

4 The Second Vatican Council (1962–5) transformed the ecumenical relations of the Catholic Church. A renewed understanding of the Church in all its dimensions as sacrament (Gk *musterion*), as People of God before it is an institution, and the life of the Church as communion (*koinonia*) in Christ through the creative activity of the Holy Spirit, was set out in the Dogmatic Constitution on the Church (*Lumen Gentium*). It was made clear in the Decree on Ecumenism (*Unitatis Redintegratio*) that ecumenism could no longer be based solely on an invitation to 'return' to communion with Rome ('unionism') such as was made by Leo XIII in his encyclical *Satis Cognitum* (1896), which was published three months before *Apostolicae Curae*, and by Pius XI in his encyclical *Mortalium Animos* (1928). *Unitatis Redintegratio* affirmed the ecclesial reality and the spiritual fruitfulness to be found in the Orthodox, Anglican and Reformation traditions:

> For those who believe in Christ and have been truly baptised are in some kind of communion with the catholic church, even though this communion is imperfect. [...]

> Our separated brothers and sisters also celebrate many sacred actions of the christian religion. These most certainly can truly engender a life of grace in ways that vary according to the condition of each church or community; and must be held capable of giving access to that communion in which is salvation. (3)[2]

In affirming the importance of ecumenical dialogue (11), the Decree on Ecumenism noted that, 'Among those [communions] in which catholic traditions and institutions in part continue to subsist, the Anglican communion occupies a special place.' (13)

Within four months of the close of the Second Vatican Council

---

2 Quotations from the documents of the Second Vatican Council are taken from Norman P. Tanner SJ ed., *Decrees of the Ecumenical Councils*, volume II (London: Sheed and Ward and Washington DC: Georgetown University Press 1990).

Archbishop Michael Ramsey met with Pope Paul VI. In their Common Declaration they committed their respective communions to 'a serious dialogue which, founded on the Gospels and the ancient common traditions, may lead to that unity, for which Christ prayed.'

The Anglican-Roman Catholic International Commission (ARCIC) began its work in 1970. Its agreed statements in three phases on the eucharist, ministry and ordination, authority, justification, the nature of the Church, ethics, the role of Mary, and synodality offer rich theological resources for Christian teaching and reflection. They testify to an intimate family likeness between our traditions which reveals a communion already shared. The process of reception remains ongoing in the lives of both our communions: some elements of the agreements already in place will surely need further work. The International Anglican Roman Catholic Commission on Unity and Mission (IARCCUM), established in 2001, has promoted the practical outworking of ARCIC's rich agreements as Catholic and Anglican bishops pursue their shared mission in their own contexts.

## The language of symbols

5 In the century since the Malines Conversations, the relationship between Catholics and Anglicans has not only developed through dialogue, agreed statements and joint declarations. An essential counterpoint has emerged in the language of symbols, chiefly through the exchange of gifts. Since St Paul VI's gift of his episcopal ring to Archbishop Michael Ramsey in 1966 (which pre-dates the first meetings of ARCIC), Anglican bishops have received pectoral crosses from popes, the Anglican priest and scholar Henry Chadwick was given a stole, and in 2016 in the church of San Gregorio al Celio Archbishop Welby was presented with a replica of the head of the crozier of Pope St Gregory the Great, which he used the next day at Vespers. The context of this presentation was the commissioning by the Pope and Archbishop of nineteen pairs of Anglican and Catholic bishops from all over the world for joint mission and pastoral work.

Visits of Archbishops to Popes, the attendance of Anglican bishops at ad limina visits and Roman Synods, the visits of St John Paul II and Benedict XVI to England and the offering of joint blessings have cast our relationship in a thoroughly new light. Such actions interpret and develop our theological dialogue. They make visible the practical implications of what we say together. We currently, however, experience a dissonance between theory and practice. The language of signs and symbols reveals a different, deeper reality about mutual recognition which extends beyond the brusque, negative theological judgment of ordination rites in 1896. We need an honest assessment of what all this means. We need an *aggiornamento* of theory and practice. The way in which we publicly and formally speak about one another should surely now reflect what has been said and done through this rich language of signs and symbols.

## Conclusion of the historical section

6 The extent to which our bishops are able to pursue joint mission, to which we are able to share in a common proclamation of the Gospel and agree on much more than simply the fundamentals of the faith, prompts us to articulate again the question posed by Archbishop Rowan Williams at a symposium in Rome (2009). Archbishop Williams argued that any detailed questions about the ordained ministry need to take place in the context of what Anglicans and Catholics have said together about the nature of the Church, baptism and Eucharist, and *koinonia*. Archbishop Williams posed the question: when so much has now been agreed on subjects of first-order importance, 'is it really justifiable to treat other issues as equally vital for [the Church's] health and integrity?' Equally, we join in asking: can statements which were made about one another's life and identity prior to our rediscovery of such a deep and shared sense of identity and mission, still be deployed as if such growth in mutual recognition, both explicit and implicit, had not taken place?

# II. THE HERMENEUTICS OF TRADITION AND SALVATION

## The Ecumenical and the Liturgical Movements

7 Whereas the previous section sketched a picture of important historical events, the purpose of the present one is to show there has also been development at an intellectual and spiritual level. For this reason, this section begins with the Liturgical and Ecumenical Movements which culminated in the Second Vatican Council, and aligns itself closely with the teachings of that Council. In the very first paragraph of the first document the Council promulgated – the Constitution on the Sacred Liturgy – it identifies as two of its aims 'to improve the standard of daily Christian living among Catholics [*fideles*]' and 'to encourage whatever can contribute to the union of all who believe in Christ.' The Council went on to say that it

'sees the taking of steps towards the renewal and growth of the liturgy as something it can and should do' (SC, 1).

The twentieth century witnessed the emergence and flourishing of the Liturgical and Ecumenical Movements. Much inspiration can be drawn from their ideas, proposals and concrete achievements. We should note that these movements were at root organically linked. Much attention was paid to worship in the Ecumenical Movement and many representatives of the Liturgical Movement were profoundly engaged in ecumenism. It is no exaggeration to say that a deepened sense of the liturgy was a motor for ecumenical rapprochement. The example of Dom Lambert Beauduin's life-long endeavour is only one of many worthy of mention in this context.

The Liturgical Movement excelled in different things. First and foremost, there was a strong commitment to the human situation of many Christians. The Liturgical Movement intended to transform the life of all the baptized by deepening their understanding of the liturgical year, the Eucharist, and the other sacraments. Second, an immense amount of work was done by scholars such as the Anglican Benedictine Gregory Dix (d. 1952) to illuminate the origins and history of the liturgy, with an emphasis on the first five centuries, and with respect to the interpretation of liturgical source texts. This scholarly work has left an indelible mark on the liturgical reforms in the later part of the twentieth century. Third, there were profound new theological and spiritual insights into the nature of the liturgy. Primary among them is the awareness that the concept of *mysterium* (*musterion*) by and large covers the meaning of the word *sacramentum*. Use of the original Greek word *musterion* became a central focus of theological thought and reflection about Christian liturgies and the potential thereof is far from exhausted – as with other rich fruits of the Liturgical and the Ecumenical Movement.

## Mystery and apostolic succession

8  A broad and deep understanding of *mystery* (*musterion*) can guide us in discussions concerning the complex reality of apostolic succession and the part played therein by both bishops and worshiping communities. Since '"what has been handed down from the Apostles" includes everything which helps the people of God to live a holy life and to grow in faith' (DV, 8), apostolic succession is above all about the sharing of the whole apostolic faith, about belonging to the community that proclaims that faith, about a common appeal to the apostles, and about communicating the faith to others. We have come to understand apostolic succession as faithful

transmission of all the various aspects of ecclesial life which constitute the Church as a living communion. The believer is invited to *participate in a mystery* – not solely to give intellectual assent to doctrine. The succession of laying on of hands in ordination to the great sees of the Church, as described by Irenaeus of Lyons, witnesses to a wider apostolic succession in faith, worship and ministry. This is a succession in the gifts and ministries given to the whole Church by the Holy Spirit. This wider understanding of apostolic succession has been crucial for the profound liturgical renewal which both our traditions have experienced and in which each has influenced the other.

## Vatican II: Revelation and history

9 The Second Vatican Council underscores the intrinsic relation between the concept of mystery and divine revelation. It speaks about a plan of revelation which 'unfolds through deeds and words bound together by an inner dynamism, in such a way that God's works, effected during the course of the history of salvation, show forth and confirm the doctrine and the realities signified by the words, while the words in turn proclaim the works and throw light on the meaning hidden in them. By this revelation the truth, both about God and about the salvation of humankind, inwardly dawns on us in Christ, who is himself both the mediator and the fullness of all revelation' (DV 2). The plan of God's revelation implies the hope of salvation for all humankind. What we know about it relies on a covenant made manifest in the history of the people of Israel and the Church. God spoke in many and diverse ways through the prophets but crucially also through Christ (cf. Heb 1:1-2), the Word of God (Jn 1:1), who became flesh and lived among us, and whose glory 'full of grace and truth' (Jn 1:14) was seen on earth. In other words, it was possible through the Incarnation to see the invisible in visible reality. It became possible to participate in the mystery of the transformation of creation in Christ and to 'discern what is the will of God, what is good and acceptable and perfect' (Rom 12:2). It became possible to present our 'bodies as a living sacrifice', which is our 'spiritual worship' (Rom 12:1).

## Vatican II: The Church as Body of Christ

10 Furthermore, the Second Vatican Council highlighted the importance of continuously looking for a better understanding of where and how the saving mystery of Christ is at work. It famously called for a scrutiny of the signs of the times in the light of the gospel (*GS*, 4) and for God's peo-

ple to work to 'discern the true signs of God's presence and purpose in the events, needs and desires which it shares with the rest of modern humanity' (*GS*, 11). It is only by doing this competently, keenly and honestly that the Church can move on its journey of hope towards the fullness of the Kingdom of God. So, 'an earnest of this hope and sustenance for the journey have been left by the Lord to his followers in the sacrament of faith' which we call the Eucharist, 'the supper of brotherly and sisterly communion and the foretaste of the heavenly banquet' (*GS*, 38).

The image of the Body of Christ, which is prominent in *Lumen Gentium*, is to be understood in both an ecclesial and in a sacramental way. As often as the Eucharist is celebrated, 'there is represented and produced the unity of the faithful who make up one body in Christ (see 1 Cor 10, 17). All people are called to this union with Christ, who is the light of the world; from him we come, through him we live and towards him we direct our lives' (*LG*, 3). 'By the communication of His Spirit, [Christ] constituted his sisters and brothers, gathered from all nations, as his own mystical body. In this body, the life of Christ is communicated to believers, who by means of the sacraments in a mysterious but real way are united to Christ who suffered and has been glorified.' (*LG*, 7). Christ is 'the head of the body which is the church. He is the beginning, the first-born from the dead,' ... 'He perpetually distributes the gift of ministries in his body which is the church; and with these gifts, through his power, we provide each other with helps towards salvation, so that doing the truth in love, we grow up in all things into him who is our head' (*LG*, 7).

## Vatican II: All the baptized participate in Christ's *triplex munus*

11 The work of Christ in and for his Church is characterized by a diversity of ministries, which, in Christian tradition, have been related to three *munera* ([sets of] gifts, functions) associated with his being Priest, Prophet and King. As *Walking Together on the Way* (2017), a document from ARCIC III, clearly puts forward (§ 52) Christ's *triplex munus* (threefold office) constitutes a model for discipleship and for imagining ways in which humankind can share in and benefit from his sanctifying grace. All the baptized are co-workers in the Lord's vineyard in different capacities. They are called to the 'apostolate', to apostolic service. 'In the Church there is diversity in ministry but unity in mission. The office and power of teaching in the name of Christ, of sanctifying and ruling, were conferred by him on the apostles and their successors. Lay people,

sharing in the priestly, prophetic and kingly offices of Christ, play their part in the mission of the whole people of God in the church and in the world' (*AA*, 2). They 'have their office and right to the apostolate from their union with Christ their head. They are brought into the mystical body of Christ by baptism, strengthened by the power of the Spirit in confirmation, and assigned to apostleship by the Lord himself. They are consecrated as a royal priesthood and a holy people (see 1 Pet 2:4-10), so as to offer spiritual sacrifices in all their works and to bear witness to Christ throughout the world. Through the sacraments, especially the holy eucharist, that charity which is the soul of the whole apostolate, is imparted to them and nourished' (*AA*, 3).

## Conclusion of the second section on theological and hermeneutical development

12 The Second Vatican Council offers a solid theological and hermeneutical basis for questioning the approach and judgment of *Apostolicae Curae*. In anchoring faith, Church and theology in God's mystery as God himself communicated it to humankind, inviting his Church to participate fully in his unique work of redemption and orienting us towards the realisation of his Kingdom, the Council promoted a powerful dynamic of liturgical renewal, mission and service to the world. The counterpart to a theology which is in this way determined both by Christology and by the action of the Holy Spirit is a comprehensive anthropology, i.e. an integral view of human persons, cultures, and societies, to which both the sciences and the humanities can fruitfully contribute. The study of how human beings interact with each other both visibly and in more implicit ways, how they employ signs and language and are sensitive to and attached to symbolic realities, supports the Church's endeavours to indicate more generously how God's grace and salvation are operative in the world. As a corollary, it makes a difference whether one looks at reality only from the standpoint of a reductive epistemology (i.e. through the perspective of what can be stated with absolute certainty as opposed to what is only probable or possible) or whether one approaches reality through a soteriological lens. The latter option equips one to do full justice to the desires, hopes and beliefs people have and to the gestures of charity which they perform. Taking into account the complex and fascinating nature of communication both human and divine is vital for the development of a more nuanced view on ministry, priesthood and communion than the

one which was underlying *Apostolicae Curae*.

# III. CHURCH, EUCHARIST AND MINISTRIES: ORDERS AND ORDINATION

## Catholic rites of ordination in the Roman rite

13  In line with the foundational hermeneutic laid out in the previous section, the present section aims at drawing primarily on the *lex orandi* of the Church to formulate an integrated vision of the sacrament of ordination embracing the diaconate, the priesthood and the episcopate. This vision gives us the basis for new proposals to heal the hurt caused by *Apostolicae Curae* and those aspects of its interpretation which harmed the very fabric of the Church. After much shared study, we feel compelled to present a view of what is entailed by ordination and priesthood which significantly differs from and even questions the view underlying the judgment that Anglican ordinations must be seen as 'absolutely null and utterly void.'

    Like all the other dimensions of the liturgical life of the Church, the liturgy of ordination in the Roman rite was significantly revised after the Second Vatican Council. This is yet another crucial factor indicating that the situation has drastically changed since 1896. It was widely agreed during and after the Council that there were serious theological reasons for improving the rites of ordination. A crucial factor making for revision was the need for a clearer focus on Christ's priesthood, replacing allegorical interpretation of various passages in the Old Testament. Another factor was the need for a more straightforward profiling of the diaconate, which could now be entered as a distinctive, lifelong ministry.

    In the revised rites, the Liturgy of the Word and the homily of the presiding bishop receive more explicit attention. The Liturgy of the Word is followed by the examination of the candidates, the litany of the saints while the candidates prostrate themselves, the laying on of hands in silence and the prayer of ordination which is an extended prayer for the Holy Spirit to make fruitful the ministry of a deacon, priest or bishop. This prayer of ordination is of central importance to the celebration and has therefore been very carefully drafted on the basis of ancient sources. Traditional explanatory rites such as the *traditio instrumentorum* (the handing over of the instruments) are less prominently profiled than before. The accompanying pastoral instructions emphasize that a time must be chosen which enables as many people as possible to attend the ceremony, for it is without doubt a high point in the forming of true communion. Moreover, the revised rites of ordination have themselves already undergone a revision.

The current text, *De ordinatione Episcopi, presbyterorum et diaconorum*, dates from 1990 and replaces an earlier *editio typica* from 1968. The present liturgical book underlines the central role of the bishop who possesses the fulness of priesthood, the priests' participation in the priesthood of the bishop, and deacons' integral participation in the Church's ordained ministry.

## Anglican rites of ordination, with particular reference to the Church of England

14  As with other Churches of the Anglican Communion, the ordination rites of the Church of England have been thoroughly revised – after consultation with Roman Catholic scholars amongst others and with a keen awareness of the critique of *Apostolicae Curae*. The revision of the Anglican Ordinals of 1550, 1552 and 1662, which in the Church of England culminated in *Common Worship Ordination Services* (2007), was intended to make clearer the ways in which Anglicans understand each ministerial 'order' to participate in the mission and ministry of Christ and to serve the life and worship of the Church. The Form and Manner of Making of Deacons, The Form and Manner of Ordering of Priests and The Form of Ordaining or Consecrating of an Archbishop or Bishop was replaced with The Ordination of Deacons, The Ordination of Priests, also called Presbyters and The Ordination and Consecration of a Bishop.

Each rite has a similar structure. There is a preface with a common introduction and a brief introduction to the order of ministry to be conferred. The presiding bishop sets out an understanding of that order which is clearly based on the New Testament, before asking a series of questions which invite the ordinands publicly to declare their prayerful commitment to various aspects of the particular ministry to be bestowed. The questions conclude with three addressed to the whole congregation: 'Brothers and sisters, you have heard how great is the charge that these ordinands are ready to undertake, and you have heard their declarations. Is it now your will that they should be ordained? (*It is.*) Will you continually pray for them? (*We will.*) Will you uphold and encourage them in their ministry? (*We will.*)' The ninth century hymn *Veni Creator Spiritus,* ('Come, Holy Ghost, our souls inspire) follows, though for the ordination of deacons it is optional, and after that comes The Litany. The ordination prayer itself mirrors the prayer over the water in baptism and the prayer of consecration in the Eucharist. It begins with extended praise and thanksgiving, before the presiding bishop moves to the laying on of hands with the words:

Send down the Holy Spirit on your servant N
For the office and work of a deacon/priest/bishop in your Church.

The prayer concludes with prayer for the Holy Spirit to make fruitful the ministry of a deacon, priest or bishop. For all three orders of ministry, this is followed by the gift of a Bible.

Over recent years, the Churches of the Anglican Communion have revised their Ordinals better to reflect local experience of the Gospel, whilst remaining faithful to Scripture and the tradition of a threefold ministry of bishops, priests and deacons inherited from the apostolic Church. This work has been done at a time when liturgical scholars have strong ecumenical links and are familiar with the fruits of liturgical reform in other Churches. Anglicans and Catholics have consulted one another and drawn upon common sources. The result has been a convergence in the structure and content of Catholic ordination rites and the rites used by the Churches of the Anglican Communion – whilst certain clear differences of emphasis remain. Most Anglican bishops and priests are now ordained using rites which have been radically changed from those condemned in 1896 as 'absolutely null and utterly void.'

## The ministry of the baptized

15 The ARCIC Statement on Ministry and Ordination (1973), which sets out a consensus shared by the Anglican and Roman Catholic members of the Commission, notes that, 'The ordained ministry can only be rightly understood within [a] broader context of various ministries all of which are the work of one and the same Spirit' (2) and that, since '[t]he life and self-offering of Christ perfectly expresses what it is to serve God and man [...] [a]ll Christian ministry, whose purpose is always to build up the community (koi*nonia*), flows and takes its shape from this source and model' (3). The ministry of the baptized, lay and ordained, is thus understood as a participation in the ministry of Christ. The ministry of all the

baptized – lay people, deacons, priests and bishops – represents for each the call of the Spirit to serve the whole body of Christ in a distinctive way.

## The diaconate

16 A remarkable renewal of the diaconate has taken place in both Anglicanism and Roman Catholicism. No longer is it seen as little more than a stepping stone on the way to priesthood. The distinctive role of the deacon has long been evident in the liturgies of Eastern Churches. As a fruit of the Liturgical Movement, it has in recent years been made clearer in western liturgies. The model for ordination to this diaconal role was the selection of the Seven, 'men of good standing, full of the Spirit and of wisdom' to serve (*diakonein*) at tables during the daily distribution of food by the Jerusalem Church (Acts 6:1ff). They 'stood before the apostles who prayed and laid their hands on them', commissioning them for their task. Writing to the Magnesians, Ignatius of Antioch declares that the ministry of the deacons is nothing other than 'the diaconate (*diakonia*) of Jesus Christ' (*Mag.* 6:1).

The Dogmatic Constitution on the Church from Vatican II (*Lumen Gentium*) set out an understanding of the diaconate which describes both the liturgical and pastoral role of deacons. It also made provision for the revival of a permanent diaconate which might include married men. This provision was further clarified and elaborated in a motu proprio of 1972, *Ad pascendum*, and a Directory for the Ministry of Permanent Deacons issued by the Congregation for Clergy in 1998. In an address to permanent deacons and their families Pope St John Paul II fittingly considered them to be 'active apostles of the new evangelization.' The revised Ordinal of the Church of England no longer speaks of 'the Making of Deacons' but the Ordination of Deacons to emphasise their place as a distinct order of ministry within the Church.

When an understanding of the diaconate, which is deeply rooted in the ministry of Jesus Christ and expressed in remarkably similar ordination rites, is shared by both our traditions, it seems untenable that there should be no mutual recognition of ministry at this point.

## Priesthood

17 The ARCIC I statement on *Ministry and Ordination* concluded that the goal of the ordained ministry is 'to serve the priesthood of all the faithful' (7). Furthermore, our communions can together affirm the liturgical and sacramental ministry of the presbyterate: 'Presbyters are joined with

the bishop in his oversight of the church and in the ministry of the word
and the sacraments; they are given authority to preside at the eucharist
and to pronounce absolution' (9). They preside when the church meets to
make 'the memorial of the sacrifice of Christ' (13) which, as the ARCIC
I statement on *Eucharistic Doctrine* says, is 'no mere calling to mind of
a past event or of its significance' (5). Both the statement on *Eucharistic
Doctrine* and on *Ministry and Ordination* use the Greek term *anamnesis* for this sacramental memorial: 'The Commission believes that the
traditional understanding of sacramental reality in which the once-for-
all event of salvation becomes effective in the present through the action
of the Holy Spirit, is well expressed by the word *anamnesis*' (*Eucharistic
Doctrine*, *Elucidation* 5) – as used in the New Testament (1 Cor 11:24-25;
Luke 22:19) and quoted at every Eucharist in the western tradition: 'Do
this in memory of me.'

The concept of *anamnesis* implies *participation* by means of the sacrament in the original event. To celebrate the Eucharist in obedience
to Christ's command is to 'enter into the movement of his self-offering' (*Eucharistic Doctrine*, 5). In presiding at the Eucharist, Catholic
and Anglican priests share a conviction that all priesthood derives from
the High Priesthood of Christ, they have a strong sense of the need for
priestly intercession in and for the community that each priest serves,
and are clear that ordination allows for entry into an 'apostolic and
God-given ministry' (*Ministry and Ordination*, 14).

## Episcopate

18 In both our traditions, the ministry of a bishop is one of 'oversight'
(Gk *episkope*), with responsibility for the flourishing of a specific local
Church: that 'portion of the people of God that has been entrusted to
their care' (*LG*, 23). For Roman Catholics, the teaching of Vatican II on
the collegial authority and responsibilities of bishops as shepherds of the
People of God (cf. LG, 18-27) has led to renewed understanding of episcopal ministry within the Body of Christ. Anglicans have benefited from
this enrichment, much of which is in accord with Anglican understanding of episcopal ministry.

The ARCIC I statement on *Ministry and Ordination* speaks of this responsibility as involving 'fidelity to the apostolic faith, its embodiment
in the life of the Church today, and its transmission to the Church of tomorrow' (9). The bishop provides sacramental leadership through presi-
dency at the Eucharist, through the blessing on Holy Thursday of chrism

and other oil which is distributed to parishes for anointing at baptisms and on other liturgical occasions, and in pastoral care.

The ministry of the bishop is symbolised liturgically by the service of footwashing. The bishop is to be a servant of unity within and among the Churches; a model of holiness through whom the people of the diocese, lay and ordained, are encouraged in their discipleship. The bishop is to maintain the catholicity of the Church, locally and more widely, by exercising 'care for all the churches' (2 Cor 11:28). The bishop is to be a faithful preacher and teacher of the apostolic tradition, bringing the good news to those who are not members of the Church and working 'to equip the saints for the work of ministry, for building up the body of Christ until all of us come to the unity of the faith and of the knowledge of the Son of God, to maturity, to the measure of the full stature of Christ' (Eph 4:12-13).

In the light of this shared understanding of episcopal ministry, it can be seen that the intention and the form of episcopal ordination according to contemporary Anglican ordinals and according to the contemporary Roman rite are remarkably similar. Both make explicit the intention sacramentally to do what the Church has always done in ordaining bishops. As a consequence, the notion that God acknowledges one and rejects the other seems untenable.

## The celebration of ordinations

19 As shown above, there are profound liturgical and theological similarities between our Churches when it comes to the rites of ordination and the understanding of the diaconate, priesthood, and episcopate. However, there are also differences, which have to do with the nature of the relation between deacons and priests on the one hand and bishops and dioceses on the other. With time, there have matured within our communions differing traditions with different customs, differences in formal arrangements and different policies. We can, however, say without reservation, that the episcopal structure of our Churches and the ministries of bishops, priests, deacons and laypersons are interpreted as playing a major role in God's plan of salvation. The practice of the Church has roots in Jesus' ministry itself, the testimony and activities of the apostles, the New Testament, the earliest Christian communities followed by a centuries-long tradition of ministerial action and theological reflection.

This layered structure is an important token of the continuity of authentic Christian living throughout the ages. It makes a living connection between Jesus' time, our time, and the time to come. When baptized Christians gather for the liturgy of ordination, when they open the Scriptures to listen to God's Word, when they have these words clarified through preaching, often by the liturgical president, when they sing psalms and hymns, when they join in prayers of thanksgiving, blessing and petition, when special prayers are said with laying on of hands for the Holy Spirit to bestow the gifts of the ministries of the diaconate, the priesthood or episcopate upon tried, examined and well-selected candidates, and when all share in the Eucharist together, receiving and forming the Body of Christ (cf. Augustine, *sermo* 272), one must conclude there is such a density of sacramental grace that a narrow focus on the question as to whether the form and formula of the ordination rite are precisely correct can actually obscure the mystical reality of what is taking place.

## The ordination of women in the Anglican Communion

20 The ordination of women in many parts of the Anglican Communion as deacons, priests and bishops has, for Catholics and for some Anglicans, raised new questions about the authenticity of Anglican ministry. Leo XIII judged that, 'ordinations carried out according to the Anglican rite have been, and are, absolutely null and utterly void.' This judgment on Anglican ordinations according to the rites of his time was quite independent of later magisterial judgments, both Catholic and Anglican, about the ordination of women. These were made on largely different grounds. We believe it would be quite wrong to use the differing positions taken on the ordination of women by our two communions as a reason not to address the adverse judgment of Pope Leo on the Anglican ordination rites that had been used up to the time of *Apostolicae Curae*. The fact that women can, in most Anglican provinces, now be ordained, does not in itself mean that the Pope's condemnation of 1896 must be applied to the present situation.

## Recognition beyond mere language

21 There is, upon close analysis, an overwhelming amount of theological evidence that the delicate issue as to whether our Churches can mutually, and fully, recognize the validity of each other's rites of ordination can finally be resolved. In spite of historical separation, the tension generated by sharp judgments and firm response and an atmosphere for too long dominated by resentment, suspicions and intolerance – which often re-

sulted in ignorance and fear of the other – the reality of such recognition is already bursting through. Even if this reality has not yet been adequately captured in the right language, even if it has not yet been asserted in the proper document, and even if it is not yet supported by an overall ecclesial discourse and shared mentality, we believe that the recognition of Anglican orders must indeed have drawn closer. The contextualisation of *Apostolicae Curae*'s most central statement is no longer a mere dream or a pious illusion. The affirmation of Thomas Aquinas that the act of faith does not halt at what can be enunciated about it but at the enunciated reality itself (*actus autem credentis non terminatur ad enuntiabile sed ad rem* – *STh* II-II q. 1, art. 2, ad. 2) is helpful at this point. Applied to our case, this would imply that the recognition of Anglican orders does not ultimately depend on any kind of statement but on a reality lived among Christians – a reality received in faith, strengthened by hope, and apprehended through love.

# IV. THE HOPE OF HEALING

## A call for reconsideration

22 The last decades have shown that theological maturing, methodological *ressourcement* (return to the sources) and mutual reconsideration of what divides us, is not only possible but has already resulted in historical agreements between Churches that have been separated for many centuries. The Joint Declaration on the Doctrine of Justification (JDDJ) between the Roman-Catholic Church and the Lutheran World Federation (1999) 'is shaped by the conviction that in their respective histories our Churches have come to new insights' (JDDJ, 7) that remaining differences in the explication of basic truths of the doctrine of justification 'are no longer the occasion for doctrinal condemnations.'

Five years before, in the Common Christological Declaration between the Catholic Church and the Assyrian Church of the East (1994), the two Churches noted that though they had been separated since the Council of Ephesus (430) by the different ways they express their doctrine concerning the divinity and humanity of Christ, they could now 'recognize the legitimacy and rightness of these expressions of the same faith and [...] respect the preference of each Church in her liturgical life and piety.' This common declaration has resulted in another historic document, the Guidelines for Admission to the Eucharist Between the Chaldean

Church and the Assyrian Church of the East (2001), which uncondition-ally recognizes the validity of the historic Anaphora of the Apostles Add-ai and Mari even though it does not contain the words of institution.

Thus, the recognition, by the Catholic Church, of the full ecclesiali-ty of the Assyrian Church of the East (2), has led to a careful study of the Assyrian liturgical texts and sacramental theology. This resulted in the judgement that 'the words of Eucharistic Institution are indeed present in the Anaphora of Addai and Mari, not in a coherent narrative way and ad litteram, but rather in a dispersed euchological way, that is, integrated in successive prayers of thanksgiving, praise and intercession.' The Ro-man Catholic recognition of the validity of the Eucharist of the Assyri-an Church of the East, which shows a remarkably flexible application of its own theological categories, was made possible practically by the ac-knowledgement of this Church 'as a true particular Church, built upon orthodox faith and apostolic succession' (2) – rather than the other way round (i.e. the recognition of the validity of sacraments leading to the recognition of authentic ecclesiality).

The Common Christological Declaration between the Catholic Church and the Assyrian Church of the East and the Guidelines for the Admission to the Eucharist between the Chaldean Church and the As-syrian Church of the East demonstrate that, where there is sufficient un-derlying convergence of theological understanding and intention, omis-sion of particular 'forms of words', however significant, need not be a bar to mutual recognition.

## A call for recontextualisation

23  As we have studied the painful historical estrangement between the Church of England and the Roman Catholic Church, we have been struck by how much change there has been in the last century. Since the time of the Malines Conversations, Anglicans and Catholics have learnt to pray together and for one another, our shared study of Scripture and tradi-tion has brought renewal, we have engaged in joint projects of dialogue, discipleship and witness, we have experienced growing friendship. In a world utterly transformed since the end of the nineteenth century, facing difficulties and threats on a scale beyond imagining at that time, we have learnt what it is to share a common hope. We long for our Churches to be able to embrace one another as sisters in Christ.

As we have reflected together, we have learnt how the condemnation of Anglican ordinations was based upon a theological method, historical understanding, church-political considerations and ecumenical approaches which were of their time. The response in *Saepius Officio* used a similar method to powerful effect. We are not of that time and we regret the damage caused should such a condemnation be allowed to remain in place and applied to contemporary Anglican ordinations. Such a notion represents a loss of hope. We believe that the condemnation of Anglican ordinations in 1896 needs to be recontextualised in part because, as we have tried to show, the focus of *Apostolicae Curae* was exclusively on Anglican rites which are now rarely used. The ordination rites of both our traditions have since 1896 been radically revised in the light of the remarkable ecclesiological and liturgical renewal of the twentieth century.

Our reflection on the Decree of Ecumenism (cf. para 4 above) has provided us with further reason to hope that the judgment of Apostolicae Curae can now be seen in a new light. We have noted the words of Unitatis Redintegratio that 'our separated brothers and sisters also celebrate many sacred actions of the christian religion [which] most certainly can truly engender a life of grace' and that, 'among those [communions] in which catholic traditions and institutions in part continue to subsist, the Anglican communion occupies a special place' (UR, 3, 13). Where such elements of the apostolic faith have been faithfully passed on over many years and have manifestly borne fruit in the life of grace – including, and perhaps especially, amongst Anglicans – it seems to us this surely points to the Holy Spirit's presence in the ordained ministry of that communion.

In the spirit of the friendship at the heart of the Malines Conversations, we have together concluded (i) that the condemnation of contemporary Anglican ordinations because of the perceived deficiencies of rites from the past needs to be re-examined. We also suggest (ii) that the implied judgment that the apostolic succession of the Church of England was lost at the Reformation should be re-examined in the light of contemporary ecclesiological and liturgical understanding of the variety of means by which apostolic succession takes place within authentic traditions of Christian life and worship.

# V. CONCLUSION

## A further step on the path of synodality?

24  Pope Francis and Archbishop Justin Welby have frequently spoken of Roman Catholic and Anglican Christians as walking together 'on the way' – commending the synodality of the Church by alluding to the likely derivation of the Greek word synod from the roots 'together' (*sun*) and 'way' (*hodos*). As we walk together, we talk and as we talk we understand the presence of Christ in new ways (cf. Lk 24:13-27). We reflect on the experience of our Churches and our experience as Christian persons. Much has changed since the condemnation of Anglican ordinations in 1896.

The Malines Conversations Group has reflected a great deal on the experiences which through more than a century have drawn our communions and their individual members so much closer together. Where we once walked apart we now walk together in friendship and love. For both our communions, it would be nothing less than a recognition of our ecclesial experience if the condemnation of 1896 were to be seen as inapplicable to contemporary Anglican ordinations. The judgment made *then* does not accord with the reality into which the Spirit has led us *now*. We do not expect that if this reappraisal were to happen ecclesial communion would immediately be restored but our two communions would have taken a significant step along the road on which we are rediscovering our commitment to one another as *sisters in hope of the Resurrection.*

# Epilogue

## ROWAN WILLIAMS

The greatest obstacle to a restored and united worldwide Christian communion is the confusion and carelessness that prevails in the realm of ecclesiology. This is a strong statement, I know, and hardly an uncontroversial one, but the discussions represented in these insightful, bold and inspiring essays seem to point inexorably to such a conclusion. Catholics and non-Catholics alike have settled too easily for versions of the theology of the Church that are either bland or formalistic (sometimes both at once). The Malines Conversations were unmistakeably shaped by the styles of theology prevalent in the early twentieth century, and their deliberations cannot just be dusted off and presented as answers to contemporary questions. But the essential job they did was to begin to ask, awkwardly and tentatively, whether the theological methods of their day were in fact adequate to a communal and historical reality far more 'polyphonic' than might be comfortable for institutions anxious about certainty of a specific sort.

And here is one of the oddities of the way in which inter-ecclesial conflict has typically been framed in the modern period, at least until relatively recently. 'How do I know whether this is a real sacrament?' is a question that locks us into a particular intellectual culture in which I am always in danger of being deceived by appearances. What I need is a set of manageable and clear criteria for assuring myself that I am not being misled. It is the kind of anxiety that energized a great deal of European philosophy from the seventeenth century onwards. Yet when you think of it in the context of Christian faith and practice, it is actually rather eccentric.

It is not, of course, that questions of the authenticity of sacraments was unfamiliar to earlier Christian generations: there was bitter controversy in the patristic era over the acceptability of baptisms conferred by supposedly schismatic bodies, an issue over which there was a striking diversity of judgements among impeccably orthodox writers. But the characteristic underlying question in the early Church was not about a search for formal features of baptism that would reassure the doubtful observer, but about the overall understanding of Christian identity within a suspect or minority group: was this body adequately embodying the Body of Christ? Or was it defining itself by something less than or other than the free gift of incorporation and adoption into Christ presently enacted and effected in the paschal transition of the baptismal rite? Augustine's treatment of Donatist baptism is sometimes seen as a watershed moment when formal sacramental 'validity' is identified as something that can be considered as an issue in itself; but it is more accurate to see his analysis as pointing out the incompatibility between a formally correct baptismal practice and a communal self-definition bound to a specific agenda in internal Church disputes – the erecting of criteria for Christan acceptability on grounds unconnected with a basic credal language about the threefold mystery into which baptism allowed our entry. The problem with the Donatists, according to Augustine, is not that they fail to perform effective sacraments but that they fail to ground their identity solely in the universal gift of adoption that baptism sacramentally confers, and look for human and contingent assurances.

This is a complex enough topic, granted; but the point is that we are not here dealing primarily with the problems of an individual believer looking for firm external criteria for assessing the efficacy of an isolated ceremony. Something has to be said about the language and 'performance' of a whole community. And as soon as the matter is framed in this way, it is less obvious that questions of ecclesial division can be resolved by zero-sum accounts of what specific tangible evidence will guarantee that you are not being deceived; it becomes necessary to ask how any supposedly ecclesial body manifests – or fails to manifest – its character *as Church*.

The Malines discussions do not quite go as far as this reframing. They tend to revert to an impressively detailed picking-over of historical and canonical material, still somewhat bound by the search for appropriate certainty; they show little awareness of any non-European dimension to ecclesial life; they barely notice the potential of Eastern Christian thought, let alone classical Reformed theology, to breaking certain kinds of deadlock; and they never quite get down to the fundamental question of what the integrity of the Church as Church consists in. But what is lastingly important in their approach is the willingness to step back from a purely self-defensive mode of argument, to the extent of assuming that both parties have things to learn and unlearn. This is to take for granted that what the Church is may be something *to be discovered* in its fullness as history unfolds, as Christians in community determine over again where the heart of their distinctiveness lies in their invitation to and confrontation of the world.

Does this mean – a sceptic might ask – that the Church's unity and integrity is always somehow provisional, subject to revision? Is there no centre of identity that allows us now to think of ourselves as participating in one continuous common life, one faith once and for all delivered to the saints? There are two possible responses to this challenge – which is a very proper one, because part of the Church's identity is its fidelity to a commission and a vision that it has not itself created or chosen; the Church is always a community existing because it has been called, blood have not revealed this to you...'). The first point is to note that to say that the Church's full identity is 'eschatological', only realized in its entirety at the consummation of all things, is not at all the same as saying that it is endlessly revisable or negotiable. Eschatology is the definitive unveiling of what has always been true, the full flowering – in and at the end of history – of a work that has been 'from the beginning'. It is the final 'Coming' of the same Christ that we know in Scripture and worship. One of the great themes of Christan Scripture is that, at the deepest level, the end is with us now: the fullness of life in the Body of Christ is not a gradual movement towards an historical goal but the active presence of a personal spiritual energy that *by its own unchanging fullness* enlarges the dimensions of the visible community in the direction of its own plenitude of blessedness and joy. The sacramental life of the Church here and now is where the Church embodies its ultimate integrity and its future fulfilment.

Thus the point underlined in several of these essays about the central significance of liturgy in thinking about the Church becomes a key to seeing the question of unity afresh. The Church is what happens when the action of the Incarnate Word creates through the Holy Spirit a network of lifegiving relationship, in which each and all grow together into their future as God's sons and daughters; and this is a relationship that extends across time as well as space. Our communion is with all who have gone before us in faith – including the saints of the First Covenant – because of this mutual connection in and through the Word that the Spirit makes and sustains. The liturgical recollection and re-presentation of this is not the performance of rites designed to guarantee that a routinely absent God becomes present but the intentional making of space for the always present God to be seen and heard in his gracious fidelity to what he has made and loved.

This theological approach, adumbrated by many of the contributions to this collection, invites us to be very cautious about any vision of unity that simply looks towards the unification of 'defective' with 'normative' communal life, with the 'normative' defined in terms of the satisfaction of various formal or institutional specifications. The 'mutual recognition' we so often speak about is less a matter of acknowledging that others meet our own familiar requirements than the recognition of how space is made for the Word of God in corporate practice, sacramental and otherwise. And this is compatible with a somewhat broader range of theological emphases and idioms than we might have thought – a point made by some of the Anglicans at Malines, especially Charles Gore. The risk of ignoring this is that we end up defending a model of the Church in which institutional homogeneity and agreement on all disputable matters become the fundamental ingredients for how we think about the Church's identity; we locate the Church's unity in our practice and language rather than the one act of the Holy Trinity through the Incarnation of the Word and the gift of his Spirit.

Hence my provocative opening comment: the risk is of thinking of ecclesial unity as something rather at a bit of a distance from the essential reality on which the Church is founded, which is the covenanted presence of God in this community, the presence made particular to each in the baptismal liturgy and renewed regularly in the re-conversion to which we are called in the Holy Eucharist, where, as those who share the table with Christ 'on the night in which he was betrayed.' The Eucharistic community is perfectly the Church precisely in its supernatural uniting of imperfect persons in a single gift and a single eschatological hope, a hope that may look as unlikely as the reconciliation between the royal sisters in Westminster Abbey. But of course one of the things that a good ecclesiology should do is to remind us just how unlikely the Church is; may this celebration and exploration of the heritage of Malines give us again the grace of being surprised by the gift of Catholic communion.

# List of Contributors

Donald J. Bolen
*Archbishop of Regina*

Sarah Coakley
*Norris-Hulse Professor Emerita of Divinity, University of Cambridge*

Francesco Coccopalmerio
*President Emeritus, Pontifical Council for Legislative Texts*

Godfried Danneels (+2019)
*Archbishop of Malines-Bruxelles (1979—2010)*

Brian Farrell
*Secretary of the Dicastery for Promoting Christian Unity since 2002*

Joris Geldhof
*Professor of Liturgy and Sacramental Theology, Catholic University of Leuven*

David Hamid
*Suffragan Bishop, Diocese in Europe*

James Hawkey
*Canon Theologian, Westminster Abbey*

Maryana Hnyp
*President of the European Network on Religion and Belief, Bruxelles*

Simon Jones
*Chaplain, Merton College, Oxford*

Gordon Lathrop
*Professor Emeritus at Lutheran Theological Seminary, Philadelphia*

Bernard Longley
*Archbishop of Birmingham*

Paul McPartlan
*Carl J. Peter Professor of Systematic Theology and Ecumenism, Catholic University of America.*

Jeremy Morris
*National Ecumenical Adviser, Church of England*

David Moxon
*Archbishop of Aotearoa, New Zealand and Polynesia (2013—2017)*

Paul D. Murray
*Director, Centre for Catholic Studies, Durham University*

Thomas O'Loughlin
*Professor Emeritus of Historical Theology, University of Nottingham*

Keith F. Pecklers, S.J.
*Professor of Liturgy and Ecumenical Theology, Pontifical Gregorian University, Rome*

Michael Nai-Chiu Poon
*Centre for the Study of Christianity in Asia at Trinity Theological College, Singapore*

Thomas Pott, O.S.B.
*Professor of Oriental Liturgy and Sacramental Theology, Pontifico Ateneo Sant' Anselmo, Rome*

David Richardson
*Dean Emeritus, Saint Paul's Cathedral, Melbourne*

Geoffrey Rowell (+2017)
*Bishop of Gibraltar in Europe (2001—2013)*

Nicholas Sagovsky
*Canon Theologian, Westminster Abbey (2004—2011)*

# List of Contributors

David Stancliffe
  *Bishop of Salisbury (1993—2010)*

Robert Taft, S.J. (+2018)
  *Pontifical Oriental Institute, Rome (1975—2011)*

Joseph W. Tobin, C.Ss.R.
  *Archbishop of Newark*

Cyrille Vael, O.S.B.
  *Monastic Association for Encounter and Dialogue, Lillois*

Clare Watkins
  *Reader in Practical Theology, University of Roehampton*

Catherine Waynick
  *Bishop of Indianapolis (1997—2017)*

Justin Welby
  *Archbishop of Canterbury*

Rowan Williams
  *Archbishop of Canterbury (2003—2012)*

# Membership of the Malines Conversation Group

## ANGLICAN MEMBERS

The Rt Revd David Hamid
  *Suffragan Bishop of the Church of England Diocese in Europe; Co-chairman of IARCCUM*

The Most Revd David Moxon
  *Former Co-Chairman of ARCIC III and former representative of the Archbishop of Canterbury to the Holy See and director of the Anglican Centre in Rome, former Primate of New Zealand;* Currently: *Hamilton, New Zealand*

The Revd Canon Prof. Dr Sarah Coakley
  *Norris-Hulse Professor Emerita of Divinity, University of Cambridge, UK,* Currently: *Washington DC, USA*

The Revd Canon Dr Jennifer Cooper
  *Canon Theologian of Newcastle Cathedral*

The Revd Canon Dr James Hawkey
  *Canon Theologian of Westminster Abbey, London.*

The Revd Canon Dr Jeremy Morris
  *National Adviser for Ecumenical Relations for the Church of England Senior Associate of the Cambridge Theological Federation, Affiliated Lecturer at the Faculty of Divinity, Cambridge University*

The Very Revd Canon David Richardson
  *Former representative of the Archbishop of Canterbury to the Holy See and director of the ACR;* Currently: *Toorak, Australia*

The Revd Canon Dr Nicholas Sagovsky
  *Former Canon Theologian at Westminster Abbey; member of ARCIC I & II;* Currently: *London, UK*

# CATHOLIC MEMBERS

Prof. Dr Joris Geldhof
> *Chair of the Liturgical Institute, Faculty of Theology and Religious Studies, KU Leuven*

Dr Maryana Hnyp
> *European Network on Religion and Belief, President; Adjunct Lecturer of Theological Ethics, Ateneo de Manila University, Philippines.*

Prof. Dr Arnaud Join-Lambert
> *Professor of Practical Theology and Liturgy, Centre de théologie pratique, UC Louvain*

The Revd Prof. Dr Keith Pecklers, S.J.
> *Professor of Liturgy and Ecumenical Theology, Pontifical Gregorian University, Rome*

The Revd Prof. Dr Thomas Pott, O.S.B.
> *Professor of Oriental Liturgy and Sacramental Theology, Pontifical Atheneum Sant'Anselmo, Rome*

The Revd Cyrille Vael, O.S.B.
> *Monastic Association for Encounter and Dialogue, Lillois, Belgium*

# OBSERVERS

The Revd Martin Browne
> *Secretary to the Anglican and Methodist dialogues at the Dicastery for Promoting Christian Unity, Rome*

The Most Revd Ian Ernest
> *Representative of the Archbishop of Canterbury to the Holy See and director of the Anglican Centre in Rome*

# COMPANIONS

His Eminence Joseph Cardinal Tobin, C.Ss.R.
> *Archbishop of Newark*

The Rt Hon The Earl of Halifax, KStJ, DL

The Rt Revd Dr David Stancliffe
> *Former Bishop of Salisbury and Chairman of the Church of England Liturgical Committee*

The Revd Em Prof. Dr Gordon Lathrop
> *Professor Emeritus of Liturgy at the Lutheran Theological Seminary at Philadelphia*

The Most Revd Donald Bolen
*Archbishop of Regina (Canada); Co-president of IARCUUM*

# PATRONS

His Eminence Jozef Cardinal De Kesel
*Archbishop Emeritus of Mechelen-Brussels*
The Rt Revd and Rt Hon The Lord Williams of Oystermouth
*Former Archbishop of Canterbury*

Printed in the USA
CPSIA information can be obtained
at www.ICGtesting.com
JSHW011149210324
59618JS00004B/26

9 780281 090358